FIND ME
THE VOTES

FIND ME THE VOTES

A Hard-Charging Georgia Prosecutor,
a Rogue President, and the
Plot to Steal an American Election

MICHAEL ISIKOFF *and*
DANIEL KLAIDMAN

TWELVE

NEW YORK   BOSTON

Twelve
Hachette Book Group
1290 Avenue of the Americas, New York, NY 10104
twelvebooks.com
@twelvebooks

First Edition: January 2024

Twelve is an imprint of Grand Central Publishing. The Twelve name and
logo are registered trademarks of Hachette Book Group, Inc.

The publisher is not responsible for websites (or their content)
that are not owned by the publisher.

The Hachette Speakers Bureau provides a wide range of authors for
speaking events. To find out more, go to hachettespeakersbureau.com or
email HachetteSpeakers@hbgusa.com.

Twelve books may be purchased in bulk for business, educational, or promotional use.
For information, please contact your local bookseller or the Hachette Book Group
Special Markets Department at special.markets@hbgusa.com.

Library of Congress Cataloging-in-Publication Data has been applied for.

ISBNs: 978-1-5387-3999-0 (hardcover), 978-1-5387-4001-9 (ebook)

Printed in the United States of America

LSC-C

10 9 8 7 6 5 4 3 2 1

Once again, to MA and Zach

—MI

To Bella and Shayna

—DK

CONTENTS

CAST OF CHARACTERS

Fulton County District Attorney's Office

Fani Willis district attorney, 2021–

Jeff DiSantis, communications director, 2021–

Paul Howard district attorney, 1997–2021

Clint Rucker chief assistant, 1995–2021

Nathan Wade chief special prosecutor, election interference case

John Floyd special prosecutor, election interference case

Will Wooten deputy district attorney, election interference case

Donald Wakeford chief senior district attorney, election interference case

Michael Hill investigator, election interference case

Tanya Miller chief senior district attorney, 2005–2013

White House

Donald J. Trump president of the United States, 2017–2021

Mike Pence vice president of the United States, 2017–2021

Mark Meadows chief of staff

Cassidy Hutchinson aide to Meadows

Pat Cipollone White House counsel

Eric Herschmann White House lawyer

Willis Family and Friends

John C. Floyd III father

Rebecca Christian Smith Emory Law School classmate

Felicia Stewart Emory Law School classmate

The 2020 District Attorney Race

Jeff DiSantis Willis strategist

Jeremy Harris Willis campaign manager

Chris Huttman Willis pollster and ad buyer

Charlie Bailey Willis adviser

Daphne and **Walter Jordan** Willis supporters

Fred Hicks consultant to Paul Howard

T.I. Grammy award winning rapper and political power broker

Angela "Amani" Davis vetter for George Soros organization

The Rayshard Brooks Shooting

Rayshard Brooks murdered gang member

Keisha Lance Bottoms Atlanta mayor

Secoriea Turner murdered schoolgirl

Secoriey Williamson father of Secoriea Turner

Charmaine Turner mother of Secoriea Turner

Omar Ivery friend of Charmaine Turner

Georgia Secretary of State's Office

Brad Raffensperger secretary of state

Jordan Fuchs deputy secretary of state and chief of staff

Gabriel Sterling chief operations officer

Ryan Germany chief counsel

Chris Harvey elections director

Carter Jones elections monitor

Bryan Tyson outside lawyer

Tricia Raffensperger wife of Brad Raffensperger

Brian Robinson media adviser

The Government of Georgia

Brian Kemp governor

Cody Hall Kemp spokesman

Chris Carr attorney general
Geoff Duncan lieutenant governor
John Porter Duncan's chief of staff
Collins Udkeigbo Duncan aide
Vince Mooney supervisor, Dignitary Protection Unit, Georgia State Patrol

Georgia General Assembly

David Ralston Speaker of the House
William Ligon senator
Burt Jones senator and later lieutenant governor
Elena Parent senator
Bill Heath senator

Members of Congress

David Perdue US senator, 2015–2021
Kelly Loeffler US senator, 2020–2021
Johnny Isakson US senator, 2005–2019
Doug Collins House member, 2013–2021
Marjorie Taylor Greene House member, 2021–
Raphael Warnock US senator, 2021–
Jon Ossoff US senator, 2021–

Republican Party

Donald Trump Jr. son of the president
Kimberly Guilfoyle Donald Trump Jr.'s girlfriend
Mark Rountree consultant
Sonny Perdue secretary of agriculture and former governor
Nick Ayers strategist
Joan Carr Isakson's chief of staff
Heath Garrett Isakson's former chief of staff
Corey Lewandowski strategist
Dave Bossie Citizens United

Fulton County Election Office

Rick Barron director

Ralph Jones chief of registration

Wandrea "Shaye" Moss election worker

Ruby Freeman election worker

Trump Election Lawyers

Rudy Giuliani New York

John Eastman Chapman University School of Law

Justin Clark Trump campaign

Robert Cheeley Georgia

Jenna Ellis Georgia

Ray Smith Georgia

Preston Haliburton Georgia

Katherine Friess Washington, DC

Jacki Pick Texas

Cleta Mitchell Georgia

Boris Epshteyn Washington, DC

Trump Defense Lawyers

Dwight Thomas

Drew Findling

Jennifer Little

Steve Sadow

At Tomotley Plantation

Lin Wood defense lawyer and owner of Tomotley

Sidney Powell outside lawyer

Michael Flynn former national security adviser

Patrick Byrne financier

Dave Hancock chief of security

Leamsy Salazar Venezuelan whistleblower (via videotape)

Gary Berntsen former CIA operative

Ryan Dark White QAnon promoter

Ron Watkins administrator of QAnon platform (via Zoom)

Doug Logan Cyber Ninjas CEO

Jim Penrose former National Security Agency official

Andrew Whitney pharmaceutical executive

Westin Arlington Gateway Hotel

Michael Trimarco businessman

Russell Ramsland Jr. Allied Security Operations Group

Phil Waldron retired army colonel

Patrick Byrne financier

Sam and **Gina Faddis** former CIA officers

Chris Smith lawyer

Howard Kleinhendler lawyer

Justice Department

Merrick Garland attorney general

Jack Smith special counsel

William Barr attorney general, 2018–2020

Jeffrey Rosen acting attorney general, 2020–2021

Richard Donoghue deputy attorney general

Jeff Clark acting assistant attorney, civil division

BJay Pak US attorney, Northern District of Georgia

Defense Department

Chris Miller acting secretary

Kash Patel chief of staff

Ezra Cohen assistant secretary, special operations

Lieutenant General Scott Berrier director, Defense Intelligence
Agency

January 6 Committee

Representative Bennie Thompson chairman

Representative Liz Cheney vice chairman

Timothy Heaphy chief counsel

MAGA Extremists

Chester Doles former Klansman

Nicholas Fuentes white nationalist

Ali Alexander Stop the Steal organizer

Enrique Tarrio Proud Boys

Stewart Rhodes Oath Keepers

Alex Jones Infowars

Cleveland Meredith QAnon follower

Journalists

Greg Bluestein *The Atlanta Journal-Constitution*

George Chidi independent journalist

Amy Gardner *Washington Post*

Sharon Reed *The Atlanta Voice*

Robert Preston Jr. *Douglas Now*

Dominion Voting Systems

John Poulos CEO

Nicole Nollette senior executive

Eric Coomer director for product development and security

The Fake Elector Scheme

Kenneth Chesebro lawyer and strategist

Mike Roman Trump campaign organizer

David Shafer chairman, Georgia Republican Party

Robert Sinners Trump campaign operative

The Phone Call to Raffensperger

Donald Trump president

Mark Meadows chief of staff

Kurt Hilbert Trump lawyer

Alex Kaufman Trump lawyer

Cleta Mitchell Trump lawyer

Brad Raffensperger Georgia secretary of state

Ryan Germany Raffensperger lawyer

Jordan Fuchs Raffensperger chief of staff

The Coffee County Breach

Cathy Latham chair, Coffee County Republican Party

Misty Hampton supervisor, Coffee County Elections and Registration Office

Eric Chaney member, Coffee County Election Board

Scott Hall bail bondsman

Alex Cruce data analyst, sidekick to Scott Hall

Paul Maggio president of Sullivan/Strickler, an Atlanta-based cyber forensics firm

Jennifer Jackson Sullivan/Strickler

Ed Voyles former member, Coffee County Election Board

At Ruby Freeman's House

Steven Lee pastor

Trevian Kutti publicist for Kanye West

Harrison William Floyd director, Black Voices for Trump

Garrison Douglas Black Voices for Trump

The Special Grand Jury

Emily Kohrs foreperson

At the Fulton County Jail

Pat Labat sheriff

Charles Shaw bail bondsman

The Body Double

"They mentioned my kids by name..."

The digitally altered voice was creepy. But it was the words that were the most chilling.

It was mid-August 2023 and Fani Willis was riding in a black SUV with Nathan Wade, the special counsel in charge of her office's investigation into Donald Trump. The two of them, with an armed driver, were on their way to a secret meeting with a potential witness. These were tense days for the fifty-one-year-old Fulton County district attorney. She and her team were in the final stages of assembling their massive racketeering case against the former president and eighteen other co-conspirators for allegedly attempting to subvert the legitimate results of the 2020 presidential election in Georgia. Trump had been riling up his supporters at raucous rallies and on social media, calling Willis a "radical," a "Marxist," a "racist," and even claiming, without a scrap of evidence, she'd had an affair with a gang leader she had once represented as a defense lawyer. All of Trump's claims were patently absurd, especially to anyone with even a passing familiarity with Willis and her record as a hard-nosed prosecutor.

Yet the taunts and the threats against the DA had been building for months, many of them rising out of the Trump investigation but some from other big cases she had brought to crack down on the gang violence that was wreaking havoc on inner-city Atlanta. At one point, she and her eighty-year-old father had been forced to move out of her house into an apartment building protected by security guards; Willis and her senior staff were assigned bulletproof Kevlar flak jackets to wear if things got really hairy. As the indictment of the former president approached, the volume and velocity of the hateful messages aimed at Willis were increasing dramatically, and the threats themselves were taking a much darker turn—more graphic, more specific.

So when Willis's cell phone rang, displaying a blocked number, she answered the call on speaker, so everyone could hear.

You know we know your address, the deep and gravelly, computer-disguised voice said. *We're going to rape you. We're going to hang you. We're going to kill you,* the caller continued, spitting out the word *n***er* for good measure. The caller hung up. Then he called back—and what really rattled Willis this time was not the racial epithet. The caller started talking about Willis's two daughters. He pronounced their names correctly and indicated he knew where they lived. For a brief moment, the unflappable DA—with nerves of steel—was unnerved. Personal attacks didn't faze her. "But they mentioned my kids by name..."

It was a terrifying sign of the times—a publicly elected local prosecutor facing threats of violence for doing her job. But for Willis, the digital message—and others like it—only made her more determined to pursue the course she had chosen. The criminal charges she would soon announce would be the most comprehensive accounting yet of Trump's post-election conspiracy, a sprawling ninety-seven-page "speaking indictment" under the state's expansive Racketeer Influenced and Corrupt Organizations (RICO) law alleging 161 acts by the former president and his confederates aimed at pressuring and intimidating state and local officials to alter vote totals. The investigation was touched off by Trump's brazen phone call to Georgia secretary of state Brad Raffensperger, telling him to "find 11,780 votes," one more than he needed to win in the state. But the call was only one part of a relentless campaign marked by blatant and documentable falsehoods, wild conspiracy theories, a computer break-in at a local election office, and an outlandish effort to anoint fake Trump electors to prevent the rightful winner of the election, Joe Biden, from assuming the presidency. While Trump's efforts were nationwide in scope, there was a compelling logic behind Willis's case: It was anchored in Georgia, a state that straddled the fault lines of American politics, and where the former president's actions were most concentrated and most furious—ground zero for what was arguably the most anti-democratic plot in American history.

But as dangerous as all of it was, the most appalling consequence of Trump's war in Georgia was the number of innocent people victimized by his reckless conspiracy-mongering. There was an eerie parallel between the ugly threats Willis was herself now receiving and the conduct she had been methodically investigating. In the aftermath of the 2020 vote, election officials at every level in Georgia had been subjected to brutal abuse, doxxed on social media, and bombarded with frighteningly specific death threats and sickening racial attacks.

And it wasn't just public servants who were in the line of fire; many of their children and parents, siblings, spouses, and colleagues were also targeted with impunity. There was Ruby Freeman, the sixty-three-year-old grandmother and poll worker who was forced into hiding because of the onslaught of violent threats she received for weeks after the election. "Do you know how it feels to have the president of the United States target you?" she asked in some of the most poignant testimony presented by the House Select Committee on the January 6 Attack. Her daughter, Wandrea "Shaye" Moss, an election official in Fulton County, radically changed her appearance to elude the mob. Raffensperger's wife, Tricia, was taunted with threats of unspeakable sexual violence. One low-level tech worker for Dominion Voting Systems, the company that supplied the state's voting machines, was so wantonly terrorized by Trump supporters that to this day he is still coping with the debilitating symptoms of post-traumatic stress disorder.

If, as the January 6 committee concluded, Trump's post-election conduct in 2020 posed an ominous threat to American constitutional government, it is also true that it met unshakable resistance from many elected officeholders from his own party, and nowhere more so than in Georgia. Raffensperger, the state's top election official and a loyal conservative Republican, had been the point person in standing up to Trump, rejecting demands from the president and his allies at every stage and never wavering despite unimaginable pressure. Chris Carr, Georgia's Republican attorney general and a former chief of staff to the state's late and much revered senator Johnny Isakson, vowed to resign before he would defend Trump's attempt to convene a special session of the state legislature to reverse the election results. Just as forceful was the state's GOP governor, Brian Kemp, who repeatedly incurred the president's wrath. "Well then, fuck 'em," Kemp said, refusing to join a Trump-backed appeal to the Supreme Court contesting the election results. In the end, Trump's efforts in Georgia failed because of an iron wall forged by the state's top Republican officeholders, their deputies, and their lawyers.

But there was undoubtedly some sort of cosmic justice in the fact that, in a state where for more than a century Black people had been denied the right to vote and suffered rigid Jim Crow segregation, it fell to a determined Black local DA to find accountability for what Trump had tried to do. Willis would still have to prove her case in court, of course, and there would likely be hurdles and multiple evidentiary challenges—just as there would also be for Jack Smith, the Justice Department special counsel who brought two other indictments against the former president, one for obstructing an investigation into the classified documents he took with him from the White House and another, much narrower case—with Trump the sole defendant—over his efforts to overturn the election on a national level. But if the Georgia case succeeds, it will be forever noted in the history books that it was Willis, a daughter of the civil rights movement, who brought Donald Trump to justice.

And perhaps that is how it should be. Instead of the taciturn Smith, a product of the buttoned-up, austere Justice Department culture, the diminutive Fulton County DA is an elected official who is earthy, often combative, sometimes controversial, and never afraid to say what's on her mind even when it offends her political allies. Donald Trump's slogan from the start was Make America Great Again. Fani Willis is a uniquely American character rooted in a community whose spirit, history, and culture he knew nothing about. Both her fans and her critics describe her as a force of nature. And as the ensuing pages will show, that is for good reason.

———

At a little before midnight on August 14, 2023, Willis stepped up to a podium at the Fulton County Government Center to unveil her charges against Trump. "Today…a Fulton County grand jury returned a true bill of indictment charging nineteen individuals with violations of Georgia law arising from a criminal conspiracy to overturn the results of the 2020 election," she said, proceeding to read off the list of nineteen defendants, clearly enunciating each of their full names—"Donald John Trump, Rudolph William Louis Giuliani, John Charles Eastman, Mark Randall Meadows," and on and on.

The throng of reporters assembled in the room dutifully recorded the historic announcement. Yet none of them would have any inkling of the dramatic scene that was about to unfold. After the press conference, Willis and her team were taken to a holding room to wait. A new piece of intelligence had been discovered on a MAGA website: *The best time to shoot her is when she's leaving the building.* The idea that assassins might be lurking outside the courthouse prompted her security team to take unusual precautions. After she finished her press conference, Willis stepped into a back office and changed out of her black business suit and into a T-shirt and sweats. A female investigator on Willis's staff, with a similarly petite frame as the DA and wearing a wig to match her hair, put on an outfit that matched what Willis had worn standing at the podium moments before. The woman was a body double, and soon she and a number of others posing as her deputies emerged from the underground garage and were driven off in a convoy of SUVs. Willis and her team, dressed as civilians, slipped out the back of the building and were whisked away to a secure hotel where for the next few days they would stay under heavy guard, waiting out the storm that was to come.

BOOK ONE

The Making of a DA

CHAPTER ONE

Badass

"I did not choose for Donald Trump to be on my plate."

What Fani Willis most remembers is what a freaking mess the place was.

It was Saturday, January 2, 2021, and Willis—wearing sweatpants and a baseball cap—showed up to inspect the cramped warren of offices in downtown Atlanta she was about to inherit in two days as the newly elected district attorney of Fulton County. Willis was appalled. She and a handful of top aides found boxes of never-closed case files—stuffed with witness statements, police reports, and prosecutors' memos—strewn all over the floors and stacked eight feet high in the doorways; one case file was randomly discovered under a fourth-floor coffee table. Then there were the piled-up boxes of personal protective equipment—ordered by her predecessor, Paul Howard, for his staff but never opened because the office had essentially been unoccupied, except for a skeleton crew, during the Covid pandemic. One local wag compared the office to *"a scene out of Raiders of the Lost Ark,"* as if Willis and her team had wandered into some long-abandoned archaeological tomb. "You couldn't even open the door" from the hallway, Willis would later recall. What leapt out most of all, she said, was "how trashed the place was."

There was something else about the shambolic condition of the office that stood out. The walls had been stripped of all their photographs—except for one rather conspicuous one. It was a shot of a beaming Willis being handed a certification of promotion by Howard, her former boss. Willis had just crushed Howard in an extraordinarily bitter campaign for DA that had been fought out against the backdrop of the national racial reckoning spurred by the murder of George Floyd in Minneapolis. There was a pointed message in that photograph that nobody missed. Howard had been Willis's mentor; she was his top deputy and protégée. Howard had promoted her, given her raises, lavished praise upon her, and assigned her the office's most challenging cases. For Howard and his allies, Willis's decision to challenge him for DA was a profound betrayal of trust. For Willis, it was simply duty calling—with no small dose of raw ambition.

Willis would retire that night to a Hooters where she had wings and her favorite drink, a lemon-drop martini with Grey Goose vodka. The next day, a Sunday, as she was preparing her outfit for her first official day as DA, the news started to break about an unusual phone call that the president of the United States, Donald Trump—who was due to leave office in just over two weeks—had made the previous afternoon to Georgia secretary of state Brad Raffensperger, imploring him to "find" just enough votes to flip Georgia's electoral votes from Biden to him. The call, she learned, had been taped, and the president's words, seeming to threaten that Raffensperger could face criminal prosecution if he did not do Trump's bidding, were being played nonstop on cable TV. There are laws on the books in Georgia against soliciting a public official to commit fraud, including election fraud. Was that what Trump had just done?

While the cable pundits dissected Trump's words and the potential implications of what he was telling the state's top election official to do, Willis began focusing on a narrower issue that only a veteran prosecutor was likely to zero in on: Where exactly was Raffensperger when he took the president's phone call? When she showed up for work on Monday, "I just remember sitting down and looking at the TV and thinking" maybe he was in Fulton County, she recalled. Her county.

Fulton County—named for Robert Fulton, the early-nineteenth-century inventor of the steamboat—is an elongated seventy-mile stretch of Northwest Georgia that includes almost all of the city of Atlanta as well as some of its surrounding suburbs, a few of them quite affluent. In fact, as he talked to the president on the phone, Raffensperger had been sitting at a kitchen table at his home on a wooded five-acre estate in Johns Creek, just a few miles inside the county's northeast border. The significance of this—even the potential enormity—was instantly apparent to Willis. "Johns Creek is one of *my* fifteen cities," she recalled thinking. A crime, or at least a potential crime, had been committed in her county.

Willis had been elected on a pledge she would restore professionalism to an office that had been engulfed in controversies and plagued by what she portrayed as colossal mismanagement under her predecessor. Most pressing, she had promised to take aggressive actions to address a staggering backlog of eleven thousand unindicted crimes, including hundreds of homicides, assaults, shootings, and sexual assaults. In sharp contrast with the wave of progressive prosecutors being elected in other big cities, Willis had forcefully pledged to crack down on an alarming rise in violent crime during the pandemic that had culminated the previous summer with the horrifying murder of an eight-year-girl gunned down by a purported Black Lives Matter protestor wielding an assault rifle. Street gangs, drugs, guns, homicides—prosecuting such crimes was the core day-to-day duty of any big-city DA, and Willis had her hands full. But once she learned Raffensperger's whereabouts, Willis immediately realized she would have to add another monumental case to her already overcrowded list of priorities: a criminal investigation of Donald Trump. "I did not choose this. I did not choose for Donald Trump to be on my plate," she would say much later. It was, she added, one more "cross to bear."

Or, as she put it, somewhat more pungently, to one of her top aides at the time: "This job is a shit magnet."

Local prosecutors are typically elected by voters. Like all law enforcement officials, they swear allegiance to the law and are duty-bound to follow judicial rules of procedure and their professional ethical code. But within those boundaries, elected DAs also reflect the will of the people and often public passions. For Black people in Georgia, the cradle of the civil rights movement, no right was more cherished or freighted with powerful emotions than the right to vote, won in a generational fight marked by state violence and searing humiliation. When Fani Willis was asked why she decided to take on the investigation of Trump's efforts to overturn the election results in Georgia, she cast her response in the context of that struggle. If Trump had been successful in his pressure tactics, she said, then millions of Georgians, Black and white, would have been disenfranchised, their votes for Biden discarded so Trump could claim victory. This was, she argued, at its core, a voting rights case.

Such framing may have been shrewd prosecutorial spin, a winning argument that she and her deputies could one day make to a Fulton County jury. But for Willis, access to the ballot was also deeply personal. She had learned as a child that the fight to win and keep that right had come at great cost. "When I was a little bitty girl, I would be dragged to the polls," she recalled, adding that her grandmother instilled in her a reverence for voting. "I understand how important the right is, so I understand how important the infraction on someone's right to vote is."

She didn't have to look far to find a role model. Her father, John C. Floyd III, a onetime radical activist from South Central Los Angeles who later would become a criminal defense and civil rights lawyer, had traveled through the South during the early 1960s, organizing and marching for voting rights. Often starting his trips in Atlanta, known then as the Black Mecca, he crossed paths with many of the most important civil rights leaders of the time, including Martin Luther King Jr., Hosea Williams, and Jesse Jackson. But his personal fury at the treatment of Black Americans and his evolving skepticism about whether the tactics of nonviolence would work took Floyd in a different direction. He drifted away from the lions of the civil rights movement into the arms of militants like Stokely Carmichael and H. Rap Brown and to a life that skirted the edges of the law.

To understand how Willis became the kind of law-and-order DA who would unflinchingly take on Donald Trump, you have to understand John Floyd's political odyssey. And in doing so you get a glimpse into his daughter's pugnacious personality and her deep-seated loathing of bullies.

"I was raised in the movement," Willis likes to say. It was an allusion to her father's civil rights bona fides, but also to his days as a gun-toting Black Panther.

John Clifford Floyd III grew up in post–World War II America in an impoverished home in South Central Los Angeles, where he'd often go to sleep hungry. "I was raised in the streets," he said in an interview for this book, explaining his grit and hardened survival skills. He lived in a house with sixteen relatives, a toilet on the back porch, and chickens in the yard. When he was six years old, his dad came home from the service and wreaked havoc in their home. An intelligent man but with few opportunities as a Black vet in the Los Angeles of the late 1940s (he eventually settled for a job as a busboy), he took his anger out on his wife and son. "My dad was a drunk and a mean son of a bitch," Floyd recalled. Looking back, he said that this was when he began resenting people who abused their authority. "I didn't like being put down," he said. Floyd started hanging out in the streets of South Central to avoid his father's beatings. An errand boy for hoodlums with names like Mile Away, because of his penchant for being far away when the police showed up, Floyd was reared by the gangs and by a shoeshine man named Pops. He started carrying a gun when he was twelve.

One break in his otherwise hardscrabble childhood was attending Catholic schools in South Central. A nun who noticed Floyd's above-average potential told him that "God had given him a gift," and that he was to use it to "help his people." He would go on to East Los Angeles College where he got his first taste of revolutionary politics, reading the writings of Mao Tse-tung and Karl Marx, while also developing a lifelong love for Ernest Hemingway. While in college he volunteered for the campaign of John F. Kennedy and then in 1962 traveled by bus with fellow activists to Mississippi to register Black voters. Floyd was shocked by the overtly cruel racism of the Jim Crow South. He'd never seen WHITES ONLY signs before, and it infuriated him. "That made me fucking crazy," he recalled. Once when he and a fellow civil rights worker were walking down a sidewalk in Jackson, Mississippi, a white man approached them from the opposite direction. Floyd's companion stepped into the street to make room. Floyd saw it as an appalling act of deference to white people, a pathetic acquiescence to the prevailing racial order. The episode was an early step on his path to radicalization.

A key turning point for Floyd came in 1965 in Memphis, Tennessee, when he took part in a sit-in at a segregated lunch counter. A sneering white man walked up to Floyd and spit tobacco juice on the top of his head. He vividly remembered the humiliation and rage he felt as the sticky liquid dripped down the side of his face. "I could feel myself getting so fucking angry," he'd recall years later. "I said 'fuck this, fuck nonviolence.'" Abandoning King's principles of nonviolent resistance, Floyd decided on a more confrontational stance. "I couldn't figure out why Black folks hadn't picked up guns and risen up."

A week after Floyd returned to Los Angeles, the Watts riots broke out. "I was there," he recalled. "I saw the fires." Whatever slight hope he may have still had for political reform from within the system was consumed by those flames of rebellion. As Floyd saw it, it was the brutality of the Los Angeles Police Department (LAPD) that provoked the riots. "We considered the LAPD to be the enemy," he said in a 2019 oral history of the Black Power movement conducted by the Tom & Ethel Bradley Center at California State University. "We just saw them as an occupying army." In February 1967, Floyd co-founded the Black Panther Political Party of Los Angeles—similar in ideology but fiercely separate from the Black Panther Party for Self-Defense that had been formed the year before in Oakland by Bobby Seale and Huey Newton. Floyd announced the new party at an event marking the second anniversary of the assassination of Malcolm X. "Malcom X is going to be our patron saint," the *Los Angeles Times* quoted him as saying to the crowd of about 250. "Our political philosophy is black nationalism."

Floyd also forged ties with a charismatic young firebrand who served with him on the new party's central committee, Angela Davis. As Floyd related it, his relationship with Davis became more than political. "I was dating Angela Davis and she and I were actually living together at the time," he recalled in the Bradley Center oral history. Davis, now eighty and a professor emeritus at the University of California in Santa Cruz, confirms this. "He is right," she wrote in an email to the authors. "We were seeing each other and did live together for a short time. If I recall correctly, our relationship lasted six or seven months—but maybe longer." Noting that "during those days, the political outweighed the personal," she added: "John was a compelling speaker and had developed a strategy for Black Liberation that emphasized politics as a realm [of] struggle."

Floyd's personal relationship with Davis was several years before she was placed on the FBI's Most Wanted list for her role in purchasing the firearms used in a courtroom break-out that killed a Marin County, California, judge. Her case became an international cause celebre and, after her capture, Davis was acquitted of conspiracy to commit murder and other charges; she later ran twice for vice president on the Communist Party ticket. Willis told the authors that, while she was aware of her father's friendship with Davis, she didn't know they had cohabitated. "My dad and his girlfriends," she said with a laugh. "You see I didn't fall out in shock here."

In the spring of 1968, Floyd and some of his fellow Panthers drove across the country to New Orleans where H. Rap Brown, the radical organization's "Minister of Justice," was on trial on weapons charges. Their mission was to provide security for Brown as he made his way to and from the courthouse each day. On the third day of the trial, Floyd and other members of the security detail were following behind in their own car as Brown was being driven to court. All of a sudden, as Floyd remembered it, about eight or nine police cars converged on Floyd's vehicle from all directions. Floyd and his fellow Panthers were ordered out of the car by the white cops and told to place their hands on the car. Then, according to Floyd, one of the officers pointed a twelve-gauge shotgun at them and said, "I'm gonna kill all five of you n***ers now and say it was an accident." Cooler heads among the lawmen prevailed and, in the end, Floyd and his comrades were carted off to the local jail where they were held on trumped-up charges of failure to pay a motel bill and possession of "marijuana greens."

Imprisoned for two months, they were released after Floyd's mother managed to hire the nephew of the judge in the case as their lawyer. The experience was traumatizing for Floyd, but he walked out channeling his anger into determination. He vowed to become a lawyer after that to protect the rights of the unjustly accused. Later that year, while still a member of the Black Panthers, he enrolled at UCLA to study law. Radical politics continued to roil the campus. Just a few months after he arrived, two Panthers, Bunchy Carter and John Huggins, were shot and killed in an altercation at a Black Student Union meeting, apparent victims of internecine strife within the Black nationalist movement. (In 1975, the Church Committee revealed that the FBI, through its COINTELPRO program, had infiltrated the campus with the explicit intention of sowing division and inciting violence among the groups.) After the shootings, Floyd put his weapons down for good.

Floyd was settling down in more ways than one. He got married in 1970. And the following year his wife gave birth to Fani, whose name came from a beloved aunt named Fanny, but was also derived from the Swahili word for "prosperous," a nod to his Black nationalist politics. Over time, Floyd drifted back into mainstream politics. He worked as a deputy press secretary for Los Angeles's first Black mayor, Tom Bradley, and he'd eventually run for state assembly, a losing effort hobbled by the fact that people didn't want to give money to an ex–Black Panther.

In 1976, Floyd landed a job in Washington, DC, as an administrative law judge with the Legal Services Corporation. Fani and her mother joined him a year later, but it was a short-lived reunion. The marriage fell apart, and Fani moved in permanently with her dad when she was in fourth grade. As a single father, Floyd had to give up his job as a Legal Services judge because it required too much travel. So he hung out a shingle and started taking court-appointed cases at DC Superior Court. On Saturdays, Floyd would bring Fani to the courthouse, where he'd pick criminal cases from the previous night's arrests. For young Fani, the close-up look at the gritty, colorful world of a big-city courthouse made an impression. Sometimes she helped organize her father's case files, which often included gruesome crime-scene photographs. (She would sometimes jokingly refer to her time organizing her father's grisly case files as "child abuse.") Other times she'd accompany him to Saturday arraignments. On one occasion, Floyd left her behind with DC Superior Court judge Joseph Hannon, a gruff but kindly Irish American jurist, while he interviewed potential clients in the cellblock. When he returned to the courtroom, he saw Fani, dressed in jeans and a T-shirt, elbows propped up on the bench, conversing with Judge Hannon. Later, Floyd asked Fani what they were talking about. She told him the judge was asking what he should do with each defendant appearing before him, let them go or "step 'em back," courthouse vernacular for locking people up. "Daddy, I know what I want to be when I grow up—a judge," Fani told Floyd. "Well, fine," her father responded. "But first you have to be a lawyer."

Floyd was a fierce advocate for his daughter. When one of her elementary school teachers insisted to Fani that her name was pronounced *FAN-nee*, Floyd drove right over to school to "set her straight on how to pronounce it." (It's *FAH-nee*, he said, not Fanny.) When the dean of the Catholic girls high school she later attended, a white man, told her she was "too smart" to attend Howard University, the elite HBCU (historically Black colleges and universities) in Washington, DC, and that she should go to the University of Maryland instead, Floyd gave him a tongue lashing that made Fani feel sorry for the man. Fani inherited her dad's combativeness. "I was always that girl with that mouth," she said.

In the end, Willis went to Howard because of its excellent academics, but also because she didn't want to attend a predominantly white institution, or "PWI" as she called them. She majored in political science and government. It was while studying there that Willis first visited Atlanta. She joined the throngs of HBCU students for Freaknik, the lively street party immortalized in Tom Wolfe's *A Man in Full*, his satirical novel of race, class, and finance in the boomtown Atlanta of the early 1990s. "It was so much fun," Willis recalled, noting that it was before the event got rough and rowdy, attracted criminal elements, and was eventually shut down by the city.

But her youth and college years in the nation's capital—which overlapped with the height of the crack epidemic—also instilled in her an appreciation for the havoc violent crime was visiting on Black communities. "I grew up in DC when it was the murder capital of the world," she said in a revealing 2023 podcast interview with iHeart-Radio. "I spent my high school going to funerals . . . And I carry some of that pain with me as a fifty-year-old woman. I still carry it because those people are not with me anymore."

When she graduated from Howard in 1993, she returned to Atlanta to attend Emory Law School. It was at Emory that she found her calling. Rebecca Christian Smith, a law school classmate from the Virgin Islands who became one of her close friends, recalled Willis's raw "male energy" and her brash refusal to take guff from anybody. "If you think you're going to mansplain anything to Fani, you better think twice," Smith said. "She was a force to be reckoned with," added Felicia Stewart, another law school friend. "She was very confident" and when taking on a task became fiercely determined and monomaniacally focused. When Willis was preparing for a moot court contest, she would cram in the library "until they locked the doors" and would assemble colleagues in sounding board sessions to test her arguments. "She wasn't playing around," said Stewart. "She didn't want to lose. It wasn't an option." With her relentless work ethic and a clear relish for courtroom combat, Willis emerged as a star in her law school class, winning the prestigious Frederick Douglass National Moot Court championship sponsored by the Black Law Students Association. It was for her arguments, appropriately enough, in a civil rights case—testing the limits of a section of the federal code, 42 USC 1983, that allows citizens to sue state and local officials who, acting under "the color of law," violate their constitutional rights.

Between her second and third year in law school, Willis drove across the country to Los Angeles for an internship. On the way she stopped in Oklahoma City. It was the end of April 1995, just a few days after

Tim McVeigh, the domestic terrorist and white supremacist, had blown up the Alfred P. Murrah Federal Building there, killing 168 people, including 19 children. When Willis arrived, smoke was still rising from the rubble of the collapsed building. A makeshift memorial of teddy bears, flowers, and pictures of the victims lined the chain-link fence authorities had placed around the crime scene. "It was horrible, horrible," Willis recalled. "To see the devastation of that building. You understood it was just death all around."

In a quirk of fate, at that very same time another person who years later would loom large in the investigations of Donald Trump was at the site of the Oklahoma City bombing, but not just as a tourist or a concerned American. Merrick Garland, then an intense forty-two-year-old top aide to the US deputy attorney general, had taken command of the Justice Department's investigation of the attack. At the time, it was the largest FBI investigation in American history, and Garland led agents and prosecutors through a near-flawless probe and prosecution that ended in the conviction and eventual execution of McVeigh. His conduct of the investigation would catapult Garland's career to a seat on the federal appeals court in Washington, a nomination to the US Supreme Court that went down in flames (after being blocked by Republicans who wouldn't give him a hearing), and, eventually, the top job in Joe Biden's Justice Department, where he had to make perhaps the most consequential decision of any attorney general in US history: whether to charge a former president with a crime.

Not long after law school, Willis got married to Fred Willis, whom Christian Smith recalled as an older "laid-back" dude with a young son who, having once been a ski instructor in Colorado, had moved to Georgia where he got a job as a videographer for the Federal Reserve Bank in Atlanta. It was clear to her and others that the young couple were on different career trajectories; the marriage lasted seven years, leaving Fani a single mother with two young daughters, six and four years old at the time. If Fred Willis did not seem especially ambitious, Fani was driven, and by this point was seriously thinking about becoming a prosecutor. Ironically, it was her father, the ex-radical and criminal defense lawyer, who was encouraging her. He argued that it would be the most direct path to achieving her childhood dream of becoming a judge. Willis had her heart set on a job at the Los Angeles DA's office after graduation. But that was right after the losing verdict in the OJ Simpson case and the office, still in disarray, was not hiring. So thanks to yet another quirk of fate—OJ's acquittal for the charge of murdering his wife and her companion, Ronald Goldman—Willis ended up with an internship at a small Beverly Hills firm that specialized in divorces, a firm by the name of Shmuckler and Associates. It was an unusual start to an ambitious legal career, to say the least.

In one sense, the internship was a blessing in disguise. Howard R. Shmuckler, the named partner, let Willis argue some of his cases in court. Willis remembered her days with Shmuckler—a kindly "older Jewish man"—fondly. "It was such an amazing experience he gave me," she said. "He would send me to court to argue things," even though, given that she hadn't even passed the bar, much less gotten her law license, she remembered thinking, "I'm not sure I should be doing this." Willis also got to spend quality time listening to Shmuckler's aggrieved high-end clients recounting the most intimate details of their marital failures and sex lives—startling new experiences for the twenty-three-year-old intern.

Willis lost touch with Shmuckler after she left, which turned out to be for the better: His relatively minor ethical transgression in letting Willis argue his cases in court only foreshadowed more serious ones, leading to his disbarment after a conviction for bankruptcy fraud. He later decamped to the Washington, DC, suburbs where—in the aftermath of the 2008 financial crisis—he was charged by federal prosecutors with running a fraudulent mortgage "rescue" company called The Shmuckler Group that scammed hundreds of clients by making bogus claims that he could lower their monthly payments. Prosecutors called him a "cunning and litigious criminal" who had shown "a blatant and repeated disregard for the law." He was convicted and sentenced to seven years in prison.

Shmuckler's legal troubles notwithstanding, Willis's time with him in Beverly Hills representing his clients made her determined to be a courtroom lawyer. After graduating from law school in 1996, she joined the small Atlanta firm of Alvin Kendall, a soft-spoken, bow-tie-wearing civil rights and personal injury lawyer who served as a mentor for a string of young Black lawyers in the city. "The big firms didn't take us back then," he explained, other than the fortunate few Black graduates of Harvard Law and other elite institutions who would be gobbled up each year by white-shoe firms like Alston & Bird. Willis was rough around the edges and somewhat disheveled in attire, Kendall remembered, even joking, "I could tell she was raised by a man." Still, he said, hiring her was a "no-brainer." Kendall also had gone to Howard and Emory Law, so that helped right off the bat. He gave her a job for $1,500 a week (plus a two-thirds cut of any case she brought in the door) and placed her in a small corner office across from another one of his mentees: the more elegantly dressed and impeccably polished Keisha Lance Bottoms, a future mayor of Atlanta and later a senior domestic policy adviser to President Biden.

Willis didn't stay long at the Kendall law firm; her most memorable case was representing an accused crack dealer who turned out to be the male stripper at her bachelorette party. And like her experience with Howard Shmuckler, her time at the Kendall law firm would not end up being the ideal résumé enhancer she might have hoped for.

Barely a year after Willis left, Kendall would be charged with a felony and get disbarred—for allegedly tipping off a drug-dealing client to an impending DEA raid. Kendall spent three years in federal prison (where, he boasts, he was an active "jailhouse lawyer" before his release and the eventual reinstatement of his law license). In due time, he would play an even more important role in Willis's life—providing her with crucial intelligence that would inform her decision to run for DA and put her on a course to investigate a former president.

After her brief time with Kendall, Willis opened up her own practice, which coincided with the birth of her two daughters. With a growing family, Willis needed a more reliable income, so she took a job in the Atlanta Solicitor's Office, which prosecutes the city's misdemeanors and other minor offenses. But the job allowed her to hone her impressive courtroom skills, preparing her for the Fulton County DA's Office, which Willis would take by storm less than two years later, in 2002, under the stern tutelage of the boss, Paul Howard. Willis was now in a new highly charged prosecutorial arena—one in which she would adopt her losing-is-not-an-option credo amid an office culture that rewarded aggressive crime fighting. It was an arena in which Willis thrived for years, but over time would sorely test her civil rights movement credentials, most conspicuously in a case that would divide Atlanta along racial lines.

———

Originally elected Fulton County District Attorney in 1996, Paul Howard was a historic figure—and a clear symbol of the political gains made by Georgia's Black citizens since the days, when, during the height of the civil rights movement in the 1960s, the state had elected Lester Maddox, a pickax-wielding arch segregationist, as governor. Howard was the first African American ever elected as a district attorney in Georgia, and he would go on to oversee the biggest and by far the most significant prosecutorial office in the state for nearly a quarter century. A proud, dour, and somewhat rigid leader (everybody in the office was instructed to call him Mr. Howard), the new DA had from the start built a reputation as a tough law-and-order man who was fully prepared to prosecute, and incarcerate, anyone and everyone who violated the law, regardless of their race or age. Just a few weeks after taking office, he indicted a thirteen-year-old Black youth, known in his neighborhood as Little B, for murder, charging him as an adult, and upon conviction sent him to prison for life. (The charges relied principally on the testimony of a local drug dealer who had initially been a suspect.) It sent a powerful message, especially to Atlanta's conservative business and political elites. Like many across the country at the time, the city's civic leaders were alarmed about rising crime rates and taken by the idea that a new breed of "super predators"—as Little B was portrayed in the press—was fueling the violence and inflicting havoc on inner-city life.

Little B was the first of many headline-grabbing cases under Howard—indictments and trials that could have provided rich material for any number of *Law and Order* episodes. (Among Howard's deputies in the early days of his tenure was a petite firebrand named Nancy Grace, who would later go on to fame pounding the table as a lock-'em-up cable TV commentator.) Howard's cases were legendary in Atlanta legal circles: Claude "Tex" McIver, a wealthy Buckhead lawyer, who shot and killed his wife from the back seat of an SUV (his initial defense, straight out of another Tom Wolfe novel, was that he had pulled the trigger accidentally because he had panicked while driving by a Black Lives Matter protest); Brian Nichols, a deranged prisoner facing rape and assault charges who escaped custody and murdered the judge presiding over his trial; Ray Lewis, the star Baltimore Ravens linebacker who was charged with a double murder that occurred during an evening of wild Super Bowl partying. Not all of Howard's cases were successful; Lewis pled to a misdemeanor and dimed out two members of his entourage who were later acquitted. But Howard was by then a fixture in Atlanta, and he would be reelected time and again, usually with little more than token opposition.

And Fani Willis, who had joined the office as an assistant prosecutor, was by his side every step of the way. She was an unusually gifted courtroom performer who wowed juries with passionate, sometimes thunderous oratory, adroitly mixed with folksy metaphors and sly courtroom tricks that were a trademark of the office's top litigators. Attempting to prove that murder suspects in one of her cases had tried to wash away blood evidence before police arrived, Willis plopped a smelly bucket of bleach on the prosecution table and wiped her hands with it—a symbol, she argued, of how the defendant tried to cover up his crime. When trying a man accused of sexually assaulting and murdering a prostitute, she brought a mannequin into the courtroom and, needling the defendant, provoked him to attack the inanimate body, essentially reenacting the crime in front of the judge and jury.

She could also be ruthless in the courtroom. Prosecuting a seventy-nine-year-old grandmother who shot her eighty-five-year-old ex-boyfriend in a lovers' quarrel at a senior living home, she tore into the defendant, ridiculing defense claims that she was a confused "sweet, old feeble lady." In fact, Willis proclaimed, the frail elderly woman was "a cold-blooded murderer." (The woman was convicted on all counts.)

Perhaps her most memorable murder trial came in a case in which she got hold of a jailhouse recording of her defendant instructing his mother to get his brother—a crack addict and a witness to his crime— to leave town. Willis was prosecuting the case, and he feared she would call his brother to testify; the last thing the defendant wanted was to have Willis grill his brother on the stand. You can't let that happen, the brother told his mother, unaware the tape was rolling. "The bitch is a genius," he said, referring to Willis.

Willis had a field day with that; she played the recording for the jury and won a conviction. Afterward, Howard—who had a habit of giving awards to his prosecutors who won big cases—presented Willis with a plaque in front of his executive staff: THE BITCH IS A GENIUS AWARD, it read. The staff erupted, howling with laughter. For years, Willis loved to show off that award.

By then, word had spread in the office that when Willis was doing a homicide case, it was well worth it for junior DAs to take time off and watch. Aside from her obvious talent, she also benefited from something else that many of the young lawyers in the office, especially women, understood implicitly. "When I walk into a courtroom, I'm always underestimated—which can be a powerful thing," she said.

In 2014, Howard launched his most consequential—and controversial—case: the prosecution of Atlanta public school teachers and administrators under RICO, the state's Racketeer Influenced and Corrupt Organizations Act. Dozens of educators were accused of manipulating students' scores on mandated tests, systematically erasing wrong answers and replacing them with the correct ones. After much internal commotion and debate, it was a case that wound up on Willis's desk—and would ultimately define her career as a deputy DA.

The cheating scandal had its roots in President George W. Bush's No Child Left Behind law, an act that kicked off the national obsession with test scores that preoccupied American educators for years. The law attempted to address slipping test scores for America's schoolchildren by introducing rigorous new standards: If schools got their test scores up, they would be rewarded with extra federal funds (and, as events played out, the teachers would get raises and bonuses). If test scores did not improve, schools would be penalized and at risk of losing federal funding. The incentives to cheat were real and perverse—and there was plenty of evidence that other school systems around the country had their own testing scandals. But nowhere did the issue get as much attention as Atlanta—or result in greater legal exposure.

There were thirty-five defendants in Howard's original indictment, including Atlanta's school superintendent, six principals, and two assistant principals as well as fourteen public school teachers. All but one were African American. None were white. All were first-time offenders. The charges deeply divided Atlanta. In North Fulton, in wealthy, predominantly white Buckhead ("the Beverly Hills of the South"), the cheating scandal was seen as a stain on the city's national reputation. But many in Atlanta's Black community were horrified at the lineup of virtually all Black defendants. "Show me a white face," the Reverend Timothy McDonald of a group called the Concerned Black Clergy told a reporter for *The New York Times*. "Let's just be real. You can call it racist. You can call it whatever you want. But this is overkill."

Why, the critics wanted to know, was Howard going after Black teachers and educators, treating them as run-of-the-mill criminals when they were simply trying to help Black students from largely impoverished backgrounds graduate to the next grade—and not suffer the stigma of being left back? And to indict them on racketeering charges as though they were mobsters or drug lords?

There was considerable dissension within Howard's office over the case. "Do we really need to display our dirty laundry?" one of the DA's deputies protested. Howard had initially assigned the case to Tanya Miller, a veteran homicide prosecutor who had previously worked in the US Attorney's Office in Manhattan (where she served with a lanky fellow assistant US attorney named James Comey). "Paul decided a Black woman needed to be the face of the case," she recalled, explaining how she was tapped for the job.

But after digging into the details, Miller decided she couldn't do it. "For me, I became a prosecutor to prosecute bad guys, child molesters, rapists," she said. "People who murdered the elderly, the worst of people's nightmares. When I put on the white hat, I did not sign up to prosecute school teachers." Miller resigned—and became a defense lawyer (and later a state legislator). So Howard turned instead to two other hard-charging African Americans on his staff: a burly veteran prosecutor named Clint Rucker and the woman who by then had risen to chief of the office's trial division, Fani Willis.

It was, for Willis, a make-or-break moment. As she would later recall, Howard had called her in and dumped the case on her lap just a couple of weeks before the statute of limitations was about to run out. Although it had been percolating in the office for some time, nobody had even bothered to pull together the evidence or assemble a list of witnesses. "They just had chaos," she recalled. "And the damn statutes are about to run, the case has been here two years and you don't have a witness list? That's got to be a joke, right? And then I realized it wasn't a joke. I used a lot of expletives for two days."

A hands-on micromanager, Willis plunged into every detail of the case. She spent countless hours driving to the homes of the students whose test scores had been doctored, sitting on the couches in their living rooms and meeting with them and their parents, who were chagrined to learn their children were being advanced in grade levels when they could barely read or write. Willis became convinced—or convinced herself—that it was the students who were the real victims of this fraud. "What I began to learn very, very quickly, is a lot of children were harmed," she said. "You know, after you sit on the couch with enough parents, who [are] not me, like, let's tell the truth—most of them were not formally educated. They did not have the means that I had. They were impoverished, but they love their children the exact same way that I love my children." She recalled one young girl who described "taking her test, and the teacher is telling her to change the answer, and she doesn't want to change the answer." And then fellow students and even some of the teachers would tell her, "'You're stupid, 'cuz you're gonna get it wrong.' That hurt that child's belief in themselves."

Willis and Rucker made the argument that the cheating scheme was a pathway to jail for young Black kids. "Look at the state's crime problem—the ones committing all these crimes—they're the kids who you let pass," Rucker said in an interview for this book. Unable to cut it once they got to high school—because they had been elevated to levels far beyond their reading levels—"they dropped out and joined street gangs, committing robberies and murders and generally made the city—in some quarters at least—unlivable."

To be sure, critics of the case said the problems of the city's Black youth had less to do with doctored test scores than generations of systematic neglect, spiraling drug use and crime, and all the other maladies of inner-city life. But the widespread cheating revealed by the scandal got huge headlines and preoccupied the media in Georgia for years. Many of the critics in the Black community wanted to blame the whole case on the state's white power structure, especially its two previous Republican governors, Sonny Perdue and Nathan Deal, both of whom had directed the Georgia Bureau of Investigation (GBI) to investigate the cheating scandal in the first place after a series

of investigative stories in *The Atlanta Journal-Constitution*. The GBI—
the state's premier law enforcement agency—ultimately produced an
885-page report that wound up in Howard's office and laid out many
of the damning details that prosecutors relied on. But there was little
question that the racial overtones were neutralized by the fact that it
was Rucker and Willis sitting side by side, heading up the prosecution
table.

———————

Big trials are like combat. Prosecutors and defense lawyers spend
months preparing for battle—marshaling their evidence, interviewing witnesses, plotting strategy. In preparing for this one, Willis and
Rucker were aided by a powerful weapon: Georgia's version of RICO,
the federal Racketeer Influenced and Corrupt Organizations Act. The
federal version of RICO had been passed in 1970, during the height of
Richard Nixon's war on crime, as a way to take down La Cosa Nostra
and drug cartels. Georgia's was one of many state laws patterned after
the federal law. But it actually went further, enumerating a longer
list of "predicate acts" that could be used to build a conspiracy case
against members of a defined "enterprise" suspected of operating for
criminal purposes. Most critically, prosecutors were only required to
show that the conspirators were working toward a common corrupt
goal—not that they actually planned the conspiracy together or even
communicated with one another.

In the Atlanta school case, "the enterprise" was deemed to be the
Atlanta Public School system itself; its superintendent, Beverly Hall,
was one of the defendants (although she was diagnosed with cancer
after the charges were brought and later died without ever going to
trial). Among the predicate acts spelled out in Georgia's RICO law
was making a "false statement or writing" that is submitted to a

government agency. The tests taken by schoolkids, because they were turned into the Atlanta school system, were judged by the prosecutors to be government documents. The teachers' erasures of their students' wrong answers—and replacements with the correct ones—were charged as a predicate false writing in a government document under RICO. It was an unquestionably creative stretch of the statute, and made the teachers, if convicted, liable for a minimum of five years and a maximum of twenty years in prison. The heavy penalties in the Georgia RICO law were a powerful lever and prompted nearly half of the original teacher defendants to plead guilty and cooperate with the DA's office. RICO also allowed for prosecutors to introduce a much broader array of evidence about the activities of the co-conspirators, showing that all of them were acting in furtherance of the overarching racketeering scheme—even if, as was the case with many of the defendants, they had nothing to do with one another.

As she was gearing up for her starring role in the school cheating case, Willis sat down for a tutorial about how to use the law from John Floyd (who shared her father's name but was unrelated), a scholarly private lawyer who was the acknowledged expert on the Georgia statute and the author of a dense textbook on the subject. Floyd had been brought in by Howard to craft the charges in the school case. "So I remember making him, like, put it on the board, break it down. Explain it to me, what is this, this, and this," Willis recalled. When he was done, "I understood what a beautiful tool [RICO] was," Willis added, and "what a great way it was to allow a jury to get to see a whole story."

It was a lesson Willis learned well—and a statute she would return to again and again. Indeed, the use of RICO against the Atlanta schoolteachers previewed another audacious RICO case that Willis, again with John Floyd's guidance, would bring nine years later—this time against a former president of the United States. And as with the teachers, her strategic deployment of RICO would produce cooperators.

The Atlanta school cheating trial began in September 2014, with Willis delivering the opening statement. She did not disappoint. Floyd described her in a courtroom as "a force of nature." Shaunya Chavis, the wife of Clint Rucker, called her a "tornado" in the courtroom, prone to theatrical flourishes, raising her voice, pounding the table, roaming the courtroom, and reaching for folksy images to connect with the jury. "They changed [the test results] from 11 o'clock in the morning to 11 o'clock at night and ate fish and grits!" she proclaimed, pacing back and forth in front of the jury, recounting what she described as "cheater parties" in which the teacher defendants would meet to alter the scores of their students. (Her language would prompt some grumbling in the Black community that she was playing on racial tropes with her reference to "fish and grits.") The cheating scheme was, she proclaimed, "a cleverly disguised conspiracy" in which the accused teachers "stole" from the students and the school system, using their "magic elixir" of altered test scores to collect hefty bonuses. One of the defendants, Shani Robinson, would later write in a book about the case that Willis had held forth "like a fire and brimstone preacher."

At times, Willis's theatricality would get her into hot water. After complaints from some of the defense lawyers, Willis was reprimanded by the judge, Jerry Baxter, for making faces and gestures during the testimony of witnesses—frowning and grimacing at times, sighing with exaggerated exasperation—in ways that were clearly visible to the jury. "Ms. Willis, you're going to have to stop making facial expressions toward the jury," he told her at one point. "Otherwise, we need to move the desk."

The proceedings dragged on for eight months, making it the longest criminal trial in Georgia history. In April 2015, the jury—six whites, six Blacks—returned its verdict: All but one of the defendants were guilty as charged. Willis and Rucker basked in the glow of their triumph. Willis stood right by Paul Howard's side, Rucker flanking his right shoulder behind him at a post-conviction press conference during which the DA publicly touted their "outstanding" performance, even leading a round of applause to thank them for delivering guilty verdicts in what he called "by far, the largest, most complex case we've ever tried in the Fulton County DA's office."

The case cemented Willis's reputation as Howard's star litigator. But a curious thing happened after the verdicts. After years of front-page headlines, the case—and the impact it had on the Atlanta public school system—faded almost entirely from the news. It was as though the whole scandal—as well as the heavy-handed prosecutions of the perpetrators—was viewed as a bit of an embarrassment for Atlanta. It was a subject few city officials even wanted to talk about. And over time, Willis would betray some defensiveness about her role. "If you're asking me if I was a sitting District Attorney would I have done that case in that way," she told interviewer Sharon Reed of *The Atlanta Voice* when the journalist challenged her about the issue in the summer of 2020, "I might not have decided to charge that case. I might have done something alternatively." But, she added, she was "unapologetic" and that "African American children were harmed" by the conduct at issue. It was a position she would stick to even when, as would soon be the case, powerful interests in the progressive movement would push her to say otherwise.

Willis left the DA's office in 2018, deciding to open up her own law office as a solo practitioner. But she remained loyal to her boss—at least publicly. At a Woman of the Year ceremony that year in which she was celebrated as one of Atlanta's "most powerful and influential" attorneys—an honor that Howard had nominated her for—Willis said that, despite occasional "heated" disagreements, "I would never work for another DA. I would never go to another jurisdiction. What I respect most about him is he always does what he thinks is right and he really fights for the victims of crime."

Barely a year later, she made the momentous decision to challenge Howard, end his career, and take over Georgia's biggest and most important prosecutor's office herself.

CHAPTER TWO

The Law-and-Order Candidate

"It was as if God was saying, 'Listen, didn't I tell you this is what you're supposed to do?' "

The pivotal moment that led Fani Willis to challenge her old boss came in December 2019, when *The Atlanta Journal-Constitution* dropped a story that stunned Atlanta's legal community. Willis was by then in private practice, working out of a rambling old house with a white-picket fence and Southern-style porch—a far cry from the gleaming glass-and-steel skyscrapers boasted by the city's prestigious law firms like King & Spalding and Alston & Bird. She was sharing office space in the house with one of her former colleagues from the DA's office, Charlie Bailey, a West Georgia farm boy with big political plans of his own. Bailey saw the *Journal-Constitution* story on his iPhone the minute it hit, and dashed up the stairs to Willis's second-floor office.

"Have you seen this?" he said, holding up the phone. Willis looked up from her work. The headline said it all. ADMINISTRATOR ALLEGES DA PAUL HOWARD SEXUALLY HARASSED HER.

"Jesus, yes I did," Willis told him. It was the era of the Me Too movement in which powerful men—Hollywood moguls, politicians, and media personalities—were being held to account for sexual misconduct and abuse. Now the times had caught up to Howard—and the accusations against him would change the trajectory of Willis's professional career, leading to a bruising political campaign that would rupture old friendships even as it brought her new prominence.

According to the *Journal-Constitution* story, a woman named Tisa Grimes, the director of human resources in the DA's office, alleged in a legal complaint that Howard had sexually harassed her over a period of nine months in 2019. Grimes, then forty-five, said Howard, sixty-eight, had repeatedly made unwelcome advances, including suggestive comments, propositioning her, embracing her, and even grabbing her buttocks. One time during an office retreat, Grimes alleged, she knocked on Howard's hotel door mistakenly thinking it was the DA's female chief of staff. Howard answered, she claimed, wearing nothing but a white button-down long-sleeved shirt—and motioned her into the bedroom. Grimes would also tell the paper she was demoted for rejecting Howard's advances. Howard adamantly denied the charges, and, through a lawyer, asserted Grimes had only come forward after she had been transferred into what she perceived as a lower-ranking position.

Willis was shocked by the allegations, but also saddened that a man whom she had long looked up to could be accused of such shabby behavior. Bailey, too, was indignant, but saw an opportunity for his good friend. "We can't have the DA in the biggest county in the state credibly accused of sexual harassment," he remembered thinking. Something needed to be done about it. An idea crystalized for him right then.

"Fani, you need to run," Bailey implored Willis.

As Bailey recalled it, Willis rolled her eyes, "Oh, come on, don't bring me into this," she said, sounding exasperated. Bailey persisted. A couple of years earlier, while they were both still at the DA's office and there was already grumbling about Howard's mismanagement, the two had briefly kibitzed about a possible challenge to the boss and concluded that it was impractical. Unless, that is, there was a scandal that would hit home with voters. Bailey reminded her of that conversation. "This is what I was talking about," he said. "This is that scandal." The episode was just the start of a drumbeat of allegations against the once all-powerful lawman that would make him vulnerable to political challenge.

As tempting as it was to run the office where she once worked, Willis had good reason to be hesitant, at least at first. How would it look for her to be challenging her longtime patron? "He was a brilliant man, he had paid me well, he had brought me into the fold," Willis would later say, reflecting back on how important Howard had been to her professional rise. And there were other factors. Willis had made a stab at running for office just the year before when, after leaving the DA's office, she had jumped into a race to fill an open judgeship on the Fulton County Superior Court.

But that had turned into a sobering experience. Willis was the top vote getter in the nonpartisan race. But, having fallen just short of the votes required under Georgia law—50 percent plus one—she was forced into a runoff. When she consulted a well-connected Georgia GOP strategist, Mark Rountree, about how best to proceed, he told her that as an African American woman, she had no chance. "It's just never going to happen," she said Rountree told her. Rountree disputes that he said that, but however he phrased Willis's political prospects in the runoff (in which plenty of Buckhead Republicans would be voting), Willis was clearly taken aback. Among her friends she counted many whites and even more than a few Republicans. Sure enough, she got clobbered in the runoff, by double digits. "Damn if he wasn't right," Willis would later say with a characteristic laugh about the consultant's prediction. "It was hard to hear that people would make decisions like that about me," she recalled. "And so, that was painful. That was painful."

In the aftermath of the race, Willis was also broke, having poured $50,000 of her own money into the campaign. Both of her daughters were in college, and her meager savings were all going toward their education. Her ex-husband Fred had run into financial troubles, had his wages garnished for failing to pay back an auto loan, and left town. "He was not a contributor," as she put it. Her nascent law practice, a paltry array of family and asset forfeiture cases, consisted of clients who often couldn't pay their bills. She was trying to make it month-to-month and feeling the heavy weight of single-parent responsibility on her shoulders.

One day, sitting at home in front of her computer, Willis sought spiritual guidance about her predicament. Raised in the more restrained Roman Catholic tradition, she had adopted some of the rituals of the Black Baptist church prevalent in Georgia. Among them was talking out loud to God. One of Willis's more cynical colleagues noted that her accounts of her monologues with a higher power played well among the city's Black ministers and their religious flock. But it was a core part of Willis's faith and one she freely spoke about in public settings, connecting her talks with God to key decisions she would make about her professional career.

"I really don't get it," she recalled saying as she sat by her laptop, seeking divine advice about her financial predicament in the fall of 2019. "I put everything in and usually when I put everything in, I win. Are you just going to leave me here?" Feeling forsaken, she pleaded for guidance that never came. "And I'm not going to tell you, like I heard some voice because I didn't hear a voice. That's what was frustrating about it," she told one interviewer in 2023. But by Willis's account, her heavenly entreaties were followed by a minor miracle. The very next day, she started getting calls from people asking her to represent them. And for the first time they were the kinds of clients who could pay their bills on time, upper-middle-class Atlantans from across socioeconomic and racial divides.

Then came another break that must have seemed like divine intervention: Earlier that year, the chief judge magistrate of the new city of South Fulton, a predominantly Black community where Willis lived, was forced to step down for signing up to do a Judge Judy–style reality TV show. South Fulton's mayor, Bill Edwards, desperately needed a replacement. One day he asked Shaunya Chavis, who at the time was working in the Fulton County communications office, if she knew who might be a good fit. Chavis and her husband Clint Rucker—Willis's old co-counsel on the school cheating case—were close friends with Willis. "What about Fani?" Shaunya said. "Well I'll be damned," Mayor Edwards responded, thinking Willis might just be the perfect choice.

She got the job. It was a part-time position, with a $130,000 annual salary that could supplement the work coming in from her legal practice. And perhaps just as important, it gave Willis the chance to achieve her lifelong dream of wearing black robes. When she was sworn in, the Ruckers organized a big banquet for Willis where her old mentor Paul Howard spoke and showered the new judge with praise and adulation.

———————

It was only a few weeks later that Charlie Bailey broached the idea of Willis running against Howard for DA and started his quietly persistent campaign to convince her to take the plunge. Her hesitancy notwithstanding, there seemed little doubt that she wanted the job, a chance to run the office where she had toiled for sixteen years. As Willis weighed what to do, another issue loomed increasingly large.

It was the first year of the Covid pandemic and crime was spiking in Fulton County. The grim trend would lead to 2020 having the highest crime rate in years, including record numbers of murders and assaults, with much of the violence driven by rampant gang activity. The city of Atlanta, whose residents represented the bulk of Fulton County's population of one million, was fast becoming—in the words of one local activist—"the murder capital of the South."

There had long been a lazy assumption among many in the media and political world that Black officials like Willis would be aligned with liberal activists who were demanding new progressive policies such as putting an end to cash bail, lightening up on harsh sentences, and eliminating the death penalty. But in the great national debate about crime and punishment, Willis did not fit the mold. She was, to be sure, a daughter of the civil rights movement whose core outlook was shaped by the struggle for African American equality and voting rights. But she was also a hard-bitten ex–homicide prosecutor who was a firm believer in what the academics loftily call retributive justice— a fancy way of saying, if you do the crime, you do the time. Willis had spent much of her career sending violent criminals, many of them

Black, to prison, arguing to juries about the grievous toll their actions had taken on victims and their families. Whatever ambivalence she may have expressed at times over her role prosecuting Black teachers and educators in the school cheating case, Willis was keenly attuned to the impact that murders, gangs, and violence were having on her county—and the demands among many, especially in the African American community, to do something about it. In due course, Donald Trump would accuse Willis of being a "radical" who cared not at all about putting violent criminals in jail. He couldn't have been more wrong.

One day in early 2020, while she was trying to decide whether to take the plunge, Willis visited her favorite nail salon for "a little Fani time," as she put it. There she ran into Daphne Jordan and her husband, Walter, who were getting side-by-side mani-pedis. Daphne was a local community activist who had been agitating for tougher anti-crime measures and more resources for local law enforcement in South Fulton ever since 2015, when a group of teenage hoods broke into her home, ransacking the place and stealing $10,000 worth of valuables. Jordan started an organization called the High Crimes in South Fulton Initiative to put pressure on local officials and the business community to deal with the mounting crime problem. A gun enthusiast, she'd also started a firearms club for women, to educate them in gun safety and self-protection. She named the club Packing Pretty and encouraged women to treat their weapons as accessories to be coordinated with their outfits and jewelry.

On this day Daphne had her holstered Walther PK380 tucked into her Louis Vuitton purse. And when she saw Willis, the crime crisis in South Fulton was very much on her mind. A few weeks before, her sister, who was working as a security guard at a local bowling alley, was shot twice in the abdomen by an eighteen-year-old fugitive wanted for murder. Daphne's sister survived, but the traumatic event gave even more urgency to her anti-crime crusade. She didn't waste any time telling Willis what she wanted.

"Girl, *pleeeeease* run for DA," she implored Willis in the middle of the salon. "He's not doing anything about crime," she said, referring to Paul Howard. "He won't meet with us, he won't talk to us, crime is out of control. Will you *pleeeease* run." Willis gave her a look like she was crazy, but the truth was that she was warming to the idea.

First, however, Willis wanted the blessing of Mayor Edwards. If she entered the race, she'd have to quit as South Fulton's chief magistrate judge, a position she'd held for less than a year. She was concerned Edwards might think she was leaving him in the lurch. Moreover, Edwards and Howard had been close friends since decades earlier, when they were classmates at Morehouse, the storied historically Black college in Atlanta.

With some trepidation she asked Edwards what he thought. "Should I do this or not?" she asked. Edwards was slow in his response. "I appointed you as my chief judge," he started. "And Mr. Howard and I have fifty years of history together." Willis was bracing for him to oppose her entering the race. But then to her surprise Edwards said he'd support her, whatever choice she made. "I'm not going to lose love for you because you made that decision." He promised to stay out of the race. And then, according to Willis, he said something even more surprising. "The truth is I've been talking to my constituents," Edwards said. "I think you'll beat him."

Then she got a tip that sealed the deal. As Willis told the story, one day she drove up to a campy, Bavarian-style resort town called Helen in the North Georgia mountains for some soul searching and talking to God, still worried about what might happen if she ran and lost. "I really don't want to be financially effed up again," she recalled thinking. When Willis arrived, she checked into a room in a cheap hotel, looked out the window, and took in the sweeping views. She rolled around the pros and cons of running for DA in her mind. She waited for God to "sit down next to her" to tell her what to do. But nothing happened. So she lay down in bed and took a nap. When she woke up a couple of hours later, there was no epiphany or bright moment of clarity about what to do.

But driving on the way back, teary-eyed with angst, she got an unexpected call on her cell phone. "You might as well run," said the man on the other end of the line. It was her old boss, Alvin Kendall, the bow-tied lawyer, now out of prison and armed with invaluable political intel that he had just picked up from a lawyer colleague. "Say what?" Willis exclaimed. With little emotion in his voice, Kendall explained: "A story is going to come out...that he can't survive."

The Atlanta Journal-Constitution was indeed preparing to drop another bombshell on Howard. It was another woman. Cathy Carter, a low-level records clerk in the DA's office, was accusing the DA in an EEOC complaint of firing her when she cut off what she said had been an affair that had lasted fifteen years. She accused Howard of "unprofessional, unethical and unlawful conduct" that included pressuring her to engage in "sex acts" at the DA's office itself. Carter gave the paper a twenty-one-minute-long recording of Howard engaging in sexually explicit and raunchy banter and planning assignations for when her boyfriend would not be around. Once again, Howard denied the charges. While ultimately admitting to engaging in sexually charged banter with Carter, he asserted that his accuser had an ulterior motive for coming forward: She had been fired not for ending a sexual relationship—but for being arrested on assault charges when she wielded a handgun in a dispute with a man over a purported $400 debt.*

Still, the details of alleged office sex in Carter's complaint were seedy enough. It was the signal Willis was looking for. "It was as if a peace came over me," she said. "It was as if God was saying, *Listen, didn't I tell you this is what you're supposed to do?*"

The next day, Willis marched into Charlie Bailey's office. "All right, let's do it," she said.

"What are you talking about?" Bailey asked with a perplexed look on his face. "Let's do what?"

"I'm running for DA. Get your guy on the phone," she ordered with a brashness familiar to anyone who ever worked with her.

Bailey's guy was Jeff DiSantis, a stocky, jaded political operative who favored cowboy boots and khakis and had a sardonic laugh that at times turned into an outright cackle. DiSantis was a well-known figure in Georgia Democratic politics. He had once been executive director of the state party and had worked on more than a dozen campaigns going back over two decades as well as serving stints in Washington at the Clinton White House and the Democratic National Committee. Bailey had already reached out to DiSantis in case Willis decided to run, and for a good reason: DiSantis had been the campaign strategist

---

* Grimes and Carter would later file lawsuits in federal court accusing Howard of sexual harassment. Howard's lawyers in both cases denied all the charges brought by both women and argued that whatever employment decisions the district attorney made were, as they wrote in a filing in Grimes's case, "based on legitimate, non-discriminatory reasons and were consistent with business necessity." As of this writing, both cases were still pending in the court.

in Bailey's losing but surprisingly close race for state attorney general two years before.

It wasn't obvious that an experienced consultant like DiSantis, who'd run high-profile statewide races and worked on presidential campaigns, would help a relatively obscure prosecutor try to get elected in a local Democratic primary for DA. But Bailey was emphatic with DiSantis that Willis was a unique talent and that this was her moment. "She's the real fucking deal, man," he insisted. "She's a badass and people love her."

So, with a slight shake of the head and a rueful smile that said, *What am I getting myself into?*, DiSantis agreed to do it. And as a first order of business, he beefed up the team, bringing in to work on Willis's campaign longtime partner Chris Huttman, a bespectacled consultant who had a nerd-like obsession with election data—a kind of Peach State Nate Silver—who was also a master at the art of ad buying. A rising young African American strategist, Jeremy Harris, signed on as campaign manager.

Willis was forging relationships that would prove key to her future political success. And for immediate electoral purposes, it made sense for her to turn to veteran Democratic operatives like DiSantis and Huttman: She was, after all, running in a Democratic primary in a solidly Democratic county. But her ties with the consultants and, even more so, to Bailey would also in time prove a double-edged sword—a weapon that Republican critics would later use to try to portray Willis as a partisan with an agenda.

———————

Willis didn't waste any time letting people know her decision and building support in the community; she proved to be a natural campaigner. One of her first text messages went out to Daphne Jordan—the pistol-packing anti-crime activist who had confronted Willis at the nail salon. "I have prayed and prayed again," she wrote in the text. "I cannot run from the responsibility no matter how personally uncomfortable. The issues are bigger than me." Then she asked for Daphne's and her husband Walter's support, and for their discretion. "OK!!!, I'm glad to hear this," Daphne texted back.

"Let's go!!!" wrote Walter.

Willis got a far less enthusiastic reception from some others in her circle. At the DA's office, her decision to run was especially polarizing. Loyal supporters of Paul Howard were outraged at what they viewed as an unforgivable betrayal. Among those who were most peeved were Clint Rucker, her co-counsel on the school cheating case, and his wife Shaunya, who had helped Willis get the magistrate's job in South Fulton. They had been friends with Willis for years. They regularly had Willis over to their home and celebrated birthdays with Willis's two daughters as they were growing up. Willis and Rucker grew so close that they called each other Brother Clint and Sister Fani. When Willis was struggling financially, Clint would help her out with small gifts.

When Willis announced her decision to challenge Howard, the Ruckers were stunned. For one thing, they were offended that Willis never bothered to give them a heads-up before going public. They'd gossiped with Willis about all the criticism of Howard and how it might affect his political future. And even after they helped get Willis the South Fulton judgeship, she'd never mentioned that she was considering running for DA. "I was just shocked," Rucker recalled. But the deeper wound was what they regarded as Willis's betrayal of Howard, a towering figure and mentor to Fani, Clint, and a whole generation of Black assistant DAs in Atlanta. As they saw it, Willis had put personal ambition over loyalty to a mentor. "Michael Jordan would not dog out Dean Smith," Clint Rucker said. "You don't go after your boss," Shaunya added.

Right after the announcement, Clint Rucker called Willis seeking some sort of explanation. She didn't pick up—and never responded to his message. They never spoke again. But Shaunya did get through—and tore into her. "I told her I was offended," she recalled. After all they had gone through together, you don't even call and tell us what you're doing, going after Howard? Shaunya said. Willis, by now singularly focused on what she saw as her new mission, was unsentimental with her old friend and blew her off. It was the brusque side of her personality—a sort of ruthlessness that could emerge when ambition met duty. Willis's response, according to Shaunya, was, "I know this is hard for you, so you don't have to confront me. I'll just un-friend you on Facebook." Shaunya was furious. *That's how you make amends? You un-friend me on Facebook?* "Boy, that's just some bullshit."

For Paul Howard, the sense of betrayal was so stinging he almost couldn't believe it was happening. In the spring, after Willis had announced she was challenging him, Howard called in Fred Hicks, a seasoned local Democratic operative, to serve as a consultant to his campaign. Their first meeting was depressing. Howard, Hicks recalled, was obsessed over the fact that Willis, his star protégée, had turned on him, and he could talk about nothing else. "I can't believe she's doing this, I can't believe she's running against me," he told Hicks. He repeated it over and over again. "I made her!" he told Hicks. He had even written a letter to help her get the judgeship in South Fulton just six months earlier. "It was almost like an *Et tu, Brute?* kind of thing," Hicks recalled.

But Willis was hitting her stride. She turned out to be a spirited campaigner and relentless fundraiser, moving easily between the church folk of mostly Black South Fulton and the socialites and well-heeled professionals of predominantly white Buckhead. There were, at first, some bumps along the road when she and the small campaign team DiSantis had assembled got into a lively dispute over Willis's incessant demands for more and more yard signs. The team's first internal polls, when they were still mostly relying on Willis's beloved yard signs, had her trailing Howard by double digits. Willis was deflated. A turning point came when DiSantis and his partner, Huttman, put together a brutal series of TV and radio ads, pounding their message that Howard was too ethically challenged to keep his job, The ads played up the sexual harassment complaints and reports that Howard was facing accusations that he had padded his salary with payments from an Atlanta city-funded nonprofit. Howard denied all wrongdoing, but the allegations did their damage. In the next tracking poll, a couple of weeks later, her numbers had shot up, surpassing Howard by a few points. "Ooh, I like this," Willis said when she saw the results.

Willis could feel the momentum swinging in her direction, but she was not about to take her foot off the gas. She hammered Howard mercilessly at every opportunity—and there were plenty of opportunities. The two squared off in multiple debates, and Willis was relentless in her attacks. At one debate at the local NPR affiliate, Willis, reading from prepared notes, went after Howard on the sexual harassment allegations, accusing him at one point of "performing a sex act on the desk." Howard's consultant Hicks, who was in the studio during the debate, was stunned. He'd never heard that before. He confronted him afterward. "Is that true?" he asked the DA. "I'm not talking about it," Howard told him. So Hicks quit the campaign.

Later Willis would acknowledge that she went into the debate with a head of steam and a plan "to be a little more vicious" than usual. She'd gotten ahold of the tape made by one of the victims of Howard's sexual boorishness—Cathy Carter, the legal clerk who had filed the second sexual harassment complaint. The recording was about as raunchy as you could get. "You know you want to give me that pussy," the sixty-eight-year-old Howard could be heard saying. "And I've got something else I could put in your mouth." For Willis, this was an egregious abuse of power. "She's like a lowly secretary; she's a single mom. She's struggling; you're the district attorney who signs her paycheck," Willis said. "He's just a bully. That's what disgusted me about it."

Willis knew how to stand up to bullies. In one defining incident during the campaign that took place behind closed doors, she showed her steel. She had gotten a request to meet with T.I., a hugely popular, Grammy-winning rapper and record executive who had emerged as a key political power broker in the city. He was incensed that Willis, thanks to her tough-on-crime stand, had been endorsed by the police union and, even more so, by Atlanta City Council member Mary Norwood, a wealthy white Buckhead activist with close ties to the Republican donor community. To curb crime, Norwood had pushed legislation to impose tighter curfews on the late-night hours of the city's nightclubs—a proposal that alarmed the city's music and hospitality industries. T.I. had it in for Norwood, a perfectly put-together stalwart Republican who looked like she'd walked off the set of the 1980s sitcom *Designing Women*. He calculated that between the cops and the Buckhead Republicans tied to Norwood, Willis had gotten some $60,000 in contributions.

T.I. offered Willis a crass deal: renounce the police union and Norwood endorsements, give back their money, and he would make it worth her while. He would endorse Willis, bringing along a sizable portion of Atlanta's vibrant rapper community and its financial largesse. "I will double your money," he told her. As for Norwood, T.I. simply said: "She doesn't like the culture; she doesn't like Black people." When his pitch was over, Willis looked straight at T.I. and said flatly: "No." Then after a long pause she told the rapper, "I represent all segments of the community. The police are part of our community and I'm happy for their support. Mary Norwood is also a member of my community."

T.I., who had had run-ins with the law in the past, including spending time in federal prison on firearms and drug charges, was not accustomed to being summarily rebuffed. Later, Willis remarked, "It's funny because I thought we were still having a meeting but he seemed annoyed and left in a huff. I don't think he was used to a woman just saying, like, no. There seemed to be some machismo going on." (Duwon Robinson, a political activist who set up the meeting for T.I., confirmed that the rapper made the offer and was "disappointed" when Willis rejected it.)

Willis had another defining encounter during the campaign that never became public and may have been even more revealing. The billionaire liberal philanthropist George Soros was pouring tens of millions of dollars into district attorney races across the country, funneling his largesse through a network of state-level and national super PACs to back progressive candidates willing to pledge to putting an end to aggressive policing and mass incarceration. A vetter for the Soros-funded political network, an American University law professor and former DC public defender named Angela "Amani" Davis (not the onetime Marxist revolutionary who had been romantically involved with Willis's father during the 1960s), arranged to interview Willis by Zoom to assess her candidacy. During the call, she questioned Willis on her position on criminal justice issues, quickly zeroing in on the death penalty.

There was no doubt that a huge contribution from Soros was at stake—"Millions and millions of dollars were on the line," Willis would tell the authors. But even though she knew exactly what the

Soros vetter wanted to hear—the organization was staunchly opposed to capital punishment—she wasn't willing to bend her position for the sake of a political donation. It was a punishment she would rarely pursue, she told Davis, but she was emphatic that there were some cases where the death penalty should be on the table. Look at the Charleston massacre where the virulent white racist Dylann Roof had gunned down nine African Americans in a church. And then: What if somebody comes into your house and "sodomizes" your children and slaughters your family? Would you not want the ultimate punishment for the killers and the sodomizers? No, Willis said, she wouldn't rule out seeking the death penalty in a case like that.

Davis moved on. What about her lead role in the Atlanta school cheating case? Did she feel bad for the educators she had prosecuted and convicted?

"I feel bad for the kids" whose test scores had been doctored, she replied.

So you don't feel empathy for the teachers? Davis wanted to know.

I feel empathy for the kids, she repeated.

What you're saying is you don't feel remorse for that case? the vetter pressed.

The truth, as Willis would soon tell interviewer Sharon Reed of *The Atlanta Voice*, was that maybe in retrospect there were less harsh ways to have addressed the problem of widespread cheating by the Atlanta teachers. But in this interview—with potentially huge campaign contributions on the table—she wouldn't bend.

I'm never changing my view, she said. The real victims were the kids, not the teachers, she repeated.

There was an awkward silence. The interview petered out. "We knew we weren't getting anything," said Jeremy Harris, her campaign manager who listened in on the interview. He was right. Willis never got a dime of Soros's money.* She had no intention of wavering from her tough-on-crime stand—a position that only hardened when, in the midst of the campaign, Atlanta was convulsed by racial protests, setting off spasms of violence, including a senseless murder that virtually assured her election.

---

* In an interview Davis confirmed that she questioned Willis on behalf of the Soros network, but added that the network does not require candidates to make pledges on any issues in exchange for an endorsement. "Our decision to support or not support a candidate is based on a variety of reasons, including their positions on all of the issues . . ." she told the authors.

CHAPTER THREE

Chaos in Atlanta

*"It's like Black lives don't matter unless you
are killed by a police officer."*

On the evening of May 25, 2020, as the Fulton County DA's race was heating up, the national conversation about race and justice changed overnight, possibly forever. Minneapolis police officers had arrested a forty-seven-year-old Black man named George Floyd after a convenience store clerk complained he had paid for a pack of cigarettes with a counterfeit $20 bill. One of the cops, Derek Chauvin, pinned Floyd to the pavement, planted his knee firmly on the suspect's neck, and held it there for an excruciating nine minutes and twenty-nine seconds even while Floyd gasped "I can't breathe" before finally losing consciousness. As the video images of Floyd's death blanketed the airwaves and social media feeds, tens of thousands of protestors across the country took to the streets. BLACK LIVES MATTER signs popped up in stores and front yards all over America and a new rallying cry— "Defund the police"—galvanized the demonstrators.

These were—for the most part—peaceful protests. But not all of them. As *The New York Times* reported at the time, the demonstrations in some cities—in Portland, Seattle, and Minneapolis—"descended into nights of unrest, with reports of shootings, looting and vandalism." At a moment that called for national healing, President Trump took to Twitter to call the protestors "thugs" and threatened to call in federal troops, adding in typical wrecking-ball fashion: "When the looting starts, the shooting starts."

But in perhaps no city did the protests have a greater—and more consequential—political impact than in Atlanta. Hundreds had poured into the streets around Centennial Olympic Park. Some of them hurled rocks and jumped on police cars, shattering windows at an Omni hotel and at the College Football Hall of Fame. Nearby, protestors broke into the CNN building, spray-painted messages, and torched an American flag. The city's mayor, Keisha Lance Bottoms—who twenty years earlier had briefly practiced law with Willis and was now on the short list to become Joe Biden's running mate—got national attention with a passionate plea for calm. "We are all angry," she said at a news conference on the evening of May 29. "This hurts. This hurts everybody in this room. But what are you changing by tearing up a city?"

Then things got worse—a lot worse.

———

On the evening of June 12, 2020, two white Atlanta police officers tried to arrest a Black man named Rayshard Brooks on DUI charges after finding him slumped in his car, fast asleep, blocking the drive-in window of a Wendy's restaurant. After Brooks consented to a test, his blood alcohol level came in at .108, well above the legal limit of .08. But when the cops moved to handcuff him, Brooks fought back. He hurled one of them to the ground and grabbed the cop's Taser, at one point turning and firing wildly at the officers. One of the officers then shot Brooks in the back, killing him instantly.

When news of the shooting broke, Atlanta was inflamed, the mayor's plea for calm forgotten. Now the city had its own George Floyd—or so it seemed to some, at least at first.

The day after Brooks's shooting, Mayor Bottoms, trying to defuse the tensions, fired the cop who shot Brooks, Garrett Rolfe, and placed the other arresting officer, Devin Brosnan, on administrative leave—without waiting for any official investigation. The city police chief resigned. That night, the Wendy's where the shooting took place was burned to the ground—and gun-toting vigilantes took over the parking lot and the adjacent street corner. They renamed the remains of the gutted Wendy's the Rayshard Brooks Peace Center, surrounding it with candles, balloons, and signs. The lot itself was proclaimed "an autonomous zone" in which "the sovereign authority of the city and state will not be recognized."

It was a de facto armed rebellion in the heart of Atlanta, and the city appeared clueless as to how to respond.

———

If there was anybody in the city who figured he could talk to the protestors at the Wendy's lot and make sense of what they were doing, George Chidi thought he was the guy. A soft-spoken, bald, and beefy army veteran, Chidi was a local activist and organizer, and a self-styled "pirate journalist" (formerly with the *Journal-Constitution*) who did regular commentary on the local Fox TV affiliate. More than that, he knew how to relate to demonstrators and was convinced that they would listen to him. Nearly ten years earlier, Chidi had made a name for himself organizing demonstrations of the Occupy Wall

Street movement in Atlanta. Yet he also played inside the lanes. He knew—and had relationships with—business and political leaders across the political spectrum. "I'm in everybody's social media feed if you're involved in Atlanta politics," he said.

But these protestors had no idea who he was—and couldn't have cared less what he might have to say to them. What are you doing here? demanded a woman who called herself Lady L, as she approached him with a group of the protestors.

You need to leave now, the protestors told him. Get out of here.

It started to dawn on Chidi what he'd gotten himself into. There were fifty or so of the protestors milling about, protecting the Rayshard Brooks Peace Center, all of them, like Chidi, African American. Some were selling Black Lives Matter T-shirts. Another had brought a grill like it was a tailgating party before a Falcons game. But the atmosphere was hardly festive. There were angry men patrolling the lot with an arsenal of assault weapons—AK-47s and AR-15s—as well as multiple handguns with scopes.

The protestors spotted Chidi's cell phone. Was he taking pictures of them? they demanded. Hand it over, one of them, a short guy in a T-shirt, said. Chidi refused.

"I'm not giving you my cell phone," he told them.

"They're standing in a semi-circle in front of me," Chidi recalled. "One of them puts his hand on his pistol and tells me, 'I'm going to count to ten and then I'm going to shoot you if you don't give me your cell phone.'"

Chidi tried to explain he was a reporter—and there were lots of witnesses around. "Look, you're not going to shoot a journalist here," Chidi told them.

The short dude started to count: "Ten, nine, eight..."

When he reached five, "I say, look fine. I'll leave," recalled Chidi.

He started to walk away, his cell phone in his pocket. Then the short guy "runs around in front of me and punches me in the face, right in my right eye. He hits me again, in the temple. Then somebody else comes behind me and hits me in the back of my head."

Chidi raised his fists, ready to swing back at them. But then he thought better of it. "Oh shit, this is stupid," he recalled thinking. He was outnumbered and surrounded. Half a dozen attackers were "hooting and hollering" and clutching their guns. Chidi decided that he'd run rather than fight. "I'm trying to escape a group of gunmen who want to shoot me."

As he hopped in his car and headed to the hospital, with a big purple bruise on his right eye, one thought popped into his head. Heavily armed gunmen had taken over a couple of blocks in the middle of the city. But there was not a police officer in sight. "Where the hell are the cops?" he thought to himself. "Because this is extraordinarily dangerous."

———————————

On June 17, five days after the shooting of Rayshard Brooks, Paul Howard called a press conference to announce that he was bringing eleven criminal charges, including felony murder, against Rolfe, the police officer who had fired the fatal shot. Rolfe's partner, Brosnan, was charged with aggravated assault. Howard invited Brooks's family to the event, as well as his nephew, the NBA star Dwight Howard. The DA portrayed Brooks as a passive victim of police violence, asserting that he had politely cooperated with the cops when they first questioned him. That was true. Brooks had cooperated—at first. But Howard didn't mention that Brooks had then resisted arrest, scuffled with the officers, hurling Brosnan to the ground and grabbing

Brosnan's Taser before he started to flee. It was later determined that Brooks was under the influence of cocaine and Eutylone, a designer drug, and a quantity of methamphetamine was found in the car. As a convicted felon on probation—Brooks had previously served time for fraud and domestic battery—he had a motive to resist. If he had been arrested, he faced the near certainty of returning to prison.

At the press conference, Howard argued that Brooks, despite wielding the Taser and firing it at the cops, posed no threat to the officers. But it was a strained argument: Just two weeks earlier, Howard had charged six Atlanta police officers with aggravated assault for firing their Tasers at two local college students. The premise of the charges in that case was that Tasers are potentially dangerous, even lethal weapons. As Chidi would later write on Substack, there was a glaring contradiction in Howard's position on the two cases. If Brooks shooting at the cops with the stolen Taser was not a threat to the two officers, "Why were other officers charged with using a lethal weapon when they Tased two college kids?"

Perhaps most concerning, at least to the cops, the Georgia Bureau of Investigation (GBI) had barely begun its own probe of the Brooks shooting, much less finished it. Such probes were standard protocol in police shootings and usually take between sixty and ninety days. Howard had brought his charges in less than a week. This wasn't a rush to judgment, it was "a rush to misjudgment," said Don Samuel, a prominent local defense lawyer representing Brosnan (who, also unmentioned by Howard, had suffered a concussion in his scuffle with Brooks). Even more pointed was the response from GBI, which quickly moved to distance itself from the case. "We were not consulted on the charges filed by the District Attorney," the agency said in a statement that day.

That night, the police began their own protest. Over the next three days, 171 Atlanta police officers called in sick. A name quickly caught on in this pandemic season for what was going on: the blue flu.

The following week, a funeral for Rayshard Brooks was held at the historic Ebenezer Baptist Church where Martin Luther King Jr. had once preached. Much of the city's African American elite was in attendance: Mayor Bottoms, Stacey Abrams, the Reverend Bernice King, and T.I. (Tyler Perry, the movie star, paid for the event.) The church's pastor, the Reverend Raphael Warnock, the Democratic Party's candidate for the US Senate, gave a eulogy. He likened what happened to Rayshard Brooks to what happened to George Floyd. "If your skin is the weapon and your complexion is the crime, what do you do to stay alive?" Warnock said to the assembled mourners. "Comply like George Floyd? Or run like Rayshard Brooks? Afraid of losing his liberty, he lost his life, running from a system that too often makes slaves out of people." The national takeaway from the event was reflected in the headline on the CNN website: RAYSHARD BROOKS REMEMBERED AS A HARD-WORKING FATHER KEPT DOWN BY A RACIST LEGAL SYSTEM.

Unmentioned in the coverage but duly noted by the cops as well as the campaign strategists for Fani Willis: Among the pallbearers carrying Brooks's casket outside the church was Paul Howard.

It was clear to Willis's team what was going on. In the first round of voting in the DA's race on June 9, Willis had beaten Howard 42.3 percent to 34.8 percent. It was an impressive showing, but Willis was short of the magic 50-percent-plus-one needed under Georgia law. A runoff was scheduled for August. Howard was now facing an uphill battle and likely ouster from the office he had held for almost a quarter century unless he could dramatically turn the race around. In recent years, Howard had been hammered for not moving aggressively enough to charge cops who had brutalized African Americans. Howard was now recasting himself—by jumping all over the Rayshard Brooks case. "He was panicked," said Huttman, the Democratic operative brought in by DiSantis to do Willis's ads and polling. "He tried to reinvent himself as this anti-police crusader...He needed something big."

As Brooks was being memorialized at Ebenezer Baptist, the situation around the burned-down Wendy's was deteriorating. In the aftermath of Howard's indictments of Rolfe and Brosnan, the city police force issued a directive that was intended to avoid a violent confrontation with the protestors but arguably only made matters worse: Stand down—and back off. If violence occurs *in an officer's presence*, they should respond, the cops were instructed. Otherwise, "we will not be overly proactive in any shape, form or fashion," read the directive from Major Kelley Collier, the commander of the zone where the Wendy's was located. "We are concerned about keeping our officers safe and healthy."

It was quietly noted among the city's politicos that there could well have been other motivations beyond public safety for the directive. Joe Biden's vetting team was now in the final stages of reviewing the candidates for vice president. Bottoms, to whom the Atlanta Police Department reported, was at this point still on a short list defined by Biden's primary pledge to pick an African American woman to be his running mate. Bottoms, who had spoken out early against Trump's immigration policies, had been an early backer of Biden's candidacy and had campaigned for him in Iowa. She had gotten a boost after her earlier plea for calm in the aftermath of George Floyd's murder; Representative James Clyburn, Biden's most influential African American supporter, had pronounced her "a tremendous candidate" for the veep pick. The prospect of a violent blowup in Atlanta—which would likely happen if Bottoms's police department confronted and arrested the protestors—was the last thing Bottoms, or the city for that matter, wanted at this fraught moment.

In the days after the stand-down directive, the Rayshard Brooks Peace Center was becoming a powder keg. The armed protestors at the Wendy's lot set up barricades, blocking entries and exits on an adjacent block. On June 19, a twenty-four-year-old woman walking along the adjacent roadway by the barricaded Wendy's lot was shot in the leg. The next night, a thirty-five-year-old man was also shot in the leg after a drive-by shooting. An eyewitness told reporters: "The police were here when the guy got shot. They saw the guy get shot. They saw the car that was shooting at us, and they didn't pursue him."

———————

Secoriea Turner was a bubbly eight-year-old, a rising third grader with a glittery unicorn backpack and a passion for slime (the gooey kid concoction) who loved posting TikTok videos of herself dancing to "Savage," the wildly popular song by the rap star Megan Thee Stallion. On July 4, her mom took her and a brother to their grandmother's house for the family's annual cookout. There were ribs, sausages, and wings as well as a jumping house for the kids where Secoriea bopped up and down for much of the afternoon. ("She loved jumping around," recalled her mother, Charmaine Turner.) That evening there were makeshift fireworks. Around 9:00 p.m., Charmaine, Secoriea, and one of her brothers piled into the family's green Jeep Cherokee, driven by a friend, Omar Ivery. They headed to Secoriea's father's house to drop off Secoriea's brother and then headed back home to Mom's. Secoriea was in the back seat as they drove by the block with the burned-out Wendy's, less than five minutes from the Turner house.

Charmaine Turner noticed two young men by the side of the lot. It was dark. The streetlights were out. They didn't see the barricade the protestors had set up at the end of the block. The two men shouted loudly and chased after the car, opening fire. Multiple shots rang out, ripping through the back of the car. "Mommy!" Secoriea cried out. Charmaine turned around to try to protect her daughter, but it was too late. She had been struck in the head. Omar tried to call 911 but couldn't get through. They rushed to the closest hospital. Secoriea was pronounced dead twenty minutes after they arrived, killed by a round from an AR-15.

This is what it had come to in Atlanta in the summer of George Floyd: an eight-year-old girl murdered by a "protestor" with an assault weapon.

The death of Secoriea Turner stunned the city. It had come amid a spasm of violence that weekend that also included a mass shooting of twelve, with two dead. A clearly shaken Mayor Bottoms held another press conference the next night, and once again pleaded for calm— and for information to help police identify the shooters of Secoriea Turner. "Enough is enough," she said. "I am just asking you to please honor this baby's life. Please, if you know who did this, please turn them in. These people are a danger to all of us."

Bottoms also spoke about the Black Lives Matter protests in response to George Floyd's killing—and how they were rightfully calling attention to years of abuse by police against African Americans. "That's an important movement that's happening," Bottoms said. "But this random wild, wild west shoot 'em up because you can, it has got to stop. It has to stop.

"You can't blame this on a police officer," she added. "This is some people carrying some weapons who shot up a car with an eight-year-old baby in the car. For what?"

Also speaking that night was Secoriea's father, Secoriey Williamson. He directed his remarks to the protestors selling Black Lives Matter T-shirts at the Wendy's lot. "They say Black lives matter," he said. "You killed your own." As he later explained, "It's like Black lives don't matter unless you are killed by a police officer."

The killing triggered a discernible shift in thinking about the events of that summer among many Atlanta residents. "The crazy thing is, after Secoriea Turner, public opinion specifically within the African American community, turned more negative to street protests," said Chidi, who wrote multiple pieces for his various outlets about what had happened. "It was a shifting moment, the public conversation started to talk about crime and matters of civil order."

It was a shift that had an impact on the race for Fulton County district attorney. Willis had ripped into Howard for politicizing the Rayshard Brooks case, noting that he was using images from the incident in his campaign ads. "Paul Howard would like to be thought of as the great prosecutor of police that do wrong," she said in one TV interview. "We can't even any more discuss if this is political." Howard, for his part, countered that it was Willis who had the ethical conflict—because she had just been endorsed by the police union. (One of the unions representing Atlanta cops had contributed $2,500 to her campaign. The lawyer for Rolfe, the officer whom Howard had charged with murder, gave her $1,000.) "When the police union endorses the DA, what that indicates is the DA will not prosecute police," he said.

But tying Willis to the police was losing its sting among Atlantans increasingly alarmed about the spike in violent crime, a shift that was reflected in her campaign's internal polling. Huttman, Willis's pollster, had included a question in a series of surveys that spring and summer that may have been the most relevant in the race: What should be the Fulton County DA's top priority: "Doing more to get gang members and other violent criminals off our streets OR spending less money locking people up for minor offenses who don't belong in prison in the first place?" Back in early May, in his first poll, 58 percent said "spend less money locking people up;" 33 percent said get "violent criminals off our streets." By mid-July, after the Turner shooting, less than half, 49 percent, said "spend less money locking people up" should be the top priority, while 40 percent said "violent criminals off our streets"— a noticeable swing in public opinion given a national conversation still dominated by the fallout over the killing of George Floyd. (Huttman's survey samples of between six hundred and eight hundred voters for his polls were unusually large for a district attorney's race.)

By the end, the outcome was hardly in doubt. Howard had already been steadily sinking under the combined weight of the allegations over sexual harassment and alleged ethical misconduct. His handling of the Brooks case—and the murder of Secoriea Turner—finished him off. On August 11, Willis clobbered Howard in the runoff, racking up more than 70 percent of the vote. It was a resounding rebuke to Howard's management of the office, but also a testament to the rising fears about street crime. Elsewhere—in Los Angeles, San Francisco, and Philadelphia—voters had been electing progressive prosecutors pledging far-reaching criminal justice reforms backed by George Soros's money. Atlantans instead had voted in a no-nonsense crime fighter. She was also the first woman ever elected Fulton County DA.

"Y'all, we made history," an exuberant Willis declared that night, promising to make her office "a beacon for justice and ethics in Georgia."*

Her victory did not go unnoticed among the supporters of Donald Trump. In fact, in one of the supreme ironies of the entire saga, it was celebrated.

"BREAKING NEWS!!!" tweeted Bernie Kerik, the former New York City police commissioner and a vocal supporter of the president who, as Rudy Giuliani's chief "investigator," would come to play a significant role in the efforts to overturn the 2020 presidential election results. "Corrupt DA Paul Howard @FultoncountyDA gets his ass handed to him by Fani Willis @FaniWillisforDA. Maybe now we can start targeting the thugs instead of the cops!"

———————

Eight months into her tenure as DA, a visibly emotional Willis announced a thirty-seven-count indictment against two members of the Bloods, a criminal street gang, for the murder of Secoriea Turner, calling it one of the "saddest cases" she had ever seen as a prosecutor. She described a chaotic scene in which the Bloods, under the guise of a Black Lives Matters protest, had taken over the lot and adjacent blocks around the Wendy's, set up barricades, and paraded around with deadly weapons. "Members of the community were allowed to

———————

* After taking office, Willis recused herself from the Rayshard Brooks case given that it had been an issue during her campaign for DA. In August 2022, a special prosecutor appointed to review the matter announced that the charges against the two police officers would be dropped, concluding that the use of force against the suspect was "objectively reasonable." Three months later, the Atlanta City Council voted unanimously to settle a lawsuit brought by Brooks's family by paying his widow $1 million, concluding during a closed-door session that the cost of continued litigation would exceed the cost of the settlement.

stand out on a street with what one of my DA's referred to as an 'AK necklace,' just brazenly holding an AK around their neck," she said.

Willis also shed new light on the apparent motivations for what had taken place after the shooting of Rayshard Brooks. Brooks himself had been a Blood, Willis said. His fellow gang members wanted revenge for his death.

Before she announced the charges, Willis had met privately with Secoriea Turner's parents, Charmaine Turner and Secoriey Williamson. The meeting was a gut punch for Willis. She had seen a photo of a beaming, gap-toothed Secoriea, her hands folded over a book on her desk, wearing the standard green polo shirt uniform of the KIPP charter school in Atlanta. It was the same school Willis's youngest daughter had attended. Secoriea was wearing the same school uniform that Willis's daughter had worn. It was "just palpable pain," Willis recalled later when she saw the photo. "So that little uniform—that's what my baby wore. The little girl, she looks like she could actually be my child."

Willis became emotional as she laid out to Secoriea's parents what her investigation had found and the charges she was prepared to announce. "She was almost trembling," remembered Charmaine Turner.

But Willis was also emphatic. "We will get justice for Secoriea," Willis told the parents. She also told them what she would soon say publicly: The case was her "number one priority."

More broadly, the killing of Secoriea Turner underscored for Willis and her deputies the plague of gang warfare in Atlanta, with its ingrained culture of vengeance and violence, that only seemed to be getting worse. It was for Willis an urgent problem she was determined to address with whatever legal means she had at her disposal. In May, she had dropped a mammoth fifty-six-count indictment charging gang members and Atlanta rappers, including Young Thug, a Grammy award winner, with participating in a years-long conspiracy to commit murder, aggravated armed assault, gunrunning, and other crimes. To bring the case, she had turned to the same "beautiful tool" she had used in the school cheating case—Georgia's far-reaching RICO statute.

The indictment was hugely controversial. It targeted Black rappers who were at the heart of Black Atlanta's musical identity—and it cited as supporting evidence the rappers' incendiary lyrics. ("I killed his man in front of his momma / Like fuck lil bruh, sister and his cousin...look at my trigger, my trigger start itching.") Critics called it an attack on artistic expression. One of the harshest responses was from Drew Findling, a swashbuckling local defense lawyer who had made a name for himself—and collected huge fees—representing rap stars, earning him the moniker "the billion-dollar lawyer." Among his clients was YFN Lucci, another prominent local rapper who had been charged by Willis in a separate racketeering case. "We don't go after Quentin Tarantino for movies filled with violence, do they?" he told a reporter while strolling down the street in his shades, the entire exchange captured on video that wound up on TMZ. "But all of a sudden, we've handpicked this music of people in the black and brown community? It's completely fucking racist, that's what it is!"

Findling would soon acquire another client, Donald Trump, who would use similar language about Willis for very different reasons.

Willis, for her part, was unapologetic.

"It does not matter what your notoriety is, what your fame is, if you come to Fulton County, Georgia, and you commit crimes, and certainly if those crimes are in furtherance of a street gang, then you are going to become a target and a focus of this district attorney's office, and we are going to prosecute you to the fullest extent of the law," she said at a press conference.

It was a standard mantra for Willis in an arena that she was used to, prosecuting murderers and gang members. But it turned out crime in Fulton County wasn't confined to the streets. It could also involve a wide-ranging campaign to steal a presidential election—a conspiracy far more complicated and time consuming to investigate, yet, as Willis would discover, more sinister and crazier than anybody imagined.

BOOK TWO

A Conspiracy in
Plain Sight

CHAPTER FOUR

A Confederate in the Attic

"We need to get this Civil War going."

It was a little before noon on January 6, 2021, when the specter of violence hit home for Gabriel Sterling. At that moment, in Washington, DC, on the Ellipse outside the White House, President Donald Trump was wrapping up his speech exhorting the crowd to "fight like hell" to block Congress from certifying the 2020 presidential election results. But Sterling was barely paying attention to the president. He was in Georgia's gold-plated state capitol, inside the office of his boss, Brad Raffensperger, as the embattled secretary of state was putting the final touches on a ten-page letter, point by point refuting Trump's claims of electoral fraud and Democratic chicanery.

Only a few weeks earlier, Sterling, a rumpled numbers cruncher with no tolerance for the wild claims of the president's supporters, had warned in a press conference that "somebody is going to get killed" if Trump didn't stop his "Stop the Steal" nonsense. Now Sterling, Raffensperger's chief operating officer, looked out the window and for a moment thought his worst fears were about to be realized. There

were men in military fatigues parading around outside Raffensperger's
suite of offices—and one of them, clear as day, was cradling an AK-47
assault rifle. "There's a militia outside!" he shouted to his colleagues.

Just then, state troopers came rushing in and alerted Raffensperger that the group's leader, one of the state's more notorious
rabble-rousers, was passing through security and entering the building, heading to the secretary of state's office. The tattooed visitor, a
professional bodybuilder, wasn't armed, but had come with a list of
"grievances" about the election that he planned to confront Raffensperger over. "I started thinking I don't want to be here when this guy
shows up," Raffensperger recalled. He had no interest in getting into a
"bar fight," he said. The state troopers briskly escorted Raffensperger
from the building—a potentially ugly confrontation narrowly averted
in the Georgia State Capitol just as the unruly crowd at the Ellipse
had started marching to the US Capitol, where they would threaten
the lives of members of Congress and fill the hallways with chants of
"Hang Mike Pence!"

The brief threat to Raffensperger that day merited scant attention
given the violence and mayhem that engulfed the Capitol in Washington, DC, that afternoon. But the episode was illustrative nonetheless
of a nasty and menacing trend that was coursing through the state's
politics. It was a trend fueled by root causes national in scope and
years in the making: an increasingly polarized electorate, the erosion
of trust in civic institutions, the advent of social media with its cor-
doned-off silos filled with hate and conspiracy theories. But there was
little question that in Georgia the toxic brew had revived the ghosts
of the state's Jim Crow past and, along the way, unleashed a bizarre
collection of extremist agitators and oddball cranks from the political
netherworld.

And no one fit the bill more than the ornery figure who had come to see Raffensperger that day—Chester P. Doles, a onetime Grand Dragon of the Ku Klux Klan and the proud descendant of a Confederate general. He was, in every sense, the proverbial Confederate in the attic.

––––––––––

"You sold us out!" said Doles when asked in an interview for this book what he planned to tell Raffensperger that day. The Georgia secretary of state, he said, was a "spineless RINO" who had "caved in to political pressure from the left" and possibly even had been bought off. Doles and a small group of his buddies in Northwest Georgia had talked about going to Washington that day to attend Trump's rally, but concluded it was likely a "trap" designed to "set up" patriotic Americans such as themselves. So they decided to make their stand at the Georgia Gold Dome instead. Doles had assembled a boisterous crowd of about forty for the event—members of a political group he had founded a few years earlier, the American Patriots USA, along with what he described as its affiliated "militia wing." Why the need for an armed militia to make his case about presumed election discrepancies? They were there, Doles said, "to protect us from Antifa attacks."

To call Doles a bigot does not quite do justice to his twisted worldview or his checkered background. One of his ancestors, Brigadier General George Pierce Doles, from Milledgeville, Georgia (the state's former Confederate capital), had commanded troops in Antietam and Gettysburg before being killed at the Battle of Cold Harbor. The general's descendants for the next four generations were active in the KKK's Invisible Empire. Chester Doles was the fifth generation and continued the family tradition. As a five-year-old growing up on Maryland's Eastern Shore, he had joined the Ku Klux Klan's "Youth Corps." As he grew older, he graduated to "Exalted Cyclops," then

"Grand Titan," then "Grand Klaliff," and finally a "Grand Dragon" for the Klan chapter covering southern Maryland, Pennsylvania, and Delaware. Doles tried, improbably, to put a benign spin on his life in the Klan, insisting it was not all about spreading terror. "We only used the robes for private ceremonies for cross burnings," he said.

After returning to his ancestral roots in Georgia, Doles—who had spent seven years in prison for beating up a Black man in the 1990s and then was locked up again some years later on federal firearms charges—would insist he had undergone a soulful conversion and forsworn racism. But that did not quite square with the public record. In the early 2000s, Doles was Georgia coordinator for the neo-Nazi National Alliance, even inviting the group's founder, William Luther Pierce, author of the race war fantasy *The Turner Diaries*, to speak at one of his meetings. (Pierce was accompanied to the event by a Holocaust-denying former Nazi SS officer who had once served as a bodyguard for Adolf Hitler.) By 2015, he had become a leader of the Confederate Hammerskins, a branch of a worldwide skinhead movement, hosting a rally outside Athens, Georgia, where he invoked the memory of "our Viking ancestors" and exhorted the crowd of about a hundred to collect their "favorite weapons" and prepare for battle. "For us, it's victory or Valhalla," he proclaimed.

And then in August 2017, Doles along with more than twenty of his Hammerskins buddies marched in the white-supremacist-led "Unite the Right" rally in Charlottesville, Virginia, where he got into a melee, throwing punches at counter-demonstrators who, he said, had started hurling brickbats and gas balloons just as he was about to shake hands with an old ally, David Duke.

Doles had been on the scene the night before when his fellow demonstrators had marched through the town carrying tiki torches and chanting, "Jews will not replace us!" Doles said he didn't join in the chant but shared the sentiment. Offering up a garbled version of the history of US immigration laws, Doles related how the country's current problems had begun years ago when Congress started letting in more people of color from Africa and Latin America rather than whites from Northern European countries. It was the Great Replacement Theory with a decided anti-Semitic twist. "You look at those senators and they were all Jewish," he said. "It just happens to be Jewish politicians for the past fifty years who came up with these open border policies."

For an interview, Doles suggested the Texas Roadhouse in the town of Cumming in "famous" Forsyth County. There was no mistaking the allusion. Forsyth County, about forty miles north of Atlanta, was long notorious for being the whitest county in the country—a distinction it achieved in 1912 when a mob of white vigilantes broke into the local jail, grabbed a Black man accused of raping a white woman, bashed his skull with crowbars, and then lynched him. In the days that followed, two more Black teenagers were hung for the same alleged rape as an estimated five thousand white onlookers who had assembled with their picnic baskets watched and cheered. What came next was one of the more shocking episodes in Georgia's venomous racial history: Virtually the county's entire Black population of eleven hundred were driven from their homes, their schools and churches fire-bombed by the white mob, an unvarnished act of racial cleansing.

As a result, Forsyth County for decades had no need for separate WHITE and COLORED Jim Crow signs for a simple reason: There were no Blacks left in the county. When the civil rights leader Hosea Williams led a "walk for brotherhood" through Forsyth seventy-five years later, he was pelted with stones and rocks by a crowd of whites that included Klan members. "I have never seen such hatred," Williams told *The New York Times* after the January 1987 melee. "I have been in the civil rights movement thirty years and I'm telling you we've got a South Africa in the backyard of Atlanta, Georgia, thirty-eight miles away."

This was a history Doles knew well.

Over a rib-eye dinner, Doles—a jug-eared man of sixty-two years with cropped white hair, a goatee, and a devil-may-care cackle—proudly displayed his ripped arms festooned with white pride tattoos. He whipped out his wallet to show off a mock credit card he keeps that reads in all caps: WHITE PRIVILEGE CARD / TRUMPS EVERYTHING. As Doles explained it, the white race was under relentless attack from Antifa. They were being backed by the Democrats whose platform, he insisted, if you looked at it "side by side," was the same as that of the Communist Party. He and his right-minded patriots needed to be ready. "We need to get this Civil War going," he said. "It's inevitable."

But Doles's confidence—and his bonhomie—cracked when a sore subject came up: his family. Doles is the father of thirteen children. Some years ago, one of his daughters had moved in with a Black man and gave birth to three of his children. Then it happened again: Another daughter shacked up with another Black man, giving Doles yet more biracial grandchildren. In the Klan's worldview, no horror was greater than the threat of miscegenation. A pained expression crossed Doles's craggy face as he related his tale of woe. He acknowledged he had a hard time dealing with his daughters' betrayal. At first, he had wanted nothing to do with them—or his biracial grandchildren. But, he said, he was coming around. As a demonstration of his new capacity for tolerance, Doles said he had recently swung by the home of one of his daughters and tossed her oldest, a teenage girl, a $100 bill for Halloween.

It would be comforting to believe that Doles is a dinosaur, a relic from a dark past whose racist and anti-Semitic views can no longer be uttered in polite company. But there was little doubt that Trump's election had emboldened him—and thousands of bigots like him. Trump "gave us hope—that maybe we can save America," Doles said about his allegiance to the forty-fifth president. "He called it like it is—he spoke for blue-collar America, for Christian America."

Doles was especially energized when Trump said after the Charlottesville march that there were "fine people on both sides." It was, as Doles saw it, a clear message to marchers like him. "Of course they wanted him to come after every one of us," he said. "Trump knew better."

Doles's enthusiasm for Trump spurred him to become active in Georgia politics. In 2019, he formed American Patriots USA to push for, among other causes, creating a "Second Amendment Sanctuary" in Georgia that would refuse to recognize any state or federal gun laws. That September, he arranged for the group to stage a pro-Trump rally in his hometown of Dahlonega, telling a reporter that the forty-fifth president was "our savior." He soon began handing out flyers and putting up yard signs as well for a local congressional candidate, Marjorie Taylor Greene. He even announced a campaign for county commissioner (an ultimately doomed move given that the state banned convicted felons such as Doles from running for office).

Doles's notoriety soon caught up with him. One of Trump's lead backers in the state, Congressman Doug Collins, pulled out of his Dahlonega rally when he learned Doles was behind it, saying there was no place in Georgia for advocates of "white supremacy." Even Greene—whom Doles said had met with him several times and had her photo taken with him—eventually had him evicted from one of her campaign events. Still, Doles's new activism had consequences. After setting up his political organization, he then created his own affiliated militia he called the American Brotherhood of Patriots.

The idea was that the Brotherhood of Patriots militia would serve as the armed wing for his pro-Trump American Patriots political organization. "It was kind of like the Sinn Féin and the IRA," he explained. The Sinn Féin was the aboveground political party that fought to end British rule in Northern Ireland. The IRA, whose members planted bombs and engaged in other acts of terrorism, was its armed paramilitary wing. Amid the battle over the 2020 election, the American Brotherhood of Patriots had joined forces with other militia groups—most notably, the state's "Three Percenters" (who had supplied security for Greene's campaign)—to push for a new cause: demanding that Georgia secede from the Union, again. It was, in effect, a new united front of far-right Georgia militias; its members underwent paramilitary training and drove around in motorcycle convoys in rural corners of the state to gear themselves up to do battle with their Antifa enemies—and anybody supporting them.

And as was clear when its members showed up with Doles at the Gold Dome in Atlanta on January 6, 2021, they brought their own air of menace to the legal and political battle over the 2020 election.

Few experienced that menace more than Brad Raffensperger. Tall, thin, soft-spoken, and unfailingly polite, Raffensperger was something of an odd duck in the state capital. He was a data-driven professional engineer (and former Sunday school teacher) who studiously avoided inflammatory rhetoric and displayed little zest for the boisterous rough-and-tumble of the state's political scene. He had first been elected to an open seat in the state legislature in 2014—a self-described "very conservative," pro-business Republican whose political hero was Ronald Reagan. Yet he took pride in his friendly relations with Democrats, some of whom he prayed with in a Bible study group every Wednesday. He also had a curious, if attenuated, history with Trump. As a young man decades earlier, Raffensperger had worked for a contractor who supplied high-strength steel to the Trump Organization for construction at the renovated Trump Plaza hotel in New York City. Raffensperger was, from a distance, taken by Trump, thinking (wrongly) that the brash, young, and apparently successful developer was a "self-made man." When Trump first announced for president in 2015, Raffensperger was among the first in the Georgia General Assembly to endorse him. "Yeah, like okay, he's a little rough around the edges," he recalled thinking at the time about the real estate mogul candidate. Then again, he figured, "I'm tired of politicians. He's a business owner. And, from afar, I thought, well, let's see how he does." Trump in time would return the favor: In November 2018, when Raffensperger was facing a runoff in his race for secretary of state, Trump weighed in from the White House, tweeting: "Brad Raffensperger will be a fantastic Secretary of State for Georgia—will work closely with @BrianKempGA. It is really important that you get out and vote for Brad."

There is no evidence that Raffensperger ever expressed doubts about Trump or his administration throughout his presidency. But it was also true that for at least part of that time, Raffensperger was dealing with the most painful of personal crises. His oldest son, Brenton, a gifted A student in school and talented oil painter, had been a chronic substance abuser who had been in and out of rehab programs since he was a teenager. He also had multiple run-ins with the law that included two prison sentences. Brenton's troubles put Raffensperger and his wife, Tricia, through the sort of pain that only a parent can know. One night they drove into town and waited outside an Atlanta crack house, fearing their son was inside. After one of his convictions for cocaine possession and a DUI in 2015, a judge ordered Brenton to buy a casket at a funeral home. He should then put it in his living room, the judge ordered, "as a reminder of the deadly consequences of your choices. I want you to be reminded every day that if you don't change your ways, you are a dead man." It didn't work. Three years later, on April 3, 2018, while he was running for secretary of state, Raffensperger got a phone call from the Atlanta Police Department. Brenton had died from a fentanyl overdose. He was thirty-eight years old.

Raffensperger and Tricia had been married for forty-four years. She is even more reserved than her husband, and in their grief they both took refuge in their faith. They had, he would later write, prayed for Brenton to heal every day for more than twenty years, to no avail. (Amid his drug addiction, Brenton had also been diagnosed with stage 3B Hodgkin's lymphoma.) At times, the Raffenspergers identified with the anguished lament of an Old Testament prophet named Habakkuk: "How long, Lord, have I called for help? And You do not hear?" But there was one small upside to the couple's personal tragedy. The experience fortified them for the election ordeal they were about to go through. His detractors would occasionally mock Raffensperger for what they viewed as sanctimonious posturing. "Oh, you mean, Saint Brad of Assisi?" one prominent Georgia Republican said with a mischievous smile when asked about the secretary of state. But there was, in the end, a steely edge to Raffensperger. As he would later write: "We've been through worse."

––––––––––––

Raffensperger wasn't the only one with a hard edge. Aside from Sterling—his chief of operations and the office "pit bull"—there was also his chief of staff, Jordan Fuchs. A cheery thirty-year-old with shaggy blond locks, Fuchs had a pleasant demeanor that disguised the sharp instincts of a savvy political operative. After serving for seven years at Mark Rountree's political consulting firm, Landmark Communications, rising to the level of vice president, Fuchs was one of the very few women in the front tier of Georgia Republican politics—an experience that sharpened her elbows and taught her that if she was to be taken seriously she would have to assert herself and punch back hard when attacked. After managing Raffensperger's race for secretary of state as a principal at Landmark, she had a falling-out with Rountree over money, in particular over whether she would get a cut of the lucrative TV ad buys placed by the firm. Fuchs left Landmark, and the newly elected secretary of state tapped her at the tender age of twenty-eight to be his chief of staff. It was a heady move for Fuchs, and she would remain fiercely loyal to and protective of Raffensperger, qualities that would soon be on full display and ultimately carry huge consequences in the vicious battle over the 2020 election.

It had been abundantly clear to Fuchs for some time that Trump was facing heavy headwinds in Georgia. In May, she had gotten an unsettling phone call from a *Washington Post* reporter. (Unlike many of her fellow Republican consultants with whom she had worked, Fuchs had friendly working relations with members of the Fourth Estate.) The reporter started asking a series of questions about the electoral process in the state. What if Trump loses Georgia? the reporter wanted to know. Could the state legislature award the state's electoral votes to Trump anyway? Fuchs was puzzled. She put the reporter on with Ryan Germany, the office legal counsel. No way, he explained. The law in Georgia was crystal clear—and had been for decades. The secretary of state tabulated the votes and presented the results to the governor; the governor then certified the slate of presidential electors "with the highest number of votes." There was no wiggle room for the general assembly to do anything different (unless it were to somehow choose, after Election Day, to change the state's long-established law about how to award electors).

But the more Fuchs thought about it, the more convinced she was that the questions hadn't come out of the blue. The only reason she was getting these questions, she concluded, was that Trump's strategists were thinking ahead and floating the idea. "It was clear to me that the Trump campaign had concluded they were going to lose and to stay in power they would have to use such a maneuver," Fuchs said.

As Fuchs saw it, the Trump team had good reason to be worried. The Georgia electorate had been undergoing a steady transformation over the previous decade and was trending increasingly blue. Some of that evolution, ironically, was the result of steps taken by Republican governors that turned out to have unintended political consequences. In 2005, GOP governor Sonny Perdue signed a law giving generous tax breaks to Hollywood movie studios that invested in the state. The incentives, intended to boost the state's economy, turned moviemaking in Georgia into a multi-billion-dollar behemoth. (Among the biggest beneficiaries of Perdue's tax breaks were giants like Amazon, Sony, and Disney, whose Marvel Studios filmed *Spider-Man*, *Black Panther*, and other blockbusters in the state.) The tax breaks also brought in thousands of new actors, directors, writers, makeup artists, and other newcomers—a huge pool of new voters with, as one Democratic operative wryly noted, "Hollywood values."

Then, in 2016, Republican governor Nathan Deal adopted automatic voter registration at state motor vehicle offices, fueling another spike in the state's active voter rolls, from 6.7 million that year to 7.6 million in 2020. The number of Black registered voters in the state rose more than 12 percent (240,000 new voters) during that same period; Hispanic voters a whopping 72 percent (108,000). These sharp increases, especially among minorities, spelled trouble for the GOP. Key regions, such as Cobb County, the Atlanta suburb that once elected Newt Gingrich to Congress, had become reliably blue. State-wide, Republicans had been losing support by 1.5 percentage points in each election cycle. If that trend continued, Fuchs concluded, Trump was in deep trouble.

On top of all that, the average age of Republican voters was getting older. By 2020, it had reached sixty-five. It was a segment of the electorate that was most vulnerable to the still-raging Covid epidemic and most likely to want to take advantage of the state's relatively lenient, no-excuse mail-in-balloting option. In March 2020, amid alarm over Covid, Raffensperger decided to mail out absentee ballot applications to every registered voter in the state. He promptly got attacked for it by the president's allies in the state. Perversely (or so Fuchs thought), Trump was shooting himself in the foot. All summer long, Trump was on a rampage about mail-in voting, calling it a "whole big scam." "MILLIONS OF MAIL-IN BALLOTS WILL BE PRINTED BY FOREIGN COUNTRIES," resulting in a "RIGGED" election, Trump tweeted in June. Thanks to mail-in voting, "2020 will be the most INACCURATE & FRAUDULENT Election in history," he tweeted on July 30, 2020. "Delay the election until people can properly, securely and safely vote???" Whatever its impact elsewhere, Trump's anti-mail-in-voting jihad was undercutting the best chance Georgia Republicans had to get their aging voters—at least those worried they might get sick from Covid—to vote that year. And as was increasingly obvious, Trump was using the issue to publicly lay the groundwork to challenge the election results, and rile up his angry army of supporters, just in case he came up short.

In the days after the election, the trend was clear. Trump's election-night lead in the state had steadily melted away as absentee ballots and the results from Democratic-leaning counties came in. There was a bit of poetic justice to the numbers: The tipping point that put Biden over the top was Chatham County, a heavily Black suburb south of Atlanta, represented in Congress by civil rights icon John Lewis, a district that Trump himself had once derided as "crime infested" and "horrible."

Inside a crowded fifth-floor conference room at Republican Party headquarters in Atlanta's tony Buckhead district, Trump's Georgia legal team was plotting its counterattack. Cleta Mitchell, a gruff, hard-right GOP campaign lawyer who for years had served as the outside counsel for the National Rifle Association and other conservative groups, had flown down from Washington with a singular directive from White House chief of staff Mark Meadows—flood the zone with lawsuits and challenge the election result at every stage. Mitchell "was pushing hard—file everything, file everywhere," recalled Bryan Tyson, a Georgia Republican election lawyer who had been hired by the campaign. As part of her team, Mitchell had brought with her a self-styled "data analyst" named Matthew Braynard, who had actually been fired by the Trump campaign in 2016 in a personnel dispute. Braynard had now wormed his way back into good graces by producing a "report"—actually, a one-page computer printout—claiming that he had found statistical disparities and other indicators proving there had been twenty-one thousand "illegal" ballots cast in Georgia, including dead voters, underage voters, and out-of-state voters. Mitchell seemed to accept the analysis. "Cleta was citing Braynard's numbers all the time," said Tyson.

But Tyson, meticulous and cautious, pushed back. Where's the evidence to back any of this up? he kept asking. The basis for Braynard's claims about out-of-state votes was that he had found voters registered in other states with similar names to Georgia voters. But, Tyson asked, how do you know the John Smith who lives in New York is the same John Smith who voted in Georgia? Have you checked middle names? Their ages and birth dates? Any other basic data that would prove it's the same voter? For Tyson's trouble, Mitchell accused him of being "disloyal" and unwilling to fight for the president.*

It was all too much for Tyson. Pressed to draft lawsuits challenging election results on behalf of Trump, he balked. "I wasn't going to sign my name to something that didn't have any evidence behind it," he said. He and two of his co-counsels soon quit the case.

Tyson didn't have much choice. He and his firm had already been retained to represent the Georgia Secretary of State's Office—the prospective defendant in any Trump campaign filing—in a separate case growing out of Stacey Abrams's claims of "voter suppression"

---

* Mitchell, in an email to the authors, disputed aspects of Tyson's account, saying she had no "preconceived notions" about filing lawsuits in Georgia until she arrived on the scene and discovered that, as she saw it, "there were more illegal votes than the margin of victory." Braynard was "only one of the experts" she relied on, and her team "did not utilize some of his data because we could not confirm its accuracy." She also said that, in her view, the "loyalties" of Tyson, long considered one of the Georgia Republican Party's top election lawyers, "were not with the GOP or the Trump campaign."

in her 2018 race against Kemp.* Once it became clear that Raffensperger would be a likely defendant in any lawsuit the Trump campaign brought, it would have been an obvious conflict for him to stay on and sue the secretary of state he was then defending. Still, faced with a choice of representing Donald Trump or Brad Raffensperger, the answer for Tyson was clear. He chose Raffensperger. In so doing, he became the first of Trump's lawyers to drop out. But there would soon be more.

Meanwhile, Mitchell was leaving nothing to chance. Even while pushing for lawsuits "everywhere," as the legal quarterback in Georgia, she was crafting a backup plan very much in line with the one Fuchs had surmised from her conversation with the *Washington Post* reporter months earlier. On November 5—just two days after Election Day—Mitchell had reached out via email to a reliably conservative law professor in California who would soon loom large in the post-election

---

* Abrams would describe her narrow loss to Kemp as a "stolen" election because her opponent had "cheated," insisting that she would back up her claims in a lawsuit filed by Fair Fight, her political organization. Raffensperger, who had succeeded Kemp as secretary of state and was required to defend the integrity of the election, would frequently point out the parallels between the Democratic candidate's claims and those later made by Trump and his allies, though clearly they were on a different scale, with no threats of violence or intimidation by the Abrams camp. Still, Raffensperger was able to claim vindication in September 2023 when, after years of discovery and a months-long bench trial, U.S. Judge Steve Jones—an African American jurist who had been appointed by President Barack Obama—rejected every single one of Fair Fight's claims of unconstitutional voting rights violations. "Although Georgia's election system is not perfect, the challenged practices violate neither the Constitution nor the Voting Rights Act," he wrote in a 288-page order that also noted that the plaintiffs were unable to produce any "direct evidence of a voter who was unable to vote, experienced longer wait times [or] was confused about voter registration status." The ruling received far less national attention than Abrams's original allegations.

battle: John Eastman, a former law clerk to Supreme Court justice Clarence Thomas. Her ask: Could Eastman provide a legal memo arguing that state legislatures could "reclaim" their "constitutional duty" to designate their own electors—regardless of state laws (such as the one in Georgia) requiring governors to designate presidential electors based on the winner of the popular vote? "Am I crazy?" she asked Eastman, a seeming sign that she realized the idea was—by contemporary standards, in a democracy—off the wall. Still, she wrote: "A movement is stirring. But it needs constitutional support."

On November 6, three days after the election, Raffensperger and Sterling had held a joint press conference on the steps of the Capitol in which they vowed to make sure that "every legal vote is counted" and investigate any claims of fraud while they conducted (given the tightness of the results) a statewide recount. But Sterling then went off message, as far as the Trump camp was concerned. "We are not seeing widespread irregularities," he told the reporters. Trump and his allies were furious. The Trump campaign announced that Congressman Doug Collins, who had just finished third in the Senate race behind the Reverend Raphael Warnock and the incumbent, Kelly Loeffler, would head up a team that would find the fraud and "prove that President Trump won Georgia." (Collins immediately showed up at the Buckhead conference room with Mitchell and Braynard. So, too, did the just-elected new congresswoman, Marjorie Taylor Greene, bearing freshly baked cookies.) That same day, Donald Trump Jr. and his girlfriend, Kimberly Guilfoyle, flew down to Atlanta and held a series of meetings at the Buckhead headquarters to fire up the troops. Don Jr. had a simple message: "People love my father because he's a fighter and now it's time for people to fight for him." Guilfoyle then whipped

out her cell phone, placed it on a chair in the middle of the conference room, and put it on speakerphone. Phoning in from his South
Carolina plantation was L. Lin Wood, the lawyer who was about to
become one of the public faces of the president's Georgia legal assault.
"I'm ready to fight for the president!" shouted Wood, a renowned
trial lawyer who was even then in the beginnings of a bizarre public
crack-up that would soon prompt Georgia state bar officials to question his sanity.

But after the office pep rally, Don Jr. held other meetings at the
Buckhead headquarters that turned into a raucous "shit show," recalled
one veteran GOP strategist who was present for the fireworks. Senate
majority leader Mitch McConnell had dispatched one of his top aides
at the National Republican Senatorial Committee (NRSC) to insist
that the party's resources, including fundraising and volunteers, be
devoted to getting out the vote for the state's two Republican senators, David Perdue and Kelly Loeffler, in an upcoming January 5 runoff in which control of the US Senate would be on the line. But Don
Jr. would have none of it; his message was "screw the NRSC," said the
strategist. Talking to top GOP officials, he demanded that state party
officials back the claims of a stolen election and put all their resources
into fighting the results for the presidency, or his father would "tank"
Loeffler and Perdue in the runoff, according to the testimony of Robert
Sinners, a Trump campaign official, before the January 6 committee.

Donald Trump Jr. would later deny he made such an explicit threat.
But his public comments seemed to suggest that this was exactly what
he had in mind. "Guess what? You're going to have another election
here in about two months that could decide the fate of the United
States Senate," he had warned his fellow Republicans at a hastily called
press conference in a parking lot outside the party headquarters. "So
we're going to be watching this nonsense."

The truth is Georgia Republican leaders at this point were living in mortal fear of alienating Trump. Although Loeffler and Perdue had both outperformed Trump on Election Day, the two senators had finished just below the 50 percent threshold needed for victory under Georgia law and were facing stiff challenges, respectively, from Democrats Warnock and Jon Ossoff. And here was the president's son suggesting his father would blow up their chances if he didn't get his way. "There was an overriding concern that we did not want Donald Trump to think that we dropped the ball—yes, we were all concerned about keeping him happy," said David Shafer, the state GOP chair. "We didn't want him getting mad at Georgia Republicans when we were trying to hold things together for the run-off." This was no easy task. Leaving one of the meetings at the Buckhead conference center that week, Shafer "looked like he'd seen a ghost," Sinners testified.

The party's chief strategists grappled with what to do. "We've got a problem," former governor (and Trump's secretary of agriculture) Sonny Perdue told Nick Ayers, an influential GOP strategist who for a while served as Mike Pence's chief of staff, and sought to resolve the dispute, according to a source privy to one of the meetings. An idea was floated during the Buckhead meetings: "Why don't we get David and Kelly to call on Raffensperger to resign?" the source recalled. On the afternoon of November 9—under intense pressure from Trump and his minions—Loeffler and Perdue dutifully fell in line: They released a joint statement calling for Raffensperger's resignation over his "mismanagement" of the election. "He has failed the people of Georgia, and he should step down immediately," the two senators said. Seventeen minutes after its release, Trump, apparently mollified for the time being, weighed in with a tweet: "Georgia will be a big presidential win, as it was the night of the Election!"

If the purpose of the statement was to keep Trump from getting "mad" at them, the maneuverings by state party officials and the two US senators had a devastating but entirely predictable side effect: Raffensperger was now squarely in the crosshairs of MAGA world, about to face furies he never imagined. So, too, was his family.

Your husband deserves to face a firing squad. So read the text message from an anonymous sender that popped up on Tricia Raffensperger's cell phone at 9:22 p.m. that night, just hours after the Perdue-Loeffler statement. The Raffenspergers were at home, in their bedroom, and stared at the phone in disbelief. The messages kept coming in, one after another, as though this was orchestrated. At 10:31 p.m.: *The Raffenspergers should be put on trial for treason and face execution.* At 10:45 p.m.: *You and your family are traitors to conservatism.* At 11:15 p.m.: *You better not botch this recount. Your life depends on it.* At 12:08 a.m.: *Suck a dick, bitch.*

And then there were equally ugly and sexualized messages in the form of fake email addresses that were interspersed with the texts: "bradandtricia@traitors.gov," "raffensperger@deathsentence .us," "hang.traitors@patriots.biz," "triciaslut@fraud.us." One even spoofed a message from Raffensperger himself to his wife: *I married a sickening whore. I wish you were dead.*

Who was sending these vile messages? How did they get Tricia Raffensperger's cell phone number? The Raffenspergers were unnerved. But Tricia knew who she blamed: the senators who were doing Trump's bidding. They had become, she thought, Trump's "puppets." Fed up, angry, and scared, she fired off her own text messages that night to both of them. The Raffenspergers knew both senators. Perdue had even attended a fundraiser for Raffensperger during his campaign for secretary of state. Tricia had had a pleasant, if innocuous, encounter with Loeffler, the wife of a Wall Street tycoon, when they were introduced at the Trump White House Christmas party the year before, just days after Brian Kemp had appointed her to fill the seat of the retiring Johnny Isakson.

Now Tricia held nothing back.

"Never did I think you were the kind of person to unleash such hate and fury on someone in political office of the same party," she wrote Loeffler in a text that night. "My family and I am being personally besieged by people threatening our lives because you didn't have the decency or good manners to come and talk to my husband with any questions you may have had. Instead you have put us in the eye of the storm.

"Unlike you," she continued, "my husband is an honorable man with integrity to do the right thing...I hold you personally responsible for anything that happens to any of my family, from my husband, children and grandchildren...What kind of person are you that you would purposely do this?...You do not deserve to be in elected office. You are not worthy of that position. Good day and Good night!"

In the days that followed, it was clear the Raffenspergers had good reason to worry about the safety of their family. The threats continued and grew more menacing. Strangers in cars started showing up in their neighborhood and lurking outside their house. The state police informed the couple that members of the Oath Keepers, a far-right militia, were casing the place. That same night, Tricia Raffensperger called her husband in a panic: Their daughter-in-law, Brenton's wife and the mother of their two grandchildren, had been out shopping and was being followed by men holding up cell phones taking photos. The next night, her home was broken into. For the Raffenspergers, it was too much. The couple had never stopped grieving Brenton's death. Now the followers of Donald Trump were targeting the widowed wife of their dead son.

The Raffenspergers were protected by state troopers who stationed a patrol car outside the house. A group of Navy SEAL veterans had also volunteered to help. But the couple made a command decision: They fled their house at 10:00 p.m. on the Friday before Thanksgiving, flying—with their daughter-in-law and two grandchildren—on a private jet to Virginia Beach, where they rented rooms in a hotel. They figured they'd stay there to ride out the storm.

———————

But the storm never subsided. In the crazed buildup to the assault on the US Capitol on January 6, capitals in states crucial to Trump's reversal of the election results were overrun with protestors—nowhere more so than in Georgia, arguably ground zero for the whole business. Far-right activists were showing up at the Gold Dome nearly every day. On November 18, an armored truck carrying Infowars conspiracy theorist Alex Jones and a young white nationalist agitator, Nicholas Fuentes, circled the building. Jones and Fuentes, joined by Stop the Steal organizer Ali Alexander, Proud Boys leader Enrique Tarrio, and Oath Keepers founder Stewart Rhodes, shouted at lawmakers through bullhorns and threatened state officials if they did not overturn Biden's victory. "If you take away our rights, and destroy our way of life, then we will shut the country down!" declared Fuentes before a rally of two hundred protestors. Alexander exhorted them to "storm the capitol." "Our country is literally fighting for its life from a multi-national global takeover!" proclaimed Jones. It turned out to be a dry run—scary but without the violence—for what would happen at the US Capitol a little more than six weeks later.

The next day, November 19, Raffensperger announced that a full statewide recount, including an audit of thousands of ballots checked by hand, had affirmed Biden's narrow victory in Georgia. It was an important milestone. Hand recounts couldn't be hacked or flipped by secret algorithms, so to credibly argue that fraud had occurred, you would have to believe that Raffensperger's staff had worked with local election workers to deliberately miscount the ballots, adding numbers to Biden's total and subtracting from Trump's. The president wasn't deterred. In a rambling conversation with White House reporters, he called the Georgia secretary of state "an enemy of the people."*

Within days, a new website popped up on far-right social media platforms: enemiesofthepeople.com. The site included a "kill list"—photographs of multiple federal and state officials who had defied Trump's demands to declare the election a fraud, Raffensperger and his deputy Sterling among them. Superimposed over Raffensperger's face was a target. Alongside it was his address and a satellite photo of his home. If you clicked on the photo, the site helpfully provided its GPS coordinates.

The initial assumption of law enforcement was that the website was the work of some enterprising MAGA loyalist. But it turned out Chester Doles and his white supremacist militia buddies weren't the only ones taking their cues from Donald Trump. When the FBI investigated the site, they traced it overseas, to Iranian cyber hackers who, acting most likely with government backing, had adopted a page from the Russian playbook in 2016 and were doing their part to stir up America's political divisions. It was yet another example of a disturbing trend in the global propaganda wars. The United States was so rife with partisan hatred, and seemingly so ready to explode into political violence, that its fiercest foreign rivals saw endless opportunities to ignite the tinderbox.

---

* In a deposition before the January 6 committee, Raffensperger was asked about what he made of Trump calling him "an enemy of the people." His response pretty much summed up Trump's entire strategy at this point: "I think he somewhere in life has this learned behavior that if he attacks people, makes up stuff and disparages them, that he'll get what he wants."

CHAPTER FIVE

The Targeting of Innocents

"They really talked about how they were going to lynch me."

The high-level pressure that had been aimed at Brad Raffensperger in the weeks after the election was only one piece of a much broader intimidation campaign targeting virtually any Georgia official, state or local, who had anything to do with the 2020 election. It was a crude, blunderbuss strategy that would quickly take on racially charged overtones. By the end of November, Trump, his lawyers, and his political allies were aiming their fire not just at Georgia's Republican secretary of state but also at a handful of African Americans who had played unsung roles in counting the votes in the Democratic stronghold of Fulton County.

One of them was Ralph Jones, chief of registration and mail-in ballots in the Fulton County Board of Registration and Elections. The soft-spoken Jones, fifty-six, was a popular figure in the office, known for his generosity and sweet disposition. A co-worker recalled that Jones was the person colleagues turned to when they were having a problem at work or in their personal lives. "He's such an empathetic listener," said one colleague.

It was an empathy—and optimism—that was instilled in Jones growing up in Collier Heights, a sanctuary of Black middle- and upper-class Atlanta where he was steeped in the city's rich if racially tortured history. Among those who showed up for his mother's Sunday-night dinners (heaping servings of baked chicken, macaroni and cheese, collard greens, and fruit pies for dessert) were prominent civil rights figures like Vernon Jordan and C. T. Martin, known as the Dean of the Atlanta City Council for his decades of service. A fixture at those Sunday-night dinners was Joseph Pierce—brother of Jones's mother and known as Uncle Pug, a student civil rights activist who, frustrated with the slow pace of change, helped launch a series of sit-ins and demonstrations that accelerated the end of legal segregation in Atlanta.

As a child in the 1970s, Jones was insulated from the indignities his parents and their generation had lived through. By 1973, Atlanta had a Black mayor, Maynard Jackson Jr., the first African American to lead a major Southern city. Blacks were a majority of the city's population, and they had accumulated wealth and power as in no other city in America. Whereas cities like Boston and Newark were cauldrons of racial tension over busing, housing, and economic inequality, Atlanta was thriving as the "Black Mecca" of the South. It, of course, faced many of the same underlying racial problems that existed elsewhere. But the Black power elite and the white business interests mostly worked together to paper over lingering racial issues and emphasize progress, economic dynamism, and Atlanta's carefully cultivated image, dating back to the 1950s, as "the city too busy to hate."

All this had given Jones an upbeat, positive outlook on Georgia's racial progress. Some regarded him as naive, but most in the Fulton election office were touched by his ability to see the good in even the most malevolent people. "I just liked to smooth things over," he said about his penchant for avoiding uncomfortable racial conflict.

But that became ever harder in the aftermath of the November 3 election. Fulton County had voted overwhelmingly for Joe Biden, giving him 72 percent of the county's vote, a blowout that helped provide his narrow margin of victory in Georgia. Just days after the election, Jones arrived at his office, fired up his computer, and checked his emails. The first message that flashed on his screen jolted him. It said: "All traitors will be punished and you will rot in jail for stealing the election." That was followed by anonymous emails and phone calls that started pouring in, one threatening to kill him and drag his body through the streets of Atlanta with a pickup truck. As ugly as those were, what really rattled Jones was how many of the self-styled "patriots" invoked the ugliest episodes in Georgia's past. When Jones picked up his office phone one day shortly after the election, the caller said in a voice edged with fury, "N***er, you're going to hang for trying to steal the election." More than a year later, in an interview for this book, Jones seemed as pained as he was incredulous: "They really talked," he said, "about how they were going to lynch me."

On the face of it, the threats to lower-level Georgia election officials made no tactical or strategic sense. Ralph Jones had no power or authority to unilaterally cast aside any votes in Fulton County. But these threats were the inevitable by-product of a reckless game plan being pursued by a trigger-happy gang of lawyers who were just then taking over the Trump legal effort. It was a crew prone to making wild, half-baked public accusations that, as Justin Clark, Trump's deputy campaign manager and chief lawyer, later testified, "believed a lot more in trial by PR" than filing serious legal challenges that had any prayer of success.

The key figure in all this was Rudy Giuliani. Nearly twenty years after adorning magazine covers as "America's Mayor" in the aftermath of the attacks of September 11, 2001, the seventy-six-year-old Giuliani was now a pale shadow of his former self. The spectacular flame-out of his 2008 campaign for president, for which he raised more than $60 million and ended up winning a single delegate, was followed by years of political exile, mental depression, and debilitating bouts of binge drinking. "He was always falling shitfaced somewhere," his then wife Judith Nathan told his biographer, Andrew Kirtzman. By the Trump years, Giuliani, once a razor-sharp US attorney, had become a boozy, financially strapped unguided missile, addicted to near-nightly Fox News hits and prone to spouting ever more convoluted conspiracy theories.

That Giuliani was still on the scene was itself remarkable. Earlier in the year, he had been singularly responsible for Trump's first impeachment, having riled up the president the previous summer with murky claims about Ukrainian shenanigans involving Joe and Hunter Biden and a supposedly disloyal US ambassador that had been largely fed to him by two Soviet-born con men. Yet Giuliani, miraculously, had managed to stay in Trump's favor, apparently by telling him whatever it was he wanted to hear about the perfidy of his political enemies. On election night, Giuliani had shown up at the White House and late in the evening, when the numbers started to turn south, told Trump in the residence to ignore the results and just proclaim victory anyway. "I think the mayor was definitely intoxicated," said Jason Miller, one of Trump's top advisers, in one of the more memorable deposition clips played by the January 6 committee. Still, Giuliani's proposed proclamation was unquestionably exactly what Trump wanted to hear.

Giuliani's newfound central role in advancing increasingly delusional theories on what had supposedly happened in the election became clear four days later when he called a bizarre press conference in front of the garage door of the Four Seasons Total Landscaping Company in northeast Philadelphia—a weeding and mulch firm down the street from a porn shop—where he upped the ante, claiming there was "a very strong circumstantial case" that as many as six hundred thousand Pennsylvania ballots had been tampered with. To provide the evidence for this alleged ballot tampering, the first speaker Giuliani called to the podium was a Republican poll-watcher who complained about being unable to get close enough to see the ballots being counted in one Philly precinct. The poll-watcher turned out to be a convicted sex offender who had served three years in prison for exposing himself to underage girls.

By mid-November, just as Bryan Tyson and his associates were bowing out of the Trump legal team in Atlanta, the emergence of Giuliani led to a blowup in the Oval Office over the campaign's strategy in Georgia. Clark, the deputy Trump campaign manager, was explaining to the president that there was no point in filing a lawsuit in Georgia until Raffensperger's recount was complete and the votes were certified. Otherwise, under Georgia law, the courts wouldn't hear the case, said Clark, who had researched the issue.

Suddenly, Giuliani, via speakerphone from the Mandarin Oriental in New York City, told the president to ignore everything Clark was saying.

"He's lying to you!" Giuliani shouted, and repeated the point over and over.

Clark, standing in the middle of the Oval Office, erupted in anger. "You're a fucking asshole, Rudy!" Clark shouted back.

An eyewitness to the scene, Vice President Mike Pence, later wrote that he would never forget the look on the face of the "normally restrained and affable" Clark when Giuliani accused him of lying to the president. "I just kind of lost it on Rudy," Clark later told the January 6 committee. "We were screaming at each other."

And with that, Clark and his top deputy Matt Morgan became the next lawyers to step aside. The following day, Trump declared that Giuliani, not Clark, would lead his campaign's efforts to challenge the election results. It was, in Pence's view, the moment the campaign's legal efforts went off the rails. "The seeds were being sown for a tragic day in January," he wrote in his book *So Help Me God*.

In taking over Trump's Stop the Steal campaign, Giuliani was now overseeing an oddball collection of legal gunslingers, including a tall, cocky Texan named Sidney Powell, who was just then starting to spread fantastical claims that Venezuelan socialists and Chinese communists had supposedly implanted algorithms in the software of a third-party vendor, Dominion Voting Systems, used in Georgia and more than twenty other states. On November 13, she vowed to Fox News's Lou Dobbs that she was about "to release the Kraken," a reference to a mythical Norse sea monster that rises from the depths of the ocean to devour its enemies. While memes of the beast went viral on Twitter, just where Powell cooked up her "Kraken" was never clear; her sources seemed to change depending on who was asking. When asked for some evidence for her assertions by Maria Bartiromo, a true-believer Fox News host, Powell forwarded an email from one of her "sources"—a mysterious woman who described herself as a "technology analyst" who passed along some highly specific but wholly nonsensical details about how the Dominion algorithm had been programmed by nefarious actors to flip 3 percent of Trump's votes to

Biden—just low enough to avoid detection. As for how Powell's informant purportedly knew all this, the woman wrote she had learned about this plan in "dreams" or "visions" that were like "time-travel in a semi-conscious state." (She added: "The Wind tells me I'm a ghost... and that no one can harm me.")

Giuliani enthusiastically joined in the fray. On the day Trump tweeted that the former New York mayor was now in charge of the president's effort to challenge the election results, he advised campaign surrogates to lean in on Powell's allegations involving the Venezuelan vote-flipping software, Dominion, and another election technology company called Smartmatic. According to an internal campaign email, Giuliani said that the Trump team should "go hard on Dominion/Smartmatic, bring up Chavez and Maduro," referring to Hugo Chávez, Venezuela's late president, and Nicolás Maduro, his leftist successor. Trump himself breezily amplified the messaging, tweeting about how Dominion was a "very suspect" company. "With the turn of a dial or the change of a chip, you could press a button for Trump and the vote goes to Biden."

On November 19, Giuliani held another press conference, this time at Republican National Committee headquarters, where, as black hair dye dripped down his face, the president's lawyer ramped up the Dominion claims—adding new and increasingly deranged details of a global conspiracy in which ballots cast on the company's machines were being shipped to secret operational centers in Europe. Then he turned over the microphone to Powell, who had become his full-fledged partner in the insanity. "What we are really dealing with here and uncovering more by the day is the massive influence of communist money through Venezuela, Cuba, and likely China in the interference with our elections here in the United States," she said.

Watching the press conference, bewildered and "freaking out" was John Poulos, the CEO of Dominion. "How do we even get our arms around this?" he recalled thinking at the time. An earnest, soft-spoken, and impeccably polite Canadian engineer, Poulos had founded Dominion in the basement of his parents' home in 2002 and, with the help of an infusion of cash from a New York private equity firm, had turned it into one of the largest suppliers of electronic voting machines in the United States. But ever since Powell had begun spreading her wild claims in interviews on Fox News and other conservative outlets, Poulos and his company had been under siege. Hundreds of death threats to Dominion employees were pouring in, forcing the company to hire a private security firm to protect them. Poulos also retained a Washington, DC, crisis communications firm with GOP ties to refute everything the president's lawyers were spreading. "Are you watching this?" Mike Shirkey, the Michigan Republican state senate leader, asked Poulos in a phone call as the Giuliani-Powell press conference unfolded. The state senator, a Trump supporter, had spent four hours on the phone with Poulos a few days earlier and had come to realize that the story being pushed by Giuliani and Powell was utterly ridiculous. "I think they're trying to start a civil war," Poulos recalled Shirkey saying to him that day. But at the time, Poulos was convinced this would all end very soon. Raffensperger's office was on the verge of announcing the results of a hand recount audit of each ballot—the "gold standard" for recounts. Surely, Poulos thought, that would make all these vote-flipping algorithm charges go away, and the president and his supporters would stand down.

Aside from the sheer outlandishness of the Dominion vote-flipping allegations, there was another part of Giuliani's history that proved directly relevant to the events that followed. Even at the height of his power as the two-term Republican mayor of New York, Giuliani had a fraught relationship with the city's African American community. He had tangled repeatedly with civil rights leaders, refused for years to meet with local Black officials, and demonstrated little sensitivity when New York police officers were accused of mistreating Black men. The most notable instance came in 1997 when the city's police officers fired forty-one bullets into the body of Amadou Diallo, an unarmed twenty-two-year-old West African immigrant. Giuliani defended the cops and ridiculed those protesting the death of Diallo. The general consensus was that the congenitally pugnacious mayor had at the very least demonstrated insensitivity, if not outright hostility, to the concerns of his Black constituents.

It was a callousness that would be on glaring display when he flew down to Atlanta in early December to press the president's case.

On the morning of December 3, Giuliani and his retinue of MAGA lawyers crossed the manicured grounds of the Gold Dome, the neoclassical landmark that houses the Georgia General Assembly. They strode past symbols of the state's inglorious past: the bronze statues of John Brown Gordon, the Confederate-commander-turned-Klansman who was a leading proponent of the South's Lost Cause mythology, and Richard Russell, the once revered senator, a staunch segregationist who for decades bottled up civil rights and anti-lynching bills through his mastery of the art of the filibuster. Giuliani and his team had been invited to address a judiciary subcommittee of the Georgia State Senate about the alleged election irregularities. To back up their spurious claims, they had come armed with a far-out legal theory and a notoriously sliced-and-diced video that would soon take on mythical status in Trump's campaign to overturn the election.

The hearing began with a prayer delivered by Senator Bill Heath, a conservative Republican who had once gained brief national notoriety for unsuccessfully pushing a bill that would have banned women from getting genital piercings. "We pray, Lord, that in this meeting today that you would give us wisdom, that if there's anything that is not truthful that might come out of our mouths I pray that you would just remove that from our minds...we pray Lord that the truth will be brought to light in this meeting."

But from the start, the hearing strayed both from the truth and from normal protocols. After making a short opening statement, the panel's chair, William T. Ligon, a hard-right Trump supporter, effectively turned the session over to Giuliani, who proceeded to run it like he was the committee chairman. Giuliani called to the stand the hearing's first witness, Ray Smith, the Trump campaign's top local lawyer in Georgia.

In a dry delivery that masked his radical intentions, Smith told the assembled Georgia legislators that, in light of all the irregularities in the election, they and their colleagues had the power—indeed, the duty—to overturn the results of the presidential election in Georgia. This was the same radical theory that just three weeks before, Cleta Mitchell had asked John Eastman to lay out in a memo.

To add further weight to the idea, Eastman later Zoomed in from a decorously appointed law library to exhort the legislature to "take back its plenary power" and overturn the election results. Under the Constitution, "the legislature gets to do what it wants," Eastman told the lawmakers, pushing an argument—known as the independent state legislature theory—that had little support among his fellow constitutional scholars and would later be soundly rejected by the US Supreme Court. The Georgia General Assembly could simply conclude that various procedures Raffensperger had adopted to deal with the avalanche of absentee ballots expected during the pandemic—including how the signatures on those ballots were to be verified—were contrary to legislative intent, Eastman argued (even though, as multiple judges later concluded, the time for Trump and his allies to challenge such issues was *before* the election, not after, when the votes had been counted and they had lost). The purported procedural missteps alone made the election "invalid," Eastman testified, adding at one point in response to questioning, "There doesn't have to be evidence of fraud."

But far-fetched constitutional theories aside, Giuliani and his team instinctively knew that only evidence of actual fraud would move the needle. And they proceeded to unveil their case, igniting an onslaught of death threats and racial attacks terrorizing Georgia election workers and their families for months to come.

Giuliani called Jacki Pick, a Texas lawyer, conservative podcast host, and Republican donor who had volunteered her services to the Trump legal team. Giuliani had selected Pick to present what he would call "powerful smoking gun" evidence of election fraud—a surveillance video from a Fulton County election facility at the State Farm Arena in downtown Atlanta.

That Trump's team even had the video infuriated Raffensperger's office. It had been supplied the day before to both Trump's attorneys and Raffensperger's by a lawyer for the Atlanta Hawks, which owned the State Farm Arena. When he learned about this, Ryan Germany, Raffensperger's chief counsel, called up the basketball team's lawyer and demanded to know why the video had not been given first to the secretary of state's office, duly authorized overseer of state elections, so its experts could review it. He wanted to be fair "to both sides," the Hawks lawyer explained. Germany knew what being "fair" meant in this brawl: a chance for the Trump team to twist the contents of the video beyond all recognition, which was precisely what it did.

Projected on a screen were excerpts from the video, selectively edited and wildly misinterpreted, that as Pick explained it showed a well-orchestrated plot on election night to illegally stack the vote tally for Biden. First, she claimed, GOP poll-watchers and reporters were "forced to leave" after "a lady with blonde braids" came out and announced, "We're going to stop counting. Everybody go home." Then, Pick said, the election workers "move into action," surreptitiously hauling out "suitcases" stuffed with thousands of ballots while nobody was looking and jamming them repeatedly through scanners. "Once everyone is gone, coast is clear, they are going to pull ballots out from underneath a table," Pick said as she narrated the video.

The grainy security footage then showed two election workers, Wandrea "Shaye" Moss—the "lady with blonde braids"—and her mother Ruby Freeman, wearing a purple blouse, dragging the "suitcases" out from under their desks and moving around the room. Pick singled out the two African American women repeatedly during her testimony, telling the senators to "keep your eyes on the lady in purple"—whom she helpfully identified as "Ruby"—and the lady with the braids, a reference to Moss, effectively putting targets on their backs.

This was all dutifully live streamed by One America News Network (OAN), a leading site in the MAGA media ecosystem. Jenna Ellis, a Trump legal adviser working alongside Giuliani, tweeted "SHOCKING...VIDEO EVIDENCE. FRAUD!!!." Trump himself weighed in. "Wow—blockbuster testimony taking place right now in Georgia. Ballot stuffing by [Democrats] when Republicans were forced to leave the large counting room," he tweeted. Before the session was over, the State Farm video had gone viral, whipping pro-Trump zealots into a frenzy. Ruby Freeman's and Shaye Moss's names were rocketing around the internet. The Trump-friendly Gateway Pundit website piled on with story after story about the two women.

"CROOK GETS CAUGHT," one of them read, displaying a photo of Freeman that looked like a mug shot.

The selective editing, Pick's tendentious narration, as well as the jumpy security cam video, had indeed made the events at the State Farm Arena that night look sinister. And privately, some of Brad Raffensperger's own aides and allies were at first worried. "What if there's something to this?" wondered Brian Robinson, a veteran GOP consultant who had been hired to assist Raffensperger's office with its "messaging." What if those really were suitcases of fraudulent ballots? Robinson wasn't the only one who briefly got nervous. Attorney General Bill Barr, who had just given a press interview saying the Justice Department had found no grounds to believe there was widespread election fraud, told the US attorney in Atlanta, Byung Jin "BJay" Pak, during a phone call to "get to the bottom of it" and report back to him.

In fact, the entire video flap turned out to be a case of bureaucratic screwups, complete with miscommunications—and a bathroom mishap—that were twisted beyond recognition. Ralph Jones, the registration chief, was at the center of it. He had arrived at the State Farm Arena facility at 10:49 p.m. and concurred with the election workers that they could pack up and go home for the evening to get some rest. They had been working for eighteen straight hours, and Jones concluded that the vote scanning could pick up again early the next morning. So some of the workers started leaving; reporters and pollwatchers who had been there observing the count, figuring the vote scanning was over for the night, left as well. Moss and Freeman stayed to close up shop. They put the unscanned ballots in large plastic ballot carrier bins, sealed them up, and placed them under desks, normal protocols to prevent tampering.

But at a command center at Georgia's emergency management center, Raffensperger was "ripped," according to the written notes of Carter Jones, a state-appointed monitor tapped to be the official observer of the Fulton County vote count. The reasons were obvious: This was a presidential election. The whole country was desperate for the outcome, and they stopped counting ballots in Georgia's largest county? "Fulton can't get anything right," an exasperated Raffensperger blurted out to his staff, according to Jones's notes. Raffensperger had immediately given a TV interview calling for Fulton County to restart the counting of the ballots. Moments later, Chris Harvey, the director of state elections for Raffensperger's office, had called over to Rick Barron, the Fulton election chief, and told him to get back to work. At 10:58 p.m., Barron, the elections chief, called Jones to pass along the secretary's directive. At that point, Moss and Freeman, now aided by Jones, began pulling the ballot box containers out from under the desks. But by then, the Republican poll-watchers and much of the press had left, unaware that the ballot counting was being resumed.

This was a hiccup in the process, to be sure. And for about forty-five minutes, before Carter Jones, the state-appointed monitor, arrived on the scene, there was counting of ballots with no observers or press watching (although the surveillance camera captured video of everything that took place). But none of this was evidence of a conspiracy to rig an election. Gabriel Sterling aggressively pushed back, holding a "Disinformation Monday" press conference a few days later, on December 7, pointing out that a review of the entire video showed nothing that Giuliani and Pick had claimed it did. The secretary of state's office along with the Georgia Bureau of Investigation and the FBI (at the direction of US attorney Pak) had by then launched an official probe following the hearing. The secretary's investigators and agents reviewed every frame of the full State Farm video and questioned election workers, including Jones, Freeman, and Moss, as well as GOP poll observers and others.

Their findings, spelled out in an internal ten-page report, were unequivocal. "There was no evidence of any type of fraud as alleged," the report stated. The "suitcases" were standard-issue ballot box containers; the ballot boxes had been opened and processed earlier in the evening, then sealed up and stored under the desks, only to be reopened for resumed counting per Raffensperger's orders after a thirty-four-minute interval. "All allegations made against Freeman and Moss were unsubstantiated and found to have no merit," the report stated.*

Pick had also claimed during the hearing that there had been a "water main break" earlier in the day that she suggested had been engineered and used "as an excuse" to clear out the arena. The saga of a supposedly phony water main break soon was circulating all over Trump world, taking on an outsize role in the unfolding of the imagined master plot, which by now had been dubbed SuitcaseGate. The water main break, it was claimed, was staged as a dastardly "false flag" cooked up by Democratic conspirators in order to shut down the count

---

* The truth is that the Fulton County election office did have a history of dysfunction and even occasional incompetence that marred its administration of elections. Its handling of the 2020 primary election was viewed by Raffensperger's office as a debacle, with far longer lines than most other counties in the state and significant problems processing mail-in ballots. Some of that was certainly the result of the Covid pandemic. Ralph Jones had fallen ill in March and another election official died from the virus in April, forcing the office to close for a few days. There were staffing shortages and significant challenges training temporary election workers because they couldn't come into the offices. Jones himself was later criticized by an independent review for his supervision of the absentee ballot process, including failing to maintain chain-of-custody records when ballots moved around the office and inadequate protection of spoiled and rejected ballots in the mail room. But there was nothing to suggest any of these shortcomings constituted fraud or had any impact on the outcome of elections.

that night and evict the GOP observers so Freeman and Moss could take out their "suitcases" and stuff the vote scanners with fraudulent Biden ballots. In fact, there had been no water main break at all—just an overflowing urinal early in the morning that had been fixed within a couple of hours and had no impact at all on the counting of ballots.

As for the supposed order directing Republican poll-watchers and the press to leave, that, too, turned out to be bogus. Two of the GOP poll-watchers admitted as much when interviewed by FBI agents and secretary of state investigators. "Both poll watchers confirmed that no one was told or instructed to leave State Farm arena," the secretary of state's report states. Instead, the GOP observers, like the few reporters present, had left of their own volition.

State senator Elena Parent, one of the two Democrats present at the hearing, had been dumbfounded by what she saw that day. "It's kind of like an Alice in Wonderland moment where you've gone down a rabbit hole and through the looking glass," she said as the hearing was winding down. She had done her best to reintroduce core facts: "We do not have evidence of widespread irregularities that would change the election and that's what you need" to even contemplate an effective election challenge, Parent intoned. "Forty judges and forty lawsuits have not found that; Attorney General Barr has not found that. Brad Raffensperger and everyone involved in elections in Georgia have not found that." But Parent made no headway with her GOP colleagues. She did, however, have an odd encounter with Trump's master of ceremonies. When the hearing ended, an upbeat and mask-less Giuliani (it was the height of the Covid pandemic) walked up to Parent and Jen Jordan, the other Democratic senator in the room, and complimented them for their contributions, spraying spittle in their direction. Parent winced behind her mask. A few days later, back in New York City, Giuliani checked into a hospital with Covid.

Moss and Freeman were astonished to find themselves accused of being at the center of a conspiracy to steal an election. Shaye Moss, with her unique blond braids and boisterous laugh, loved her job as a registration officer at the Fulton County election office, and she was good at it. She was a data-entry whiz—Barron called her a "savant"—when it came to processing voter registration numbers. Wandrea "could process applications twice as fast as the next fastest," Barron recalled. Moss didn't always get along with her co-workers and sometimes had an "attitude" according to Barron. But she was devoted to her work and was a stickler for the rules, once turning in two co-workers who were shredding voter registration applications to reduce their workload.

Her mother, Ruby Freeman, began as a temporary election worker a few years earlier after retiring from her job at a 911 call center for Fulton County. On the side she had a pop-up fashion boutique called LaRuby's Unique Treasures, after the honorific she was known by in her Georgia community: Lady Ruby. Colorful and feisty, Freeman liked to mix it up with people who crossed her. But both she and Moss believed their work counting election ballots was part of a higher duty instilled in them by Ruby's mother, whose refrain was: "If you don't go vote, then I don't want to hear you complaining."

It was not lost on Freeman that her mother had grown up at a time when the state of Georgia conspired to deprive Black people of their right to vote. "We showed up on election night proud to be playing a small role in American democracy," Ruby Freeman would later testify to the January 6 committee. "Our work honors...those who fought and sacrificed to make sure that all people have the right to vote in America."

Freeman and Moss had no idea what sacrifices they were about to make for their service.

————————

The Trump camp was just getting started stirring up hatred against the two women. On December 5, Trump traveled to Valdosta, Georgia, for a rally that was ostensibly to boost the candidacies of the two GOP Senate candidates. Instead, Trump spent most of his time airing his grievances about the "stolen election." When he did invite Kelly Loeffler and David Perdue onto the stage to make remarks, they were drowned out by shouts from the audience of "fight for Trump." Then Trump directed the audience to look up at a "very, very powerful and very expensive screen." He was showing OAN coverage from the previous day that included excerpts from the State Farm video.

The fabricated accusations of voter fraud were bad enough. More insidious and cruel was the persistent insinuation that somehow Black people were the main perpetrators of electoral corruption. It began with Trump, who brazenly targeted urban areas with majority or large Black populations as hotbeds of vote rigging, tweeting about imagined "mountains of corruption" in cities like Philadelphia, Detroit, and Milwaukee. But it was primarily Giuliani who carried that slanderous, racially freighted message to Fulton County.

What is perhaps most striking about all this is how cavalier Trump's lawyers were about whether any of their allegations were actually true, much less backed by evidence that could hold up in court. At 12:54 p.m., on December 7, 2020, one of Trump's most trusted advisers, Boris Epshteyn, reached out to Giuliani and others on the legal team in a text thread saying that he had gotten an "Urgent POTUS request" and he needed "best examples of 'election fraud' that we've alleged that's super easy to explain. Doesn't necessarily have to be proven but does need to be easy to understand. Is there any sort of 'greatest hits' clearinghouse that anyone has for best example? Thank you!!!"

Giuliani replied three minutes later at 12:57: "The security camera in Atlanta alone captures theft of a minimum of 30,000 votes which alone would change result in Georgia. Remember it will live in history as the theft of a state if it is not corrected by State Legislature."

Three days later, on December 10, Giuliani, still recovering from his bout with Covid, testified via Zoom before the Georgia House Governmental Affairs Committee. Once again he leaned hard into the baseless theory of election fraud, singling out Moss and Freeman, crudely stereotyping the two Black women as akin to drug dealers. "I mean, it's obvious to anyone who's a criminal investigator or prosecutor that they are engaged in surreptitious, illegal activity," Giuliani said. "And they're still walking around Georgia. They should have been questioned already. Their homes should have been searched for evidence." Again he played the grainy surveillance footage, claiming it showed them exchanging USB memory sticks as if they were "vials of cocaine and heroin." (Moss would later testify to the January 6 committee that what her mother was handing her was not a memory stick but a ginger mint.)

Giuliani's testimony unleashed a new salvo of threats and racist messages over the coming days. Strangers showed up at Moss's grandmother's house and tried "to bust the door down and conduct a citizen's arrest of my mom and me." Freeman told the FBI and Georgia investigators that she had received "over 500 emails [and] text messages," according to a summary of her interview in the secretary of state's report. A commenter on the right-wing social media site Parler, referring to Freeman and Moss, wrote: "The coon cu..s should be locked up for voter fraud." A Facebook post said "YOU SHOULD BE HUNG...FOR YOUR CRIMES." A text message that popped up on

Freeman's phone read: "We know where you live, we coming to get you." Menacing Christmas cards started arriving in the mail. "Ruby please report to the FBI and tell them you committed voter fraud. If not[,] you will be sorry," one read. "You deserve to go to jail, you worthless piece of shit whore," read another. Strangers began knocking on their doors at night. Unsolicited pizza orders from a nearby Papa John's were sent to Freeman's house. A fake Instagram account was set up in her name in which she purportedly confessed to committing election fraud—along with a phony mug shot. (After agents got a search warrant for the Instagram account, the FBI tracked down the perpetrator, who acknowledged he had made the whole thing up.) Moss would change her appearance to avoid being terrorized; Freeman, at the urging of the FBI, went into hiding for two months.

Much later, Freeman recounted what she and her daughter had gone through in some of the most terrifying testimony ever delivered to a committee of Congress.

"There is nowhere I feel safe. Nowhere," she told the January 6 committee. "Do you know how it feels to have the president of the United States target you?"

CHAPTER SIX

The QAnon Commission

"Where we go one, we go all."

As the pressure on Georgia officials intensified, the cries from the Trump crowd got even more exotic. And leading the charge was L. Lin Wood, the flamboyant Georgia defense lawyer whom Donald Trump Jr. had brought into the battle at the Buckhead GOP headquarters just days after the election. It was an odd move by the president's son. In bringing in Wood, he had hitched his father's post-election efforts in Georgia to a high-profile, if increasingly unstable, commander who had fallen into the bizarro world of a deranged conspiracy cult.

On Wednesday, December 2, Wood, wearing his red MAGA hat, appeared at a rally in Atlanta alongside Sidney Powell and her client Michael Flynn. He exhorted the crowd to surround the governor's mansion and blow horns. "I want you to go to the Governor's mansion. I want you to circle it. I want you to blow your horns until Brian Kemp comes out and orders a special session of the Georgia legislature!" he exclaimed.

Wood was calling on the Trump faithful to take part in a "Jericho March." It was a Stop the Steal twist on the Old Testament story in Joshua in which God commanded the Jewish priests to march around the ancient biblical city seven times blowing their rams horns, or shofars, to vanquish the corruption and iniquity within its walls.

The lawyer had embraced an apocalyptic strain of Christian nationalism, along with belief to a theological certainty that Donald Trump had won the election. When a voter at the December 2 rally asked Wood for guidance on how to respond to friends who thought the claims Trump had won the election were "crazy" conspiracy theories, he didn't hesitate in his answer. "Tell them they said the same thing about Jesus," he said.

Wood's language and messianic tone had begun to reflect the strange beliefs of QAnon, a cult-like far-right movement fueled by the conviction that a cabal of satanic, cannibalistic pedophiles was conspiring to destroy Trump's presidency. QAnon's followers took their cues from an anonymous supposedly high-ranking government official known as "Q" (a reference to somebody who purportedly had a high-level Energy Department security clearance) who shared updates in internet chat rooms about the latest developments in the supposed "deep state" plot. According to the QAnon crowd, global forces in the Democratic Party, Hollywood, and the media were trying to cheat Trump, their revered hero and the savior of the country, out of his rightfully won second term.

Wood stood out as a symbol of the symbiotic relationship between QAnon and Trump world. He had become a true believer. "This is the battle between good and evil," Wood proclaimed at his Atlanta rally, where the crowd was filled with avowed QAnon followers. "This is the battle between truth and lies."

By then Wood had added the QAnon slogan WWG1WGA—
"Where we go one, we go all"—to his Twitter profile. But his immersion
in the QAnon swamp would turn out to be even deeper than that.

Q postings had first popped up in the dark corners of the internet in
late 2017. At the time, the droppings from Q and his followers seemed
too ridiculous to be taken seriously. Among them, for example, was
the idea that there was a cavernous network of tunnels beneath New
York City's Central Park where young "mole children" were being
held in cages, having been bred and raised for sexual slavery. Still,
by the time of the 2020 election, Q devotees had become an unmistakable part of the Trump coalition. They were a noticeable presence
at Trump rallies, carrying signs, chanting Q slogans, and wearing Q
T-shirts. Whenever Trump went off on one of his wild rants—such as
when, without a scrap of evidence, he spent a week on Twitter accusing MSNBC host Joe Scarborough of having murdered a young female
member of his congressional staff—Q partisans in chat rooms would
boost and amplify the boss's messaging. Trump in turn would retweet
the postings of QAnon-linked accounts—more than three hundred
times, according to one tally.*

By August 2020, Trump was finally asked to respond to questions
about the cult. "I don't know much about the movement other than
I understand they like me very much, which I appreciate," he said
at a news conference. "I heard that these are people that love our

---

* As a further sign of his willingness to cultivate the cult's supporters, in February
2020 Trump pardoned Angela Stanton King, an Atlanta-area promoter of QAnon
theories who had spread the idea that the Wayfair furniture chain was secretly trafficking children on its website. Stanton King, the goddaughter of a niece of Martin
Luther King Jr. who had been convicted in 2004 for her role in a car theft ring, was
then invited to the White House, where she joined other Black supporters who
prayed for the president.

country. I don't know anything about it other than that they supposedly like me. "

A reporter, apparently astonished at the president's failure to distance himself from such lunacy, followed up. "The theory is this belief that you are secretly saving the world from this satanic cult of pedophiles and cannibals. Does that sound like something you are behind?"

"I haven't—I haven't heard that. But is that supposed to be a bad thing or a good thing?" Trump said to much laughter. "If I can help save the world from problems, I'm willing to do it."

These were Trump's first public comments on the subject, and they were of a piece with his later remarks about the Proud Boys militia during a presidential debate. "Stand back and stand by," he had said, when pressed by moderator Chris Wallace about whether he would condemn the extremist, gun-toting Proud Boys. The dangers of Trump's wink and nod to the Proud Boys would become clear after the 2020 election, when its members cased the home of Brad Raffensperger and then showed up in significant numbers for the riot at the US Capitol on January 6. But the earlier comments about QAnon may have been just as consequential.

At its core, the QAnon followers were wedded to the idea that the country was hurtling toward an apocalyptic battle in which America's very existence was at stake. It was a view not only embraced but actively promoted by Wood at the very moment he was emerging as among the most visible public faces of Trump's legal effort in Georgia. On December 14, he tweeted a seeming prescription to prepare for civil war, or perhaps Armageddon. "Make sure you have PLENTY of water, food, flashlights & batteries, candles, radio, 2nd Amendment supplies." And the next day, he posted on his Twitter account photos of Kemp and Raffensperger wearing red Chinese Communist Party masks. "They will soon be going to jail," he wrote. A few weeks later, he put a bull's-eye on Vice President Pence. "He will face execution by firing squad." The post got the attention of the Secret Service, which dispatched agents to South Carolina to question Wood at the local sheriff's office. His posting about Pence being executed was just "hyperbole," he told the agents.

What had happened to Wood? He had once been one of the country's most celebrated and feared attorneys, known for his take-no-prisoners approach to litigation and relentless attacks on the government and media. He had represented Richard Jewell in several high-profile defamation suits against an array of media outlets after the FBI wrongly accused the security guard of setting off a bomb at the 1996 Olympics in Atlanta. Similarly, he had been hired by the family of JonBenét Ramsey to pursue libel cases when they were suspected of murdering their daughter. (The Ramseys were never charged.) More recently, he had briefly represented Kyle Rittenhouse, the seventeen-year-old who had been charged with and acquitted of killing two Black Lives Matter protestors in Kenosha, Wisconsin, and Nicholas Sandmann, the MAGA-supporting teen whose confrontation with a Native American man on the Washington Mall had gone viral.

There was a common thread running through Wood's cases, one that hinted at his eventual susceptibility to Trump's extreme politics of grievance, and ultimately to QAnon. He was taking on clients who perceived themselves to be vilified and mocked by powerful elites—the government, liberals, the mainstream media, global corporations, and more. Wood saw himself in the vanguard of a struggle that was bigger than law and politics; it was about the survival of the country.

But it was also true that by the time of the 2020 election battles, Wood's personal and professional life was in turmoil. His erratic behavior and conspiracy-laden outbursts had estranged him from his adult kids and grandchild. His law partners had sued him, describing middle-of-the-night maniacal and abusive behavior. "You all better get on your knees and pray to Almighty God that He now asks me to show you mercy," Wood wrote in one email to one of his law partners amid a dispute about attorney fees. "If he does, I will show it, if he does not, I will deliver a fiery judgment against you on earth. Who the fuck did you think you were dealing with?"

Some traced his descent into the swamp of conspiracy theories and paranoia to a high-profile defamation trial he lost to Elon Musk in December 2019. Wood was representing British cave diver Vernon Unsworth, whom the Tesla owner had mocked on Twitter as "pedo guy" after he criticized Musk's involvement in the rescue of twelve Thai boys and their soccer coach who had been trapped in a flooded cave in 2018. In an audio recording not long after Wood lost the trial, he accused his law partners and his son Matt of conspiring to "fix the jury and the whole Unsworth case in a special op." (Two years later he'd dox Matt—his own son—on his Instagram account, citing Jesus Christ as a justification.)

Dave Hancock, a former Navy SEAL and security consultant whom Wood had hired to harden his phones and computer networks against intrusions from what he perceived to be deep-state enemies, saw a man "in deep distress." When they first met at Wood's Buckhead home in March 2020, Hancock was starstruck by the famed lawyer. But then, according to Hancock, Wood launched into a convoluted claim about a plot against him by Mark Zuckerberg, Peter Thiel, and Elon Musk. The tech entrepreneurs, Wood said, had conspired with the CIA and his children, using subliminal Facebook messaging to convince him to go to a psychiatrist. It was, he claimed, a "special op" meant to discredit him and keep him from being appointed to the US

Supreme Court. (Wood would soon start tweeting baselessly about links between Chief Justice John Roberts and Jeffrey Epstein, the mysterious jet-setting financier whose sex trafficking conviction had made him an object of the QAnon crowd's obsession.)

Still, for all of his fevered imaginings, Wood was a case study in how even the most extreme, fringiest characters could find a firm toehold in Trump world. A prolific tweeter, Wood developed relationships online with Rudy Giuliani and Michael Flynn. Some of his high-powered clients, like Steve Wynn, the billionaire casino mogul and Trump adviser, provided further entrée. It also didn't hurt that earlier that year Wood had donated $375,000 to the Trump Victory Fund, partly in the hope of winning a posthumous Medal of Freedom for Richard Jewell. That never happened. But on March 11, 2020, Trump reciprocated and invited Wood to the White House for a meeting at the Oval Office. Wood later posted a picture of himself on Twitter beaming as he stood next to the forty-fifth president, who was sitting and smiling behind the Resolute Desk.

In April 2020, Wood purchased a sprawling thousand-acre former plantation in South Carolina's Lowcountry. Tomotley, as it was named, boasted an elegant avenue of oak trees, their twisted branches draped with Spanish moss, leading to a grand Craftsman-style house. Enslaved people had harvested rice and other crops on this lush property until it was burned down by Sherman's troops at the end of the Civil War. But soon enough Tomotley would rise again as a key command post in a new American insurrection—the plot to overthrow a legitimate election and keep Donald Trump in power.

———————

That spring, Hancock traveled to Tomotley to install elaborate physical and digital security measures to protect Wood against the shadowy forces he claimed were out to get him. Wood, according to a member of Hancock's team, was convinced that members of the FBI or Antifa (the villains would change according to his moods) were lurking on the grounds outside Tomotley plotting to snatch him. He fretted that enemies might be poisoning his breakfast. By late October, just days before the election, Wood had reached a low point and his ravings were becoming too much for Hancock to handle. By then Wood had started and served as president of a nonprofit called the FightBack Foundation, to raise money to resist assaults on constitutional rights—with his client Kyle Rittenhouse serving as the prime victim. Hancock was placed in charge of the foundation but quickly got disillusioned. So, too, did Rittenhouse, who fired him, calling him "insane," adding "because he was, like, going on with all this QAnon stuff." Rittenhouse's mother later cited another reason for Wood's firing: She had suspected—quite rightly as it turned out—that Wood was using the foundation's funds for himself.*

One afternoon, Hancock questioned a $100,000 expenditure from the Rittenhouse fund. Wood told Hancock not to question how he conducted his business. When Hancock said there needed to be "accountability," Wood pointed skyward and said that was his "accountability,"

---

* Out of $6.8 million the foundation ultimately raised, more than a third, $2.8 million, went directly to Wood, the nonprofit's president, for "security" and "legal fees," according to a review of the group's tax returns. But the legal fees appear to have had little if anything to do with upholding Rittenhouse's rights. Instead, Wood—who played no role in Rittenhouse's defense at trial—redefined the foundation's purpose on its website more broadly as paying for legal resistance to the "the unconstitutional actions taken against Trump-supporting lawyers such as Lin Wood," which he described as "the defining civil rights issue of our time," thereby using the nonprofit to pay his personal legal expenses. At the time, he was facing a lawsuit filed by his ex-partners and disciplinary actions by the Georgia State Bar.

insinuating, according to Hancock, that he was the "son of God." Hancock called Wood "ridiculous," and a "clown," at which point the sixty-seven-year-old trial lawyer reeled back and socked the former Navy SEAL in the jaw. ("Not exactly a Mike Tyson hook," Hancock would later say.) Wood then grabbed the holstered 9mm pistol off Hancock's belt and began waving it around in the air. Local sheriff's deputies arrived on the scene soon thereafter, but by then the altercation had died down. Wood told the officers that "it was only an argument between friends," according to a Beaufort County police report. For his part, Hancock declined to press charges. He loaded up his Chevy Silverado pickup and drove out of Tomotley, never to see Wood again. But crucially, he maintained access to the email server at Wood's plantation, the contents of which would provide an invaluable window into the planning and plotting that would take place there. (Later, he would share a cache of emails, texts, memos and audio tapes with Willis's investigators and the authors of this book.)

In the weeks before the election, Wood often sat in a wing-back chair in his master bedroom overlooking the lake, taking long drags on his vape and obsessing over his Twitter feed. Ever since he'd begun tweeting about the politically charged Rittenhouse case, he'd noticed that his number of followers had increased exponentially. He went from 60,000 followers in the period before Rittenhouse's arrest to nearly 250,000 in the weeks after. Watching the numbers skyrocket was like a dopamine fix for Wood, recalled Hancock. More than that, it seemed to feed his growing messiah complex. Hancock recalled Wood suggesting that his Twitter followers were like his disciples—that he was spreading God's message through social media. Then again, noted Hancock wryly, Wood had one advantage over Jesus Christ in spreading the gospel: The son of God did not have a Twitter account.

It was during this period that Wood bonded with Flynn and his lawyer, Sidney Powell. They'd become online allies after Wood began tweeting his support for Flynn during the criminal case against him first brought by special counsel Robert Mueller in his investigation of Russia's involvement in the 2016 election. Flynn, Trump's first national security adviser, had initially pleaded guilty to lying to the FBI about a conversation he had with the Russian ambassador to Washington after the election. Then the retired general fired his original lawyers, hired Powell, and tried to withdraw his plea—a move that was resisted by the Justice Department and the federal judge in charge of his case.

"Persecution of Gen. Flynn is low point in history of federal judiciary," Wood wrote in one tweet. Soon Wood, Flynn, and Powell were texting one another on a regular basis.

Wood's conspiratorial tweets in the immediate aftermath of the 2020 election would also attract the attention of Trump's top advisers. "Every lie will be revealed. The coup will fail. Pray," one of them read. It was postings like this that prompted Donald Trump Jr. to bring Wood into the fold, inviting him to join the series of rally-*cum*-legal-planning-sessions at the Republican headquarters in Buckhead. Wood could hardly contain his enthusiasm. "I just landed in Atlanta," Wood wrote to an associate on Friday, November 6. "Trump campaign has summoned me to help."

If being invited into the campaign's legal inner sanctum by the president's son himself wasn't heady enough, what came next must have been positively intoxicating. The next day, while puttering around his Atlanta home, his cell phone rang. It was Trump's executive assistant calling from the White House. She asked him to hold for the president, who moments later came on the line. According to an account of the call Wood gave at a backyard gathering at Tomotley in March 2023, Trump, not surprisingly, started by asserting he'd won the election.

"I did not lose and I will never concede," he said. Wood said he responded: "Mr. President, don't you ever concede. You won this election by a landslide." Then, according to Wood, Trump asked him what he thought of Kelly Loeffler and David Perdue, the two Georgia GOP senators who had been forced into runoffs by their Democratic opponents and whose races would determine the control of the US Senate. "I think Kelly Loeffler's a communist," Wood said, about the wife of the chairman of the New York Stock Exchange. As for Perdue, Wood said, "I think he's wishy-washy and I wouldn't trust him." Trump thanked Wood and promised to be in touch.

Wood had already been preparing to file his own lawsuits, separate and apart from the Trump campaign's legal efforts, challenging the election results in Georgia. But with the president's blessing, he was now a charter member of Trump's outside legal team, a self-styled "elite strike force" that over time would be more accurately described as the gang that couldn't shoot straight.

The strike force had initially been set up by Giuliani in Washington before the election to help him examine the contents of Hunter Biden's laptop, the hard drive of which he had obtained in late August 2020 from a computer repairman in Delaware and which he hoped would be an "October Surprise" ensuring the forty-fifth president's reelection. Flynn could have been a potentially huge asset to his team given that, aside from having served as director of the Defense Intelligence Agency under President Obama (before getting fired), he had been a general in Iraq and Afghanistan, where he was known for his expertise in exploiting computers for intelligence. But Powell, his lawyer, said she needed to keep her client out of the Hunter Biden operation so as not to jeopardize his ongoing legal battle to withdraw his guilty plea. Instead, she insinuated herself into Giuliani's separate project to overturn the election that he launched after November 3. Soon enough, though, Giuliani started to chafe at Powell's overbearing and publicity-grubbing style. (He may also have been concerned that she was horning in on his Fox News airtime.) So, in an early sign of the internecine squabbles to come, he asked Michael Trimarco, a New York businessman who was also a client of the former New York mayor, to find a place where the group could relocate—in part to keep Powell at bay while Giuliani himself worked out of the upscale Mandarin Oriental in DC.

On November 11, Trimarco secured rooms at the Westin Arlington Gateway hotel in nearby suburban Virginia. It was there that a motley group of lawyers, cyber sleuths, businesspeople, ex-military men, and intelligence operatives began their frenzied quest to keep Donald Trump in power by proving that the election had been rigged. Among those who set up shop at the Westin were Powell, Trimarco, and Patrick Byrne, the wealthy former CEO of Overstock.com, who would end up bankrolling much of the effort. Also lending a hand were Sam and Gina Faddis, both former CIA officers who had worked in the agency's directorate of operations. Two of the more gung-ho members of the Westin team, in addition to Powell, were Phil Waldron, a retired army colonel who owned a bar in Central Texas, and Russell Ramsland Jr., the head of a Dallas-based cybersecurity company called Allied Security Operations Group or ASOG, and a failed congressional candidate. Ramsland had been suspicious of the Dominion machines even before the 2020 election. After the 2018 election, he had urged candidates to challenge the results of their elections, citing the voting equipment's supposed vulnerability to hacking. But none did. At an airplane hangar outside Dallas, Ramsland offered briefings to anyone who would listen. Few would, although one of the exceptions was Sidney Powell.

In the days after the 2020 election, the group began vetting tips and brainstorming cloak-and-dagger operations to seize evidence that would prove their case. Throughout, the group was fixated on OPSEC—operational security—concerned that they were being followed and under surveillance. Participants recall that it was Gina Faddis who infused the Westin meetings with a sense of paranoia. She insisted that cell phones be placed in microwave ovens during sensitive meetings. Soon she and the others started noticing a suspicious white van parked outside of the hotel. Throughout, a beefy security guard—an executive with the security and military contractor originally known as Blackwater Worldwide—kept a watchful eye on the comings and goings of the Westin group.

A few days into the Westin operation, Trimarco was on a family getaway in the Poconos when he got a call summoning him back to Virginia. Powell, Waldron, and Ramsland needed to meet with him urgently. He cut his trip short, to the consternation of his wife, and returned to the Westin command center. It was then that the trio briefed Trimarco and his lawyer Chris Smith on a plan for a "black op" that could blow the lid off the whole "stolen" election, according to a previously unreported account Trimarco and Smith gave the authors.

The idea was to tap ex-intel operatives who would break into election offices in swing states and seize Dominion voting machines and servers so they could prove the equipment had been hacked by foreign powers. "What the fuck?" Trimarco recalled thinking during the meeting as images raced through his mind of shadowy special forces types in black ninja outfits busting into election offices "like it's fucking Zimbabwe."

But this wasn't some overseas commando raid. The group was focused on the six states with the closest margins, including Michigan, Arizona, Pennsylvania, and Wisconsin. Yet Powell and her team quickly landed on Georgia as the most practical state for the operation, in part because of its proximity. It didn't hurt that its state government was entirely in Republican hands. "Georgia was the one," Trimarco recalled. They were especially focused on a couple of rural counties where friendly Trump supporters ran the election offices and might be helpful. Waldron and Ramsland estimated the entire operation would cost roughly half a million dollars, recalled Trimarco.

But there was a catch, Ramsland said, according to Trimarco's account. The operatives would need "hunting licenses" in order to fulfill their mission. Now Trimarco and Smith, who sat in on the meeting, were puzzled. Hunting licenses? What in the world were they talking about? Before Trimarco could ask, Powell chimed in. Pardons, she said, from President Trump. "I need six to eight pardons," she added, scribbling the numbers down in her notepad. But these weren't ordinary pardons for past misconduct; they would be "preemptive pardons," she explained, an advance permission slip from the president to protect the operatives from criminal prosecution in the future should any pesky prosecutors go after them for breaching an election office and stealing the data. Powell wasn't the only one pushing the idea. Another member of her ragtag team—Andrew Whitney, a British pharmaceutical executive who had met with Trump at the White House to peddle a purported Covid cure—made it explicit in an email to Lin Wood. "What we need is a 'hunting license' that provides top cover for ops," he wrote Wood.*

The group wanted Trimarco to get Giuliani's sign-off to bring the plan to Trump. As bonkers as he thought the plan was, he held his tongue and agreed to run it by the former New York City mayor. The next day, Trimarco went to see Giuliani at Trump campaign headquarters, accompanied by Howard Kleinhendler, another lawyer he'd brought into the Westin project. Trimarco told Giuliani about the plan and the presidential "hunting licenses" they would need. Giuliani then called in his own chief investigator, Bernie Kerik, the former New York City police commissioner and ex-con who'd served in the military, and asked him if he'd ever heard of "hunting licenses" in this context. He had not.

Giuliani dismissed the idea as over the top. But what was clear by now was that conspiracy theories involving the Dominion voting machines were going to be central to the efforts to overturn the election—and Trump's operatives were so obsessed with proving their theories that they were willing to go to extreme, even extra-legal lengths to get their hands on the evidence.

Too extreme for some. Trimarco's lawyer, Chris Smith, had initially believed that there might be some validity to Trump's claims of election fraud, but he was not on board with talk of "hunting licenses" and seizing election machines. "When I first started this endeavor, I recognized that it was either the greatest conspiracy in our country's

---

* Powell herself would refer to her interest in "hunting licenses" in her January 6 committee testimony, but in a different context. She described them as the equivalent of "search warrants" that could have been authorized by Trump had he invoked an executive order declaring a national emergency in the event of foreign interference in a US election. But Trimarco insisted that the discussion of hunting licenses referred to preemptive pardons.

history or the greatest debacle from a legal perspective," he said. "I recognized that there may have been some smoke out there but there just wasn't any fire. At the end of the day, I was thankful I walked away when I did."

In the second week of November, Lin Wood made what was perhaps his most important contribution to the effort: He offered up his secluded Tomotley estate in South Carolina to serve as the new headquarters where the whole crew could assemble. Within days, the gang started flying in: Powell, Flynn, and Overstock's Byrne, along with others from the national security and cyber world: Doug Logan, the CEO of the cybersecurity firm Cyber Ninjas; Jim Penrose, a former NSA cryptographer; and Sam and Gina Faddis, the veterans of the CIA's directorate of operations. Members of the team had blasted out a "call to action" to their massive social media followings seeking examples of voter fraud. Wood was fired up by the results. In an email to Powell, he wrote, "Just a sample of info I am receiving from my Tweet. Tell General Flynn his digital warriors are working hard and producing excellent results." As an avalanche of dubious, and in some cases outright bizarre, tips flooded in, Penrose, the ex-cryptographer, set up a war room in Wood's living room with computer banks, printers, and whiteboards to cull and organize them. "It looked like Election Central," Wood later told a reporter.

The events at Tomotley are laid out in detail in Hancock's cache of thousands of emails, text messages, audio recordings, videos, and memos. One typical message sent to Penrose, the former NSA cryptographer, touted a Chinese Communist Party whistleblower promising to expose supposed vote flipping by Dominion.

Another sent to Wood from someone who identified himself as

Douglas J. Keenan in the UK claimed that the designer of the Dominion software was a Serbian who was also the person behind Guccifer 2.0, whom US officials identified as the nom de plume of the Russian operative or operatives who had hacked the Democratic National Committee and Hillary Clinton's 2016 campaign. It, of course, didn't matter to the conspiracy theorists the improbable likelihood that the same individual or persona who had hacked the DNC to help Trump defeat Hillary Clinton would now be supposedly working on behalf of Joe Biden to defeat Trump.

But the pièce de résistance—or so the Tomotley crew thought—came the day another former CIA operative, Gary Berntsen, and a colleague showed up with a videotaped deposition of Leamsy Salazar, a former security chief to the late Venezuelan president Hugo Chávez. Salazar, a defector-turned-DEA-informant, claimed to have been present at a "secret meeting" in Caracas more than ten years earlier at which Chávez entered into a "pact" with Smartmatic executives—whose names he could not remember—to program the company's software to flip election votes in Chávez's favor, and that Smartmatic later shared that software with its "partner" firm, Dominion. The claims were instantly debunked—by no less than the Trump campaign itself. Within a day, the campaign's research department produced an eighteen-page document pointing out that, while it had once shared common machines years earlier in an election in the Philippines, Dominion was not a partner of Smartmatic; it had no corporate connection with the company whatsoever, and there was "no evidence" that Dominion used Smartmatic's software in the 2020 election in the United States.*

---

* An affidavit from Salazar—with his name redacted—was filed as an exhibit in federal court in a lawsuit Wood brought seeking to throw out the Georgia election

But Powell was pumped. She and Lin Wood dubbed it "the holy grail of evidence," according to one account. This seemed more credible than the tech analyst's "The Wind tells me I'm a ghost" email she had previously sent to Maria Bartiromo when the Fox News host asked for evidence to back up her Dominion claims. Powell called the White House. That night, Trump himself called back. Powell, like Wood, was never a formal member of Trump's legal team and by this point was already on the outs with Giuliani. But as the events that day showed, she had no trouble getting the president on the line.

Hey, the guys came through, they got the stuff, we need to send it to you, Powell told the president about the hot new videotape, according to a source at Tomotley who monitored the conversation. *Good job,* said Trump, who "seemed excited," according to the source. Powell instructed a tech consultant to put the Salazar video on a flash drive. A jet was chartered—and the flash drive with the Venezuelan defector's account was flown straight to Washington for delivery to the White House.

The teachings of QAnon remained a persistent undercurrent throughout the Tomotley interlude. Wood and Flynn were regularly tweeting

---

results. The case was dismissed within a week by a federal judge who found that it had "no basis in fact or in law." In February 2021, Smartmatic filed a $2.7 billion lawsuit against Powell and Giuliani as well as Fox News and several of its anchors for repeating the lawyers' claims about vote flipping. The suit noted that Smartmatic, a global election company, had no connection to Dominion, and while three of its founders were Venezuelan engineers, it had no ties to the Chávez and Maduro regimes. As of this writing, the case is still pending. For its part, Dominion in April 2023 won a $787 million settlement from Fox News over its airing of bogus election claims about the company.

out and retweeting the crazed beliefs of the cultish clique. In one message, Wood called on Trump to release all evidence connected to Jeffrey Epstein, so that "ALL individuals connected with pedophilia could be brought to justice for their crimes against children." That included Chief Justice Roberts, a particular obsession of Wood's. "I believe Chief Justice John Roberts & a multitude of powerful individuals worldwide are being blackmailed in a horrendous scheme involving rape & murder of children captured on videotape," Wood proclaimed in one tweet that predictably enough offered nothing in the way of evidence to back it up. (Wood claimed in his tweets to have files containing the purportedly damning videos, but they were protected by an "encryption key" that he would only hand over to Trump, Flynn, or Powell.)

Where was Wood getting all this information? One key source was apparently Ryan Dark White, a twice-convicted felon who had served twenty-seven months in federal prison after being charged in 2015 by federal prosecutors in Baltimore with health care fraud and illegal possession of an arsenal of guns and ammunition.

As part of his case, a DEA agent portrayed White as an audacious con man. In a sworn affidavit, the agent wrote that White had collected at least ninety-five hundred pills of Zohydro, a powerful opioid, paid for by Medicare, by feigning that he suffered from ALS, or Lou Gehrig's disease; he would walk slowly with a cane as if in considerable pain when visiting doctors and pharmacists. And then, as observed by the agent, with prescriptions in hand, White would then discard the cane and walk and talk freely.

Upon his release from prison in 2017, White emerged as a QAnon oracle, claiming to be a deep-state whistleblower who had been framed by the DEA for his efforts to expose a shocking conspiracy to assassinate members of the Supreme Court—with the active assistance of

Chief Justice Roberts. White, who tweeted under the since-suspended handle @johnheretohelp, would soon show up at Tomotley and, at Wood's request, spend more than an hour in front of a video camera for a tape that could potentially later be used in a court filing. Speaking in a low Joe Friday just-the-facts tone, White laid out a fantastical evidence-free story: that a "dirty tricks squad" headed by former deputy attorney general Rod Rosenstein had murdered former Democratic National Committee staffer Seth Rich because of his imagined role in leaking internal party emails to the Russians. (The Rich case, fueled by Russian propaganda, was one of the prime conspiracy theories that circulated in the aftermath of the 2016 election.) White also claimed the "dirty tricks squad" had blackmailed Roberts and Vice President Pence with secret surveillance tapes of them engaging in gay sex with underage boys, liaisons arranged by Epstein.

"John is a truth-giver," Wood tweeted about his newfound informant, referring to White's Twitter handle name of @johnheretohelp. "Many high-ranking officials must go to prison. Including John Roberts. Level of evil in our government officials is frightening."

On November 15, the Tomotley crew gathered around for a Zoom meeting. That day's special guest was Ron Watkins, who was calling into the video conference from his home in Japan. Watkins, whose online moniker was Code Monkey, was a mega-celebrity in the QAnon world and appears to have been key to the entire operation. His father, Jim Watkins, a Philippines-based pig farmer, was the owner of 8chan (later renamed 8kun), the anonymous message board that had become a cesspool of hatred and racism and was the principal platform for the QAnon masses. It was also the platform where the mysterious Q posted his "Q drops," the cryptic messages decoded by the cult's followers. As the administrator of 8chan, Ron Watkins may have been more instrumental than anybody in spreading QAnon messaging. There was even much speculation that Watkins was actually Q himself. (In fact, Watkins seemed to acknowledge in the last episode of an HBO documentary series on QAnon that he was posting as Q. Then he quickly took it back. He wasn't Q, he said, but he did proclaim himself to be "the new Rosa Parks" of the digital civil rights movement.)

Ever since Election Day, Watkins had positioned himself as a so-called white-hat hacker and voting technology expert who could expose fraud despite no apparent expertise in the subjects. Now he was being piped in via Zoom to the president's team—Wood, Powell, and the other members of the Tomotley crowd—offering his insights into what steps they needed to take to document the stolen election and save the world. As if to underscore the intertwining of QAnon and the White House effort, Trump called in to Tomotley on the same day, speaking to Powell while Wood excitedly listened in. Three days later, Trump retweeted a clip from a One America News Network interviewing a supposed "cyber analyst" discussing flaws in procedures by Dominion. The cyber analyst was the QAnon man, Ron Watkins.

The pace of the work at Tomotley was frenetic. Powell, according to testimony she would later give to the January 6 committee, worked alone in an office off the living room, while two young associates from her firm would shuttle in and out with new evidence and tips. Flynn would pop in to see how he could help and what she needed. What was he working on?

"Logistics," Powell later testified in a deposition.

But the logistics Flynn was handling, it turned out, went well beyond supporting litigation. Flynn woke up at dawn each morning, quietly plying his trade, working multiple cell phones, keeping to himself, speaking in hushed, conspiratorial tones, gaming military options.

Within weeks, he would drop the hushed tones and talk openly about the need for the president to declare martial law and call on the

US military to seize the election machines for a redo of the election. The plans for doing so would be laid out in a draft "executive order" that was written in part by Andrew Whitney and edited by Flynn at Tomotley; a version of the order would soon be presented to Trump at the White House.

As for Powell, she too would periodically get worked up over random pieces of "evidence" that came in through the pipeline. At one point, after flying into the local airport, she held up a plastic bag full of ripped-up papers she had just been handed by a "source," telling the crew it was "shredded ballots" that would prove there had been a plot to rig the election. She dumped the shredded papers on the floor and directed the assembled team of security professionals and guards to get on their knees to start piecing them together. When they did, they discovered they weren't ballots at all. "They were informational flyers" listing polling stations and other dos and don'ts about the election, said one of those who had the time-consuming job of painstakingly piecing together the shreds of paper.

Powell's conspiratorial mindset seemed to have no limits. She reached out to Ezra Cohen, the assistant secretary of defense for special operations, during this period to try to enlist his help in instigating a covert operation to expose a plot to steal the election that supposedly involved CIA director Gina Haspel. As Cohen recalled it, he was sitting in the Pentagon when Powell called his direct desk line—a number he had given out only to his wife and a handful of very senior intelligence officials. In her Texas drawl, Powell told him that Haspel had been kidnapped and was injured in Germany while on a secret mission to seize Dominion machines—not to prove the fraud but the opposite, to destroy the evidence that the machines had been programmed to switch votes from Trump to Biden. Powell wanted Cohen to dispatch the Navy SEALs to stop Haspel. "She wanted to know whether we could send special forces to capture her," Cohen said. Cohen got off the phone as quickly as he could.

The stories about Haspel in Germany soon bled into a related tale—actively promoted in QAnon chat rooms—dubbed Italygate. The idea was that two employees of an Italian aerospace company had been reportedly imprisoned in Naples for hacking into military satellites in order to flip votes from Trump to Biden, an operation supposedly being run by a CIA operative working out of the US embassy in Rome. Chris Miller, the acting secretary of defense, actually got a phone call about all this from White House chief of staff Mark Meadows, asking him to look into it—a request he assumed came from Trump himself. Miller, just to cover himself, had instructed an aide to look into Powell's nonsensical story about Haspel, the CIA director, being kidnapped in Germany. And now this Italy stuff? "It was batshit crazy," Miller recalled about the story Meadows was relating. He wasn't the only one to have that reaction. About the same time, Meadows forwarded a YouTube video about Italygate—which was fast making the rounds in QAnon world—to Jeff Rosen, the acting attorney general, who forwarded it to his deputy Richard Donoghue. "Pure insanity," Donoghue wrote back in an email.

Still, once again Miller at the Pentagon did his due diligence. He and his newly appointed chief of staff, Kash Patel, a Trump loyalist who had previously worked as a top aide to Republican congressman Devin Nunes, together got on the phone and called Lieutenant General Scott Berrier, the director of the Defense Intelligence Agency. Berrier, a career military officer, was all business as he took the request from the SecDef and his top aide to contact the military liaison at the embassy in Rome and get to the bottom of this latest crazed conspiracy theory. "He was 'Yes, sir. No, sir,'" recalled Miller. A few days later, the DIA chief reported back. Yes, there were two guys in prison in Italy on hacking charges. But it had nothing to do with the 2020 election. There was, Berrier said, "no legitimacy to this."

"Sidney Powell @SidneyPowell1 is going to confront the devil in GA this week. So are many others. Some who have been quiet are about to speak out. The devil has no idea what he is about to face in GA. We The People are going to confront the devil, too."

So proclaimed Lin Wood on Twitter on November 20. The Georgia litigator, convinced he was immersed in a spiritual battle, was previewing the prospects for the much-anticipated Kraken lawsuit by Powell exposing the Dominion fraud—including the company's supposed links to Venezuelan socialists and Chinese communists. "Georgia is probably the first state I'm going to blow up," Powell boasted to Newsmax the next day. (Powell was filled with martial metaphors; in one email she sent to Wood about her coming legal assault, Powell said, "I am loading a larger version of the Enola Gay," referring to the B-29 bomber that dropped the atomic bomb on Hiroshima.) She added that Kemp and Raffensperger needed to go because "they're in on the Dominion scam." It was an allusion to her completely bogus accusation that the governor and secretary of state had taken bribes in exchange for awarding the state's vote-counting contract to Dominion. Touting the coming lawsuit as "biblical," Powell went on to say: "Georgia is extremely bad. We've got ballots being shredded, ballots being thrown into trash bags... votes being switched, the algorithm being run... you name the manner of fraud and it occurred in Georgia." When she finally filed her lawsuit in federal court in late November, the filing was a mishmash of conspiracy theories, full of misspellings and incomplete sentences.

But its most notable element may have been one of her listed "expert witnesses": QAnon impresario Ron Watkins. While outwardly it may have seemed as if the Dominion conspiracy claims were an utterly quixotic strategy to convince the courts to reverse the election results, there was a certain method to the madness. Giuliani never believed they would prevail in the courts; he understood that unelected judges would be loath to overturn the will of the people. His strategy depended on convincing state legislators in the key states that the election had been rigged. The lawsuits provided a platform for a persuasion campaign that would leverage every bogus claim and conspiracy theory—from dead voters to vote-switching Dominion algorithms.

With that, the Trump forces could implement John Eastman's plans, which were just then taking shape: to reject the certified Biden electors in the battlegrounds states on January 6, opening the door for Trump to be installed for another term as president.

Wood gave the whole game away. In one email to Powell on November 11, he had acknowledged that the legal fight was a tool for their public pressure campaign. "I have so much data for you," Wood told Powell. "But we're not going to need it. We just have to look like we're pursuing litigation. Ha!"*

The threat of violence and the menacing presence of Oath Keepers

---

* Wood did not respond to multiple requests for comment about his post-2020 election activities. He did provide the following general statement to the authors about his role in the Tomotley meetings: "I know very little about what Sidney [Powell] and Mike [Flynn] (and those who came with them) were doing at Tomotley when they sought my hospitality and asked if they could come work here. I was busy on my own projects which were personal to me and did not involve them." In comments to other journalists Wood has maintained that he had nothing to do with Powell's "Kraken" lawsuits, despite the fact that his name appeared on those pleadings. According to Wood, that happened without his knowledge.

had forced the Raffenspergers to flee their home over Thanksgiving. But the holiday at Tomotley was a festive affair. Wood, Flynn, and other members of the Tomotley crew had dinner at Cotton Hall, a property adjacent to the plantation that Wood also owned. Flynn had much to be thankful for.

The day before, Trump had announced on Twitter that he was pardoning Flynn, stopping a three-year federal prosecution brought by Mueller dead in its tracks. It was a celebratory moment, and as the guests prepared to sit down for dinner, Flynn carved the turkey.

Meanwhile, Trump kept in touch with the whole crew. The next week, he called down to Powell and Wood while they were gathered with Flynn in Atlanta for their "Jericho March" horn-blowing rally. On the call—captured on a tape obtained by the authors—Trump bucked up his legal gladiators. "Go knock 'em dead," the president told Wood. He railed about the just-confirmed narrow defeat of Michigan Senate Republican candidate John James to Democratic senator Gary Peters. Trump saw in that race a scenario identical to what he imagined had happened to him in Fulton County—a last-minute infusion of fake ballots that altered the outcome.

James "was celebrating his victory—and then they said, 'Sir, 25,000 votes just came in,'" Trump told the lawyers. "He was with his parents—African American, celebrating his victory. And they said, 'Sir, 25,000 votes—they just found—and they happen to be for a guy nobody ever heard of named Peters.'" (The president seemed unaware that Peters was actually the incumbent US senator from Michigan.)

Trump and the lawyers discussed reaching out to Senate GOP leader Mitch McConnell, apparently to get him on board with challenging the outcome of the Michigan race in court even though, by this point, James had already conceded. "I'll call McConnell," Wood said on the tape.

"Mitch is a quiet guy, but he wields a pretty good stick," Trump said. "He just wants to win this thing."

"We're going to get you more congressional and Senate seats. We can't let the rip-off..." Powell pledged.

"Stay strong," said Wood.

"I will," said Trump as he hung up.

———————

While Powell, Wood and the others were relishing the attention, they were also spreading terror with impunity to innocent people caught up in the web of conspiracy theories and lies.

One set of social media postings turned into a national inflection point in the post-election madness. And it turned out to have been triggered by a QAnon operation from the start.

In late November, Watkins called on his 325,000 Twitter followers to conduct surveillance of Dominion facilities throughout Georgia and livestream evidence of suspicious conduct. Then he thought he had discovered something. Around midnight on December 1, Watkins tweeted from Japan what he described as a "smoking gun video" of a young Dominion worker in his twenties, supposedly altering Georgia voter data by "plugging in an election USB drive into an external laptop."

It was a completely bogus claim not backed up by anything visible on the video. The young man was simply trying to read the data on his computer. But coming from Watkins, the tweet was like rocket fuel for the conspiracy theorists. It quickly got thousands of retweets. The video was uploaded by another QAnon influencer onto YouTube. Soon enough, an army of Q-connected cyber sleuths had unmasked the Dominion tech's identity, unleashing a torrent of death threats against him, including a superimposed animated image of a noose slowly and ominously swinging outside his home.

For Gabriel Sterling, Raffensperger's chief operations officer who had been charged with implementing the state's contract with Dominion, it was all too much. Nicole Nollette, a senior executive at Dominion who oversaw the company's Georgia operations, called Sterling in a near panic hours after Watkins's tweet. Nollette, who herself had been harassed and doxxed, was a hard-nosed former US Navy officer who had served at a NATO base in Greece. But now, said Sterling, her voice was shaking as she alerted him to what was happening to the young man. Sterling looked it up on his phone and was horrified. "May God have mercy on your soul," read one of the messages to the contractor. "You have committed treason."

"I'm done," Sterling recalled thinking. "I'm done." It's what prompted him, just after seeing the viral tweets, to give his impassioned press conference on the steps of the Gold Dome that got instant national attention.

Sterling's voice was filled with fury as he recounted what had happened to the contractor, an immigrant from what he believed to be a North African country—the harassment of his family, the noose, and the demands that he be hung for treason. Sure, election officials such as he and Raffensperger could expect blowback in a hotly contested election, he said.

"But this kid? He took a job. He just took a job and it's just wrong. I can't begin to explain the level of anger I have right now over this... This has to stop!"

Sterling continued, "Mr. President, it looks like you likely lost the state of Georgia. We're investigating. There's always a possibility. I get it, and you have the right to go through the courts. What you don't have the ability to do, and you need to step up and say this, is stop inspiring people to commit potential acts of violence."

And then came his most memorable words: "Someone's going to get hurt. Someone's going to get shot. Someone's going to get killed."

In little more than a month, Sterling would be hailed as a prophet. Powell's much-touted Kraken lawsuit in Georgia, and a similar one in Michigan, would go up in smoke, summarily dismissed by multiple federal judges. As for Wood, his QAnon-inspired lawsuits, too, would get thrown out. In January 2021, the Georgia State Bar informed the famed litigator that it had opened up an inquiry into the state of his mental health, requesting that he submit to an evaluation by a state-approved psychiatrist.*

---

* Wood tried to challenge the inquiry in court, but rather than submit, in July 2023, he surrendered his license to practice law in the state of Georgia.

CHAPTER SEVEN

The Republican Stone Wall

"I will resign before I do that."

In December 2019 Donald Trump did something totally unexpected: He invited Johnny Isakson to the White House, ostensibly to honor him on his last day in office as the senior US senator from Georgia.

Trump's gesture at magnanimity was surprising if only because it would be hard to find two political figures more different than Trump and Isakson. Then seventy-five and suffering from the advanced stages of Parkinson's disease, Isakson was a throwback: a soft-spoken, silver-haired moderate Republican of the old school whose gentlemanly approach to politics was the polar opposite of the smash-mouth bombast that defined the Trump presidency. "He broke everybody down into two categories—friends and future friends," recalled Joan Carr, Isakson's chief of staff. "When he saw a Democrat, it was an opportunity to get a bill passed." Each year, on Martin Luther King Jr.'s birthday, Isakson could be found sitting in the front row at the Ebenezer Baptist Church, locking arms and holding hands with the parishioners, listening to the ceremony and the sermon by the Reverend Raphael

Warnock, and—unlike most of the politicians—staying for the whole service. After one such event, Warnock approached Isakson with a delicate subject: He was looking for a pardon for his brother—a former Savannah cop who was then in federal prison for taking payoffs from a drug dealer. Could Isakson help? "You have never called me for anything," Isakson responded, and immediately agreed to do what he could, putting Warnock in touch with the president's son-in-law Jared Kushner.*

It was no secret in Washington that Isakson could barely hide his disdain for Trump's habit of insulting and demonizing anybody and everybody who crossed him. For the most part, Isakson held his tongue—because that's what Isakson usually did—but not always. After the white supremacist rally in Charlottesville, Virginia, in August 2017, when Trump said there were "very fine people on both sides," Isakson decried the event before the Georgia Chamber of Commerce, invoked Martin Luther King Jr.'s letter from the Birmingham jail, and warned that "what happened in Charlottesville was in Virginia, but it might as well have happened here." When Trump referred to Haiti, El Salvador, and African nations as "shithole" countries, Isakson said Trump "ought to be ashamed of himself" and called for him to apologize to the people of Haiti "and all of mankind."

Isakson, the chairman of the Senate Veterans' Affairs Committee, hit his breaking point in August 2018 when Trump once again denigrated his good friend in the Senate, John McCain, upon the occasion of the Arizona senator's death. As he was on his way to a meeting in the Capitol, Isakson was informed by a reporter that Trump had

---

* It's not clear if Kushner acted on Warnock's request. His brother never got a pardon. But a year later, he was let out from federal prison under an early-release program prompted by the Covid pandemic.

refused to order flags outside the White House be lowered in McCain's honor. "He did what?" Isakson asked in disbelief. Isakson turned and headed straight to the Senate floor, where he paid tribute to McCain, who spent five and a half years in a North Vietnamese prison camp, and, without actually naming him, unloaded on Trump with words that at that point no other GOP senator would dare utter. "Anybody who in any way tarnishes the reputation of John McCain deserves a whipping," Isakson said. And then, in a clear reference to Trump's diagnosis of bone spurs that allowed him to avoid serving in Vietnam War, he added: "Most of those who would do the wrong thing about John McCain didn't have the guts to do the right thing when it was their turn."

By the summer of 2019, Isakson was fading. He had cancer, was suffering from back injuries, and had taken a nasty fall in his apartment, fracturing four ribs. His Parkinson's was getting worse—at first, he needed a cane, then a walker, then a wheelchair to navigate the hallways of the Capitol. In August, citing his "health challenges," Isakson announced he would retire at the end of the year, three years before his term was up. It was a fateful move. Few Republicans in Congress had done more to stand up to and push back against Trump than Isakson, Georgia's senior senator.

On December 30, the day before he would leave the Senate, Trump asked Isakson, his family, and his senior staff to join him in the Oval Office. *How nice*, thought Carr, Isakson's top aide. *Trump is letting bygones be bygones.* But what the senator and his entourage assumed would be a touching moment commemorating the senator's more than forty years of public service quickly turned into something very different—an extended grievance session for Trump to vent about who Georgia governor Brian Kemp had appointed to replace him.

Trump was gracious at first. As the Isakson entourage of about twenty-five filed into the Oval Office, Trump helped steady the aging senator, placing the hand of Isakson's son, John Isakson, an Atlanta businessman, on his father's shoulder to help him stand for a photograph without his walker being visible. Three chairs were set up in front of the Resolute Desk: one for Isakson, another for son John, and a third for Jack Isakson, the senator's fourteen-year-old grandson. Trump looked straight at Jack. "What's it been like having an icon for your grandpa?" Trump asked him. "You're a good-looking boy. You should run for office some day. And I tell you what. If you run I'll endorse you—and you'll win!"

Carr, standing right behind the senator and his grandson, thought to herself with some amusement: *Is there anything more Trump-like than this?*

What Trump really wanted to talk about had nothing to do with the future political prospects of Isakson's grandson—or, for that matter, anything to do with the retiring, much-admired Georgia senator, either. When Isakson announced his retirement, it had fallen to Kemp to name his replacement. Trump demanded that Kemp pick Georgia congressman Doug Collins, who had become a regular on Fox News defending Trump night after night during his first impeachment trial. But Kemp, a tough-minded former construction company owner and a conservative stalwart, was at this point chafing at Trump's directives. It was an attitude that sources close to him say was encouraged by the governor's wife, Marty, a strong-willed adviser who had gotten fed up with Trump constantly taking credit for Kemp's 2018 GOP primary win and his later victory over Democrat Stacey Abrams in that year's general election. Rather than follow Trump's dictate, Kemp opened up the process to applicants—even setting up a computer portal for aspiring senators to submit their résumés—and eventually settled on Kelly Loeffler.

In strictly political terms, the choice seemed to make sense. Loeffler was a woman—and that could be helpful with moderate voters in the critical Atlanta suburbs. Even more, she was fantastically wealthy; she lived in a sprawling $10 million Atlanta mansion, was married to energy trader Jeffrey Sprecher, the chairman of the New York Stock Exchange, and she co-owned the Atlanta Dream, the city's professional women's basketball team. That meant that when she would be up for election in 2020, she could be a "self funder," a prospect that was especially pleasing to Republican Senate leader Mitch McConnell's political operation and, not coincidentally, would also free up more GOP donor funds for Kemp himself, who would be on the ballot at the same time.

But for Trump, this was a betrayal. When Kemp had brought Loeffler to the White House earlier that month to inform him of the decision, Trump erupted with a string of expletives. Now three weeks later, he was still stewing.

"Now, Johnny, what do you think about that awful appointment that Kemp made of that Kelly Loeffler?" Trump, visibly angry, said to the senator. "What's wrong with your governor?"

Isakson pushed back gently. "I've known Kelly for a long time. She's a good person."

Trump wasn't interested. His face grew red and he started shouting, startling his guests. "I made Brian Kemp! He wouldn't be governor if it weren't for me! He was losing by 75 points until I endorsed him! Does he not understand I'm the most popular Republican in Georgia?"

"Actually, I'm the most popular Republican in Georgia," Isakson interrupted.

Trump would have none of it. He turned to one of his top aides, Kellyanne Conway, who reassured him that his poll numbers were very good in Georgia. And on he went, demanding to know how Kemp could "dare" to defy him.

"There was no stopping it," recalled Carr. "This was supposed to be about Johnny. He's in front of all our friends. And he made it all about him. It was all about trashing Kemp. We were like, 'Oh my God.'"

Isakson said little then or in the year that followed as Trump ran for reelection and refused to accept his defeat. Isakson was by then in pain and woozy from medication. With his filters lowered, he blurted out ever more harshly about Trump. "The more outrageous Trump became, the less Dad liked it," said John Isakson. "He became more and more frustrated."

"He was distraught," recalled Heath Garrett, another former Isakson chief of staff and his longtime political consultant. "He couldn't believe what Trump was doing to the Republican party" and even more to his "beloved state of Georgia." In his many years of working for Isakson, Garrett said, he had never heard him use a curse word. But when Trump attacked the election results, Isakson dropped his guard. "This is complete bullshit!" he told Garrett when Trump claimed the election was stolen.

There was a poignancy to Isakson's despair. Garrett recalled a conversation in which he suggested they needed to do a better job of figuring out how to recruit more ethical young people to get involved in public service. Isakson was deflated. The nastiness, the personal attacks, the threats, the crazed conspiracy theories—he was sickened by it all. Sitting in his favorite rocking chair in his post-Senate office, Isakson paused with a pained expression on his face. "I don't know that I could tell anybody they should do this anymore," he finally told Garrett.

In December 2021, Isakson passed away and the tributes poured in from both sides of the political aisle. "Georgia has lost a giant, one of its greatest statesmen," said Kemp. "One of Georgia's finest," added Warnock. John Lewis, the civil rights icon, called Isakson a "brother." Tweeted Stacey Abrams: "With every interaction, my respect for him grew and never wavered. I was honored to call him a friend."

The tributes continued for weeks, right up to a moving memorial service at the Peachtree Road United Methodist Church in Buckhead. More than twenty US senators showed up for what became a bipartisan salute to a man whose passing had a sad end-of-an-era feel to it. Isakson, soft-spoken and dignified, was gone; the most high-profile Georgian in Washington was now the loudmouthed, conspiracy-obsessed MAGA provocateur just elected to the House, Marjorie Taylor Greene.

There is no record that Trump, by then an ex-president, ever commented on Johnny Isakson's death, and when it came time for the funeral, he was nowhere to be found.

———————

Trump's meeting with Isakson was revelatory, exposing the president's raw fury toward Kemp for refusing to bend to his wishes—a hostility that would shape the critical weeks at the end of 2020 when the president and his allies made Georgia the setting for their last stand.

By then, the lawsuits being filed by the motley crew of lawyers— Cleta Mitchell, Lin Wood, Sidney Powell, and Rudy Giuliani—were being rejected left and right, not just in Georgia but in every battleground state from Arizona to Michigan to Pennsylvania. So with time running short and their options dwindling, the Trump team began resorting to ever more extreme tactics. At the top of the list was the idea first floated by Mitchell in her post-election email to John Eastman and echoed by Trump lawyer Ray Smith at the December 3 legislative hearing—that the Georgia General Assembly should reconvene and invoke its "plenary power" to choose its own electors, regardless of what the actual election results were. All that was needed was for Kemp to invoke "emergency" powers and call the legislature into special session.

The plan, on its face, was a repudiation of the very idea of democratic elections. Legislators were supposed to meet in special session and substitute their own preferred candidate for the one chosen by the voters? How would that have any public credibility? And yet talk of such a move had been circulating for weeks. "People were chirping about that within twenty-four hours" of the election, recalled Georgia attorney general Chris Carr, a former Isakson chief of staff himself before passing the baton to his wife after he became the state's chief legal officer two years earlier. He called up Kemp, Lieutenant Governor Geoff Duncan, and Raffensperger and let them know that, as far as he was concerned, the plan was nuts. He wouldn't even try to defend it in court. "Let me be crystal clear, I will not defend any attempt to remove the duly elected electors," he recalled telling them. "I wanted our team to win, but this is fundamental. This is how we elect a president. I will resign before I do that." Kemp, Duncan, and Raffensperger were in total agreement, Carr said. "Absolutely not," Kemp replied, in response to the idea that he call a special session of the legislature.

And yet the special session idea just "took on a life of its own," said Duncan. "You know, just throw in a little magic pixie dust on everybody's desk and all of a sudden Donald Trump can, you know, stay the president. And so it just kept gaining momentum."

One month after the election, the general assembly and the state's elected leaders were preparing to gather in Athens—hometown of the University of Georgia—for a conference known as the Biennial to discuss the state's business for the upcoming legislative session. But in the run-up, the heat was on among Trump's allies to demand a special session and have it announced in time for the Biennial. Trump himself stepped up the pressure, calling then Georgia House Speaker David Ralston to get him behind the effort. (Ralston gently blew Trump off. "I will do everything in my power that I think is appropriate," he told him, refusing to make the commitment the president wanted.) Trump was also calling down to state senators to get them on board, recalled Duncan, another sign of his willingness to personally engage at the most granular level if it meant he could cling to power. One of his principal contacts was Burt Jones, a state senator whose father, Bill Jones, was a wealthy oil man and GOP donor. (Both father and son would soon be invited guests at Mar-a-Lago.) Jones and three other state senators—Brandon Beach, Greg Dolezal, and Bill Heath (who had loosely presided over the December 3 session that Giuliani had hijacked)—were circulating a petition calling for a special session. Since Kemp had at that point become, in the words of one Georgia pol, "Enemy number one," the Trump team was looking to generate pressure to get Duncan to bend, or at least get him to stop going on cable TV deriding the president's fraud claims. In the days before the Biennial was set to begin, Jones and several of his petition allies went to see Duncan in the Gold Dome. "There were several instances of them coming into my office and sitting down and saying, 'Hey, you, you know you really need to consider a special session, right?'" Knowing where Duncan stood, they tried to soften the extreme nature of their proposal a bit. It didn't mean the legislature necessarily had to actually replace the Biden electors, they argued. It could be a chance to at least explore and debate the election fraud claims, and then see where that took them. It was cast as "it's just an opportunity for us to talk about it," Duncan said.

But talk about what? Duncan, a telegenic former minor-league baseball pitcher, had made it his mission to liberate his party from the iron grip of Trumpism. He had no patience for any of this. "I didn't philosophically agree with reconvening the legislature to go contemplate conspiracy theories that my son's third-grade class could debunk in ten seconds," he said.

On Thursday night, December 3, there was a four-car smash-up on a deserted stretch of highway in South Georgia. Three of the cars were engulfed by flames. Killed in the crash was Harrison Deal, a twenty-year-old staffer to Loeffler, who had been on his way to Savannah to do advance work for a Mike Pence rally scheduled for the following night. The lanky six-foot-four Deal, known for his infectious smile and upbeat attitude, had been the longtime boyfriend of Lucy Kemp, the second of the governor's three daughters. Everybody assumed they would get married. The Kemp family was devastated. The next day, the Kemps put out a statement on the governor's Twitter account. "Words cannot express how much Harrison Deal's life, love and support meant to us . . . Harrison was the Kemp son and brother we never had."

Apparently, nobody at the White House had thought to check Kemp's Twitter account. The next day, Trump called—but it was not to offer his condolences. Pretending that he had not been railing about Kemp for months, calling him "hapless" on Twitter, and telling aides he was a "moron," Trump started out asking the governor how he was doing. Kemp told him it had been "a rough twenty-four hours."

Trump assumed Kemp was talking about poll numbers. Had he gotten some bad numbers? he asked Kemp. No, Kemp explained, "we lost a close friend of the family."

After briefly offering his sympathies, Trump got down to business. What about calling that special session? What about demanding a statewide audit of all mail-in ballots to document all those phony ballots that were counted? Trump at first tried cajoling the governor, telling him it would redound to his political benefit if he called a special session because, after all, everybody knew about all the fraud. But Kemp held firm and refused. It would never hold up and would distract from the upcoming runoffs where control of the US Senate would be on the line. Trump exploded, shouting at Kemp that his refusal would doom him when he ran for reelection. "There was lots of yelling and cursing," said one person briefed on the call. Kemp barely got a word in edgewise. Then the call ended abruptly. "This was not a condolence call. This was Kemp being chewed out by Trump," Cody Hall, the governor's spokesman, said in a statement at the time.

"Chewed out" may have been an understatement. "I've never been talked to like that by anybody in my life," Kemp later confided to a close associate. But he also told friends something else: "I didn't give a shit about what he had to say."

On December 6, the day after Trump's call, Kemp and Duncan moved to put the matter to rest. Just as the Biennial session was convening, after consulting with Carr, they put out a press release officially rejecting the special session proposal as "not an option that is allowed under state or federal law."

"State law is clear: the legislature could only direct an alternative method for choosing presidential electors if the election was not able to be held on the date set by federal law," Kemp and Duncan said in their statement. "In the 1960s, the General Assembly decided that Georgia's presidential electors will be determined by the winner of the state's popular vote. Any attempt by the legislature to retroactively change that process for the November 3rd election would be unconstitutional and immediately enjoined by the courts, resulting in a long legal dispute and no short-term resolution."

The Kemp-Duncan statement was clear and unequivocal. Trump and his allies were on notice. In the view of Georgia's top two elected officials, as well as the state's chief legal officer, what the White House wanted to do was outside the boundaries of federal and state law.

But there were yet other far-fetched options that soon came into play. If Kemp and other governors were refusing to call special sessions, why not get the Supreme Court to order them to do so? On December 8, Texas attorney general Ken Paxton—joined by eighteen other Republican attorneys general—filed an extraordinary petition with the high court asking it to enjoin officials in Georgia, Pennsylvania, Michigan, and Wisconsin from certifying the election results and directly send the matter back to their respective state legislatures (all conveniently controlled by the GOP) to appoint new electors.

The audacity of the move was striking. Elections are conducted by states, under their own rules as dictated by their respective legislatures and administered by their own state and local officials. There was no precedent for one state, such as Texas, going to court to invalidate the results of an election in another state, such as Georgia, conducted under Georgia's rules. But even more so, the idea that it was Paxton who would be upholding the integrity of a presidential election seemed ironic in the extreme.

Paxton, a hard-right evangelical activist, may at that point have been the most ethically compromised attorney general in the country. He had been under indictment since 2015, charged by Texas prosecutors with three felony counts of securities fraud. Yet for reasons that mystified the Texas legal community, the case had languished in the state's conservative courts for years over multiple procedural issues. In the fall of 2020, the FBI opened up a new investigation of Paxton. Eight former top deputies had quit, accusing Paxton of abusing his office to block an investigation into a real estate developer who had been a campaign donor (and who had given a job to a woman with whom the attorney general was allegedly having an affair). As he prepared his office's case to overturn the 2020 election, Paxton was facing a potential federal indictment—one that, it was widely noted, could magically go away in an instant with a Trump pardon.*

The Texas lawsuit put Chris Carr in the most awkward of positions. The former Isakson staffer had just been elected chairman of the Republican Attorneys General Association. The first week in December, Trump invited all its members to the White House, a political move aimed at getting them all on board with the Supreme Court case. Carr obviously couldn't go. Once the case was filed, it would be his job to defend Georgia's election results. While at the White House, after being summoned to a meeting with Trump, Paxton was overheard telling some of his attorney general colleagues, "I'm about to take care of the Chris Carr problem." The remark immediately got back to Carr in his office in Atlanta. Moments later, Paxton called him

---

* In May 2023, the Republican-controlled Texas House voted by an overwhelming 121–23 margin to impeach him over the misconduct allegations, and he was temporarily suspended from office. At trial before the Texas Senate in September 2023, Paxton was acquitted on all charges, and he resumed his duties. But as of this writing, the FBI probe was reportedly still continuing.

and left a message on his voice mail: "Hey Chris, hey man. Can you give me a quick call? I need to talk to ya." About an hour later, he called again. "Hey man, I really need to talk to you. Come on, buddy. Give me a call."

Wisely, Carr never returned the call.

––––––––––

But Carr was getting other calls from his fellow Republican attorneys general telling him they were being pressured to sign on to Paxton's Hail Mary. They wanted his take. Carr did take those calls and laid out the state's position that the lawsuit was "legally, factually and constitutionally wrong." Then, on the evening of December 7, he got alerted by Senator Perdue that Trump wanted to speak with him. Apparently, Trump was upset after it was suggested—most likely by Paxton—that Carr was initiating the calls to his fellow attorneys general and lobbying them to reject the Supreme Court suit.

As first reported by the *Journal-Constitution's* Greg Bluestein, Carr had just gotten home from Publix with a chicken dinner for the family to eat while they all sat down to watch *Elf*, the popular holiday favorite. But instead, he had to wait around for over an hour before the White House switchboard put the call through. When it did, Trump made a stab at being avuncular.

"Chris, I've heard good things about you. But you can't be calling your colleagues."

"I'm not affirmatively calling anybody," Carr said. But, he explained, when they reached out to him, he had to brief them on why the Georgia fraud allegations were meritless. Trump didn't get angry but vainly tried to litigate the matter, bringing up the various debunked fraud claims, including, of course, the State Farm video that was by now a holy talisman for the White House. "He talked about the suitcases. And I said, 'Sir, I'm pretty sure this has been investigated,'" Carr recalled. Trump then raised other claims. One in particular stood out: reports that there were voting irregularities in Coffee, a small rural county in southeastern Georgia. "Look into it," Trump told him. It was the first indication that strange and soon-to-be-revealed events in Coffee were on the president's radar screen.

After a while, there was a pause, "and I'm thinking I got to get out of this," Carr recalled. So he tried to change the subject. "Mr. President, I voted for you twice for two reasons—your economy and judges, and I really thank you."

"Yeah, I did a hell of a job on both of those."

When Carr relayed the exchange to his wife, Joan, she couldn't help but think, again, *Is there anything more Trump-like than this?*

The day after the Texas lawsuit was filed, the Trump campaign filed its own amicus brief in support with the Supreme Court. So did more than one hundred Republicans in the House.* In a tweet, Trump called it "the case that everyone has been waiting for."

As soon as it was filed, Carr and his team of lawyers got busy crafting their response to the Texas case. It was a forceful smackdown of the lawsuit's fraud claims and pointedly rejected the "breathtaking remedies" (overturning a presidential election) it sought. Carr was

------

* The ringleader in organizing Republican members to sign the brief was Rep. Mike Johnson of Louisiana, who sent around an email seeking signatures under the subject line: "Time-sensitive request from President Trump." In the email, Johnson wrote that he had just gotten a phone call from Trump and that "he specifically asked me to contact all Republican Members of the House and Senate today and request that all join on to our brief. He said he will be anxiously awaiting the final list to review." In October 2023, Johnson was elected Speaker of the House.

quite proud of it. But before it was filed, he consulted with Kemp to advise him what he was preparing to do on behalf of the state of Georgia.

"Do you believe this is right?" Kemp asked him.

"Yes it is," Carr replied.

"Well then fuck 'em," Kemp said.

On December 11, three days after Ken Paxton filed his lawsuit, the Supreme Court briskly rejected it without granting a hearing. "Texas has not recognized a judicially cognizable interest in the manner in which another state conducts its elections," the court said in an unsigned order.

The case "that everyone has been waiting for" was no more. Trump was furious—and his reaction was telling. "The president's just raging about the decision and how it's wrong and why didn't we make more calls and just his typical anger outburst at this decision," Cassidy Hutchinson, chief of staff Mark Meadows's top aide, later testified about encountering Trump in the Rose Garden that day. "He had said something to the effect of, 'I don't want people to know we lost, Mark. This is embarrassing. Figure it out. We need to figure it out. I don't want people to know that we lost.' "

———

A little before noon on December 14, John Porter, chief of staff to Lieutenant Governor Geoff Duncan, got a call from Greg Bluestein, the ace political reporter for the *Journal-Constitution*. It was a big day around the Gold Dome. Amid fear of MAGA protestors descending on the Capitol, there was unusually tight security. Sixteen Democratic electors were ushered through side entrances into the Senate chamber to formally cast their ballots for Joe Biden and Kamala Harris, officially locking in Georgia's electoral votes. One of them, Stacey Abrams, the party's failed 2018 gubernatorial candidate, said it was a moment she had "dreamed about" since childhood.

But Bluestein wanted to know about something odd that was going on in Room 216, down the hallway from Porter's office. Bluestein had noticed that David Shafer, the portly chair of the Georgia Republican Party, and other GOP operatives were gathering for what appeared to be a meeting that wasn't on anybody's schedule. When Bluestein tried to enter, he was told it was a meeting for "educators" and was asked to leave. Educators?*

"What are Shafer and all those guys doing in the Capitol?" Bluestein asked Porter. Porter didn't know and hadn't heard anything about it. So he dispatched a staffer, Collins Udkeigbo, to go down to Room 216 and find out what was going on.

A few minutes later, Udkeigbo came back with an unsatisfying report: Nobody would tell him anything. "I tried to enter the room and was told it was a closed-door meeting," he said. "I do remember trying to get my head inside the door. They asked me to leave." There was, he also recalled, somebody standing by the door to block anybody from entering.

What was going on behind that closed door was part of a grand plan that had been hatched weeks earlier by one of Trump's lawyers, Kenneth Chesebro, inspired by Eastman, encouraged by Giuliani, and blessed by the president. The idea was to have Trump electors

---

* Bluestein wasn't the only journalist to learn about the events in Room 216. George Chidi, the independent journalist who the previous year had been chased away from the Rayshard Brooks Peace Center, had also been tipped off to the meeting from a source inside the office of Speaker of the House David Ralston. When he found the room and walked in, he too was told the assembled group was holding "an education meeting." "A guy got up and walked me out the door," he testified, adding that the conspirators then "posted a guy out front" to keep others out.

assemble in the state capitals of seven battleground states that Trump had lost and designate themselves as the bona fide electors from their states, to be counted as legitimate when Vice President Mike Pence presided over the counting of the electoral votes before a joint session of Congress on January 6, 2021.

In many ways, Chesebro was an improbable figure to wind up at the center of this plot. A Wisconsin native and Harvard Law School graduate, for most of his life he had been a staunch Democrat and an avatar of the liberal legal establishment. During law school he served as an assistant to Laurence Tribe, the constitutional law professor and liberal icon, holding his own with some of his star assistants, including future Supreme Court justice Elena Kagan and future president Barack Obama. Chesebro even worked with Tribe in his representation of Al Gore during the disputed 2000 election, where he cut his teeth on thorny questions about recounts and presidential elector disputes.

But about ten years later, his personal life—and political ideology— took a sharp turn. He split from his wife of twenty years, began heavily (and very successfully) investing in Bitcoin, and adopted a lavish lifestyle that exposed him to new people and radically different points of view. Soon enough he was devoting himself to right-wing legal causes, including in 2018 representing Senators Ted Cruz and Mike Lee before the US Supreme Court in a voting rights case. By the 2020 election, his transformation from Larry Tribe disciple to MAGA legal warrior was complete, making Chesebro—with his background in election disputes—the ideal guru for the Trump campaign's fraudulent fake elector plan. (As if to underscore Chesebro's commitment to the cause, video would later emerge of him, wearing a red TRUMP 2020 hat, outside the US Capitol on January 6 in the middle of the riot, although there was no sign he actually joined the rioters inside the building.)

Chesebro's plan for Trump electors was channeling a vision for

changing the election results that had been laid out early on by Eastman. And it rested on a strained reading of an obscure footnote in
American electoral history. In the razor-tight race in 1960 between
John F. Kennedy and Richard Nixon, the first returns out of Hawaii
showed a tiny margin for Nixon of 141 votes. The state's acting Republican governor certified the result. But with the margin that slim, a
state judge ordered a recount. The count was still under way when
the Nixon electors assembled on December 19 to officially cast their
votes for the Electoral College. By then, the Kennedy slate had actually pulled ahead by about forty votes in the ongoing recount. So,
with not unreasonable hopes that they would ultimately prevail, the
Kennedy electors met the same day and proclaimed themselves the
legitimate winners. On December 28, the recount was finished. Kennedy had won by 145 votes. The state's newly elected governor, also
a Republican, signed a new certificate endorsing the Kennedy slate as
the real winners.

In what two legal scholars later called "perhaps the most gracious
act of his long tenure in public office," Nixon, presiding over the Electoral College count on January 6, 1961, chose the Kennedy slate over
the previously certified slate pledged to him. In fact, it was an uncon-
troversial choice that got scant attention at the time. With Kennedy's
overall victory secure, with 303 electoral votes, Hawaii's 3 electoral
votes made no difference either way.

For Chesebro and Eastman, this was ample precedent for the
Trump team to follow the Kennedy playbook from 1960. Except the
historical analogy was deeply flawed. There was no margin in any of
the states that was remotely as close as in Hawaii. Even more important, there were no ongoing recounts. No judge, state or federal,
had weighed in to question any of the results in any of the states. No
state official, as Hawaii's governor did in 1960, certified the Trump

electors or even suggested they would be open to consider certifying them—absent a confirmed popular vote victory. With the Texas suit tossed by the Supreme Court, there was also no pending lawsuit that had the remotest chance of success. Some of Trump's lawyers, informed of the plan, wanted nothing to do with it. "I'm out," Justin Clark, still formally the campaign's general counsel's office, told Chesebro after learning what he was up to. There was, he later explained, "no contingency where these votes would count." Two of his deputies in the Trump legal office took the same position and withdrew from any participation in the scheme.

Still, the Chesebro plan was implemented with military-like efficiency. Chesebro distributed documents for the fake Trump electors to sign and gave them step-by-step instructions on where to meet, how many copies to sign, and where to send them after they did so. ("Pretty simple!" he wrote in emails.) Giuliani tapped a campaign operative, Mike Roman, to oversee the scheme and set up an "Electors Whip Operation" to round up all the Trump electors, track them to make sure they showed up on time, and find replacements if any of the electors balked.

Roman had his work cut out for him. In Pennsylvania, the Republican Party's chief counsel wanted to know if the electors would be indemnified by the campaign in the event "someone gets sued or worse (charged with something by the AG or someone else)." In Michigan, one Trump elector, the former secretary of state, refused to attend, saying she "was uncomfortable with the whole thing." Former Pennsylvania congressman Tom Marino backed out because "I'm a constitutionalist" and if the country's attorney general, Barr, hadn't found any fraud, "that's good enough for me."

And in Georgia, there was John Isakson, the son of the recently retired, ailing senator who had sat right in front of the president the year before while he went on his rant about Brian Kemp. In the run-up to the election, Isakson, being a loyal Republican, had held his nose and agreed to be a member of the Trump slate of electors. But when he was asked to show up at the Capitol for a meeting of the electors on December 14, he flatly refused. Isakson was done with Trump. He would later say he didn't even understand what exactly the Trump campaign wanted him to do but he instinctively knew it was sketchy. "I didn't want to be a part of it," he said. "The whole thing bothered me." It was, he thought, little more than "political gamesmanship."

The two key figures in Georgia for the alternate elector plan were Shafer, the party's chairman (a Trump loyalist who had actually lost to Duncan in the lieutenant governor's race two years earlier) and Robert Sinners, a young former congressional aide and Trump campaign official who was tapped to serve as the operational manager for the scheme in the state. On December 13, the day before D-Day, Sinners sent an extraordinary email giving specific instructions for the next day—with a stern admonition to keep quiet about it.

"I must ask for your complete discretion in this process," he wrote in his email, which he later said was done under the direction of "senior campaign officials" and Shafer. "Your duties are imperative to ensure the end result—a win in Georgia for President Trump—but will be hampered unless we have complete secrecy and discretion." When the electors showed up at the Capitol the next day, they were to tell the security guards they had an appointment with one of two state senators, Jones or Beach. **"Please, at no point should you mention anything to do with Presidential Electors or speak to the media,"** he wrote in bold. Shafer later reinforced the message. "Listen. Tell them to go straight to Room 216 to avoid drawing attention to what we are doing," he texted one of the electors.

The next day, the group assembled and dutifully sat around a

U-shaped table to sign the assorted documents that Chesebro had distributed declaring themselves "the duly elected and qualified Electors
for President and Vice President of the United States of America from
the state of Georgia." With an extra creative flourish, Shafer listed
himself as "the chairperson, Electoral College of Georgia"—a position
that does not actually exist—in a cover memo that was later sent along
with the documents to the National Archives, the US Senate, Raffensperger's office, and the chief federal judge in Atlanta. As he did so, the
veil of secrecy was lifted. Shafer let reporters into the room and gave
public interviews confirming the meeting; Sinners later testified that
his email urging "complete secrecy" was intended to protect against
anti-Trump protestors disrupting the solemn business at hand. As
for the purpose of the whole affair, Shafer insisted it was being done
on a "contingent" basis in case a court somewhere ruled in Trump's
favor. Ten days earlier, on December 4, the Trump campaign had filed
yet another lawsuit in Fulton County based on the same discredited
claims of illegal votes and other alleged procedural irregularities that
had already been thrown out. "In order for that lawsuit to remain
viable, we were required to hold this meeting to preserve [Trump's]
rights," Shafer told a local TV station.

Shafer and his lawyers would later argue that he was relying in
good faith on the advice of Trump's legal team when he presided over
the fake elector scheme. The idea that the fake elector ringleaders
were following a script laid out by some of Trump's lawyers was, on
its face, a plausible argument even if the campaign's still-extant lawsuit, based on the error-riddled analysis about out-of-state, underage,
and other "illegal" votes of Matt Braynard and another Trump data
cruncher, was going nowhere in the state courts and would soon be
withdrawn. Yet Shafer's claim that the elector scheme was being pursued solely to preserve legal rights was belied by the plain language in

Chesebro's memos and emails. In one, he wrote that the Trump electors in the battleground states could retroactively be recognized "by a court, the state legislature *or Congress*" (emphasis added). The Congress option turned out to be the real game plan. On December 13, Chesebro had emailed Giuliani with the subject "Brief notes on 'President of the Senate' strategy." The alternative Trump electors could, he argued, be put in front of Vice President Pence when he presided over the formal January 6 session under the theory that "he, and he alone, is charged with the constitutional responsibility not just to open the votes, but to count them—including making judgments about what to do if there are conflicting votes."

As constitutionally dubious as that claim was, there was an ever bigger problem with the elector scheme that would in time focus the attention of Fani Willis's prosecutors in Fulton County. The papers signed by the Trump electors in Georgia contained nothing about them acting on a contingent basis in the event of a favorable future ruling in a lawsuit. The Trump elector papers in two of the states—Pennsylvania and New Mexico—did contain such language. But the documents in Georgia (as in Arizona, Michigan, Nevada, and Wisconsin) mentioned nothing of the kind. In official-looking documents submitted to Congress and government offices in Washington and Atlanta, including the chambers of a federal judge, they proclaimed themselves "duly elected" electors when they had been elected by nobody but themselves.

For some, like John Porter, a veteran GOP consultant who had been Duncan's top aide, the fake elector scheme was the moment the Trump Stop the Steal campaign hit rock bottom. "What the fuck now?" he recalled reacting when he learned what was really going on in Room 216. "The floor for what they would do and how far they would go just kept getting busted through."

Even Sinners—the operational chief of the scheme in Georgia—came to view his role with regret. More than a year later, when it came time for him to testify to the January 6 committee, he said he would never have had anything to do with it had he known that three of the Trump campaign's top lawyers—Clark and two of his deputies—had questioned its legitimacy.

"We were just useful idiots or rubes at that point," he said. "I was ashamed."

CHAPTER EIGHT

The "Perfect" Phone Call from Hell

"Fellas, I need 11,000 votes. Give me a break."

Why Georgia?

It was a question that hung over the relentless campaign by Trump and his allies to flip the outcome of the state's vote. Like Hawaii's three electoral votes in 1960, Georgia's sixteen electors would not have altered the outcome of the presidential race. After the real electors assembled and voted in state capitals on December 14, Trump was stuck at 232 electoral votes—38 short of the 270 he needed to be reelected as president. Yet Trump's fierce determination to change the results in the state—what Representative Bennie Thompson, the chairman of the January 6 committee, later referred to as his "particular obsession" with Georgia—had little to do with Electoral College math. This was personal for Trump, for all intents and purposes, a vendetta. In his mind, he had been wronged. Georgia officials whom he assumed he had in his pocket had screwed him and he was going to go to whatever lengths it took to make sure he was made whole.

But it was also, in its way, a cover-up for his campaign's own bungling. Georgia had been reliably red for years, having voted Republican in eight of the last nine presidential elections. But the GOP margins had been steadily shrinking as Georgia's electorate underwent a dramatic transformation—more Blacks, more Hispanics, and an influx of liberal voters with "Hollywood values" from the movie industry who had flocked to the state thanks to those generous tax breaks initiated by former Republican governor (and later Trump's secretary of agriculture) Sonny Perdue. Trump had carried the state with 51 percent in 2016. Kemp, in 2018, had barely beaten Stacey Abrams for governor, eking out a win by less than 1.5 percentage points.

Yet despite the warning signs that Jordan Fuchs and others had flagged in the months before Election Day, the campaign's top officials had been slow to realize just how much trouble Trump was in, especially after he went on his public jihad about mail-in ballots during the Covid pandemic. Trump had hardly campaigned in the state until the last weekend before Election Day when a last-minute rally was hastily staged in the northwest city of Rome—Marjorie Taylor Greene country—to fire up the troops. By then, it was too late.

After the election, Trump and his warriors were consumed by a domestic political version of the old Cold War domino theory: If they could just get Georgia to flip, it would create enough momentum that other states would fall and the president would be swept back into power. Corey Lewandowski, who had served as Trump's first campaign manager in his 2016 race, recalled how the day after the election—while Donald Trump Jr. was headed to Georgia—he got a call from the president's second son, Eric Trump, dispatching him to Pennsylvania while his longtime sidekick, David Bossie, Trump's deputy campaign manager in 2016, was ordered to Arizona where the Trump campaign clung to the idea that Fox News's election night call that put the state in the Biden column was wrong.

All three states—Pennsylvania, with twenty electoral votes, Arizona with nine, and Georgia with sixteen—had to end up in the Trump column for the president to prevail. And the president and his confederates pressed their case relentlessly in all three (as well as Wisconsin). In Pennsylvania, for example, Trump called Jake Corman, the GOP president pro tempore, while Giuliani left repeated voice mails for Bryan Cutler, the Republican Speaker of the House. Arizona House Speaker Rusty Bowers got two calls from Trump and separate calls from Giuliani and Eastman pressing him to back fake electors in the state. And in late November, Trump and Meadows hosted Michigan GOP lawmakers—including Senate leader Michael Shirkey and Speaker Lee Chatfield—to push their fraud claims and get them to change the state's election results. But Trump and his election warriors were convinced that Georgia—where the margin was the tightest and the levers of state power in the legislature and the executive branch were all safely in GOP control—gave them their best shot. Throughout the post-election fight, it was targeted as the first and most important domino that could fall. "That's why Georgia was important," Lewandowski said.

Jordan Fuchs, Raffensperger's street-smart deputy, recalled getting a phone call from a Pennsylvania political operative in the weeks after the election, telling her the state's Republican leaders had cut a "deal" with the Trump campaign that they would consider pushing for their own special session if Georgia were to switch. There was never any corroboration of such a deal. Sterling, whom Fuchs told about the call at the time, suspected that it was just a line by top Pennsylvania lawmakers to get Trump off their back so they didn't have to call a special session themselves. In fact, they had firmly resisted such a move for the same reason that Kemp and Georgia legislators had: State law mandated that electoral votes were awarded to the winner of the popular vote, not allocated based on the whims of legislators. No matter. Trump and his lawyers clung to the Georgia domino theory, convinced that through sheer willpower they could make it happen—and that could set off a cascade of falling dominoes in the other battleground states. By late December, the president, according to the testimony of a senior Justice Department official before the January 6 committee, was "laser-focused" on Georgia.

What Trump hadn't counted on was the resistance of Kemp, Duncan, Carr, and, most of all, Raffensperger and his two deputies, Sterling and Fuchs.

On the morning of December 22, a black SUV, surrounded by vans carrying a crew of Secret Service agents, pulled up to the Cobb County Civic Center outside Atlanta with a VIP passenger: Mark Meadows. The White House chief of staff had shown up in Georgia unannounced to personally observe an audit under way of how election workers had checked the signatures of mail-in ballots to verify they matched those when the voter first registered.

Meadows was there because the so-called signature match issue was playing an ever more central role in the Trump campaign's arguments. The previous spring, Raffensperger had agreed to an out-of-court settlement with the Georgia Democratic Party to resolve a contentious issue in the continuing legal fallout over Kemp's narrow victory over Abrams in the 2018 gubernatorial race.

After her defeat, Abrams had refused to concede and claimed she was the victim of systematic "voter suppression." One issue she and the Democrats had raised was the state's signature match policy, which required the signature on the outer envelopes containing mail-in ballots—in which the voters sign an oath certifying they are a legally registered voter—to match those already on file from the same voter with a state agency, such as the signature recorded when the person registered to vote or when they got their driver's license. In 2019, the Georgia Democratic Party filed a lawsuit alleging that the policy was discriminatory, leading to cases where a single poll worker could arbitrarily block a vote from being counted on the grounds that the voter's signature on the ballot didn't appear to match their signatures on file, an inherently subjective judgment.

To settle the lawsuit and take signature match off the table in 2020, Raffensperger in the spring had agreed to revise how the state verified the signatures on mail-in ballots while keeping the underlying match policy in place. It was the kind of negotiated deal that takes place every day in courtrooms across the country. Under new guidelines sent to local election offices, Raffensperger and the State Board of Elections recommended that three election workers review a signature before a ballot was rejected—an extra layer of protection to protect validly cast votes. The agreement also called for a voter whose signature was questioned to be notified by phone, email, or text within three days. After Trump's defeat, his campaign cried foul, claiming that Raffensperger's settlement was "illegal" and had gutted a policy that was mandated by the state legislature and, though it had no actual evidence of this, had allowed thousands of fraudulent Biden ballots to be cast. Trump himself in November had tweeted that the court settlement—which he wrongly referred to as a "consent decree"—had made it "impossible to check & match signatures on ballots and envelopes, etc. They knew they were going to cheat. Must expose real signatures!"

Hence Meadows's surprise visit. In light of Trump's claims and to ensure public confidence in the process, Raffensperger, with the assistance of the Georgia Bureau of Investigation, had directed an audit in Cobb County of the handling of the signatures on a sample of fifteen thousand mail-in ballots. The White House got its hopes up, convinced that the audit would find proof of fraudulent mismatched signatures, giving the president's lawyers new ammunition to challenge the Biden victory in court.

Tipped off to the visit shortly before his arrival, Fuchs rushed to the scene and got there just in time for an uneasy confrontation with Meadows. As she saw it, the very idea that a White House chief of staff would fly down to Georgia to look over the shoulders of election workers trying to do their job smacked of intimidation. As soon as she arrived, the thirty-year-old Fuchs positioned herself in the doorway to the audit room blocking Meadows, more than twice her age and towering over her, from entering. "My singular purpose was to make sure he's not inside the room," Fuchs said.

Meadows protested he hadn't come to disrupt anything. "I'm not making any allegations as much as I am trying to get to the truth," Meadows said. He just wanted to watch how the audit was being conducted, he explained. On the spot, the resourceful Fuchs invented a new policy for secretary-of-state-supervised post-election audits. Because there was an official investigation under way, only law enforcement was permitted to enter the room, she told him. No outsiders, even from the White House. In this, she got a helpful boost. Vic Reynolds, the longtime chief of the Georgia Bureau of Investigation, was there—and somewhat more softly backed Fuchs up on Meadows not coming in. Maybe it's better if you wait outside, he told him. Meadows was not happy. "Mark kept trying to edge his way in," Fuchs recalled.

When that didn't work, he managed to give the auditors an ano-dyne pep talk from the doorway, telling them they were serving the cause of American democracy. Fuchs didn't buy it. "His real purpose was to talk to the investigators and persuade them there was fraud."

What possessed Fuchs to confront the White House chief of staff? She, like Raffensperger and Sterling, had been through the wringer for the previous seven weeks, subjected to unrelenting attacks and whisper campaigns, accused of being corrupt RINOs and traitors to their party, with much of the flak coming from longtime friends and political allies. Fuchs was attacked most notably when Lin Wood, fir-ing shots left and right from his Tomotley redoubt, accused her of being the behind-the-scenes manipulator of Raffensperger...and of having been a "witch."

Woods had picked up on an episode from Fuchs's past that she had come to regret. For a brief period as a teenager, she had dabbled in the occult, immersed in the cosmology of witches and warlocks, an interest that grew out of her reading of the Harry Potter books. Her parents, evangelical Christians, pushed her to go public as part of an organized campaign to ban the phenomenally popular books due to their purported satanic influences over the minds of young children. As a fifteen-year-old girl, Fuchs testified before a Gwinnett County school board hearing in suburban Atlanta about how the Harry Potter books made witchcraft seem "mystical, exciting and innocent," caus-ing her and her friends to cast spells and perform a séance in gym class. Her testimony got statewide media attention and was later high-lighted in a report from a far-right Christian group that quoted a Vati-can exorcist as saying, "Behind Harry Potter hides the signature of the king of darkness, the devil." (The school board rejected the book ban after its lawyer pointed out that if it were to remove all books that discussed witchcraft it would also have to ban *Macbeth* and *Cinderella*.)

Fuchs had long since outgrown her interest in witchcraft. She graduated from high school, attended the University of Georgia, and joined College Republicans. She later landed a Council of Foreign Relations fellowship in Washington and worked on Capitol Hill for a Republican congressman before moving back to Georgia to pursue her fledgling career as a GOP consultant. But in the overheated post-election atmosphere, Wood took off after Fuchs and sought to portray her as Raffensperger's devil-worshiping Svengali.

"Do you believe @JordyFuchs age 30 with 1 year of government experience should have negotiated Dominion deal & thereafter essentially run GA Sec. of State Office?" he tweeted on December 16. "Something ain't right in GA." And then he added: "Jordan Fuchs @JordyFuchs has admitted publicly on Facebook that she was at one time a practicing witch. Yes, a Wicken [sic]. I do not respect that belief."

As upsetting as it was for Fuchs to have this incident from her past dredged up, she now had well-honed instincts for smacking back. "Little man ego will always have issues with female leadership. Just ask @LLinWood former law partners...and ex wife," she wrote on Twitter. And then, in another tweet tagging Wood: "Have you ever met a man with a tiny man ego? How do you manage little man syndrome? Asking for a friend."

It was part of the ethos of her trade—let no charge go unanswered, and make sure you get the last word. Fuchs by then viewed herself as being in the middle of a political war for which there was only one acceptable outcome. Her mindset was best explained in a revealing interview she gave some time later with a University of Georgia student who questioned her over Zoom about her advice for young women who wanted to make it in the world of politics. What makes it worth it for you? the student asked her. Fuchs didn't mention the post-election battle with Trump world, but she might as well have.

"It's the win," she replied. "Once you win, and once you get a client into office, the win clears all memory of anything horrible that happened in a campaign—working late, long hours, the attack ads you have to deal with, the whisper campaigns—all of that goes away with the win. And that's what really keeps me going in all this."

In the battle over the 2020 election, Fuchs was determined to stand up to Donald Trump's pressure—and to win.

Outside with Fuchs during her standoff with Meadows was Frances Watson, the secretary of state's chief investigator. Seemingly impressed that such a high-ranking official from Washington would fly down to watch her at work, Watson, a former homicide detective in DeKalb County, posed for a photo with Meadows. The White House chief then asked for and got her card with her cell phone number. Fuchs, watching all this, didn't like it. If they were all in Washington for an official White House visit, sure—have your photo taken with the chief of staff. But not under these circumstances. There was ongoing litigation. Watson was a senior employee of the office that Trump's campaign was suing. Watson was overseeing an official state audit in which Trump's White House had a singular interest. "I thought it was inappropriate," she said about Meadows's entreaties to Watson.

The next evening, around nine thirty, Watson was at home in bed when her phone rang. It was the White House switchboard asking her to hold. The president wanted to talk to her. Instinctively, Watson, the ex-cop, taped the call.

"Hello, Frances. How are you?" Trump said in a casual, friendly tone as though there was nothing unusual about the fact that he was calling her.

"Hello, Mr. President, I am actually doing very well," Watson replied, seeming to suppress laughter at the very idea she was having this conversation.

Trump continued with the sweet talk. "Well, you have a big fan in our great chief, our chief of staff, Mark. I just wanted to thank you for everything. He told me you've been great."

Getting to the point, Trump said, "Look, this country is counting on it"—referring to the Cobb County audit. "So I won Florida in a record number, Ohio in a record. Texas in a record, Alabama by forty, forty points. And I won everything but Georgia and, you know I won Georgia by a lot and the people know it. And you know, something happened. I mean, something bad happened."

Trump brought up Fulton County, which he was now fixated on thanks to Giuliani's wild claims about Ruby Freeman and Shaye Moss before the state legislature weeks earlier. Trump wanted Watson to quickly finish up the Cobb County audit and expand it to include next-door Fulton County. He even started giving Watson instructions about how to do it. She needed to start looking at signatures from past years and comparing those with the signatures on the envelopes of ballots mailed in for the 2020 election.

"You know, I hope you're going back two years, as opposed to just checking, you know, one against the other, because that would be a signature match that didn't mean anything," Trump said. "But if you go back two years, and if you can get to Fulton, you're going to find things that are gonna be unbelievable, the dishonesty that we've heard from them . . . But Fulton, Fulton is the mother lode, as the expression goes."

The call didn't last long, a little more than six minutes in its entirety. Watson tried her best to be diplomatic throughout.

"Well, Mr. President, right, yeah, I appreciate your comments, and I can assure that our team and the GBI...that we're only interested in the truth and finding the information that's based on the facts," said Watson. The audit team had been working "twelve, sixteen hour days...

"I know you're a very busy, very important man, and I'm very honored that you called. And you know quite—"

"It's so important what you're doing," Trump interrupted.

"Quite frankly, I'm shocked that you would take [the time] to do that, but I'm very appreciative."

Trump wasn't through. "You know, you have the most important job in the country right now, because if we win Georgia, first of all, if we win, you're going to have two wins...the people of Georgia are so angry at what happened to me. They know I won, won by hundreds of thousands of votes. It wasn't close."

There were no overt threats, only talk of the kudos that would come her way if she did what the president wanted. "When the right answer comes out, you'll be praised...Anyway, but whatever you can do Frances. I would be—it's a great thing, it's an important thing for the country, so important. You have no idea, so important, and I very much appreciate it."

Watson didn't know what to say other than to wish Trump and his family "a very healthy and happy Christmas."

But Trump had one more seemingly offhand question. "Do you think they'll be working after Christmas, to keep it going fast? 'Cause, you know, we have that date of the sixth, which is a very important date." By this, he meant January 6, the date the Electoral College votes are officially certified by the Congress.

When Watson assured him they would be working hard on the audit through the holiday, Trump wrapped up with a friendly, if highly unusual, offer. "Call anytime you need, if you need help, call me."

Watson was getting antsy—and had no intention of taking the president up on his offer. "I just wanted to get off that phone as soon as possible," she told a colleague after the call.

That night, after the president's call, Watson called Fuchs and told her about the conversation. The next day, based on Watson's account but before she'd had a chance to listen to the tape, Fuchs recounted the call to *Washington Post* reporter Amy Gardner. The *Post* account was a big story; the president had called a Georgia state investigator to influence the outcome of an official state audit. But the story overstated what Trump actually said. It said Trump told Watson to "find the fraud" and she would be a "national hero" if she did. He didn't use those precise words. The actual ones—and the mere fact of the phone call in the first place—were damning enough. Still, the *Post* had to run a correction.

For Fuchs, it reinforced an important lesson. The tape, with the actual words, was critical.

As for the whole country counting on the results of the audit, it didn't have to wait long. Six days later, the Georgia Bureau of Investigation announced that it had reviewed the entire sample of 15,118 ballots in Cobb County and found "no fraudulent absentee ballots."

This was, as Raffensperger later noted, "the third strike against voter fraud claims in Georgia." It was not the end, however, of the White House's efforts to prod Watson to find the supposed "dishonesty" in heavily African American Fulton County that so consumed the president. On December 27, Meadows texted Fuchs with an extraordinary proposal: What if the Trump campaign paid for the secretary of state's office to conduct a Fulton County audit? "Is there a way to speed up Fulton county signature verification in order to have results before Jan 6 if the Trump campaign assist financially," he wrote her.

With Trump making little headway in getting Georgia officials to do his handiwork, the effort to flip the election results was entering its final, manic phase. On December 18, core members of Lin Wood's Tomotley team—Powell, Mike Flynn, and Patrick Byrne—came to the White House with an outlandish plan of action: Trump should declare that there had been foreign interference in the US election, install Powell as the White House "special counsel," name Flynn as "field marshal," create a federal "strike force" to seize the election machines in six counties across the country, livestream a recount in those counties via the internet, and then, assuming the search for fraud hit pay dirt, "rerun the election" in battleground states—all before a new president could be inaugurated on January 20, 2021.

To give their brazen plan the patina of legal cover, they presented Trump with a draft "executive order" that, if signed, would have authorized the Defense Department to deploy military troops to confiscate election machines and other voting equipment anywhere in the country. It was another version of the memorandum first drafted at Tomotley one month before—and it underscored the determination of the Powell team to get its hands on the Dominion machine software. In the end, Trump didn't sign the executive order, after White House lawyers forcefully pushed back on the idea. But he did tell Powell he was naming her White House special counsel that night, only to pull "the appointment"—if that's what it really was—a couple of days later when it became clear that she and Giuliani could by this point barely stand the sight of each other.

There had been much shouting and many threats during the Oval Office meeting. While Trump sat behind the Resolute Desk, the Tomotley crowd and Pat Cipollone (Trump's White House counsel) and two of his deputies shouted insults and cursed one another. At one point, Byrne—a strapping guy who towered over most others in the room—got up and stood toe-to-toe with Cipollone, "prepared to bury my knuckles in his throat." Powell and Flynn accused the White House lawyers of abandoning Trump. White House lawyer Eric Herschmann told them to "shut the fuck up." He'd later tell the January 6 committee the meeting was "nuts."

Giuliani at first had joined the meeting by phone before deciding he needed to show up in person. In keeping with the overall tone, the former New York City mayor called the White House lawyers a "bunch of pussies" for failing to stand up and fight for the president. Still, Giuliani wasn't on board with the military option. For all the talk of martial law and decreeing new elections, with their echoes of Latin American banana republics, Giuliani was focused on a more subtle plan to gain access to the Dominion machines. Giuliani, according to one friend, saw himself as the "adult in the room," dismissing eccentric schemes like Powell's "black op." Though in the end, his alternative plan of action—obtaining what he called "voluntary" access to the machines with the connivance of Trump-friendly local officials—would attract the intense interest of Fani Willis and her investigators.

But long before that would happen, the campaign to subvert the 2020 election would take yet another sharp turn into constitutional craziness.

The roots of what became a plot to subvert the Justice Department could be traced back to December 14, the same day as the fake electors meeting, when Attorney General Barr told Trump to his face that his fraud claims were "bullshit" and resigned. Trump named deputy attorney general Jeffrey Rosen as acting AG and Richard Donoghue as his deputy.

Trump at first tried to get Rosen and Donoghue on board with denying the validity of the election. In a December 27, 2020, conference call with the two, he raised a host of far-fetched claims: that Dominion software had flipped votes from Trump to Biden in a county in Michigan; that a tractor trailer carried thousands of suspicious absentee ballots from New York to Pennsylvania; that there were "suitcases" of illegal ballots on the Fulton County video, by now a hearty perennial in the president's litany of imagined abuses. As the January 6 committee later documented, Rosen and Donoghue—with Barr gone, they were now the two top officials at the Justice Department—had told Trump at least four times that what he and Giuliani kept saying about the Fulton County video was flat-out false. "It wasn't a suitcase," Rosen had told him in a phone call on December 15. "It was a bin. That's what they use when they're counting ballots. It's benign." Donoghue reinforced Rosen. "I told the President myself...several times, in several conversations that these allegations about ballots being smuggled in a suitcase and run through the machines several times, it was not true, that we had looked at it...we interviewed the witnesses and it was not true."

Trump waved it all aside. "You guys must not be following the Internet the way I do," he said. As for the propriety of what he was proposing—having the Department of Justice declare the election invalid—Trump was remarkably candid: "Just say the election was corrupt and leave the rest to me and the Republican congressmen." That is, Donoghue later emphasized in sworn testimony to the January 6 committee, "an exact quote from the President."

The next day, a mid-level Justice official, Jeffrey Clark, sent Rosen and Donoghue the draft of a startling five-page letter for them to sign. It was focused on Georgia. Addressed to Governor Kemp and the leaders of the general assembly, it asserted that the Justice Department was investigating "various irregularities" in the 2020 election, and in light of "significant concerns" about what had happened in Georgia and other states, the department "recommends" that the legislature should immediately reconvene and consider selecting the Trump electors over the Biden electors to send to Congress for the official January 6 counting of the vote. (The letter was attached to an email from Clark that also suggested there was evidence that a Dominion voting machine had "accessed the Internet through a smart thermostat with a net connection trail leading back to China.")

Who was Clark and why was he sending the letter? He had been a corporate lawyer at a prestigious law firm, Kirkland & Ellis, representing the US Chamber of Commerce in challenging environmental regulations, and BP in lawsuits over the *Deepwater Horizon* oil spill. In the Trump administration, Clark was initially tapped to serve as assistant attorney general in charge of the Justice Department's environment and natural resources division, but had been recently elevated to acting chief of the department's civil division—a position that gave him no authority over presumed election law violations. A Trump ally in Pennsylvania, Representative Scott Perry, had recommended Clark to the president, leading to a meeting with Trump at the White House. Nobody had told Rosen and Donoghue of the meeting—a clear violation of long-standing department policy sharply restricting contacts between department officials and the White House without senior-level approval.

When Rosen and Donoghue saw Clark's letter, they were furious.

Virtually nothing in it was true: The Justice Department wasn't investigating anything in Georgia and its officials on the ground—the US attorney in Atlanta and the FBI special agent in charge there—had *not* expressed "concerns" about what had taken place in the election. "There is no chance that I would sign this letter or anything remotely like this," Donoghue emailed Clark in response. There was simply no authority for the Justice Department to do what Clark was proposing. If pursued, Donoghue later testified, the draft letter "may very well have spiraled us into a constitutional crisis."

There was also a growing realization inside the Trump team that they may well have crossed a line that would get them in future trouble. "I have no doubt that an aggressive DA or US attorney someplace will go after both the President and his lawyers once all the dust settles on this," Eastman wrote, prophetically, in an email to two of the president's lawyers on December 31, 2020.

The fixation on Georgia reached its apex on January 2, 2021. The situation at that point was looking increasingly desperate for the president. The Electoral College vote was locked in. The Trump campaign's lawsuits were going nowhere. Not a single legislative leader in any state had signaled a willingness to call a special session. The clock was ticking toward January 6, when Trump was planning a Stop the Steal rally outside the White House in the hope that a giant public outpouring would bolster his last implausible move: getting Vice President Pence to unilaterally reject certifying Biden electors in the contested battleground states once friendly Republican members of Congress objected to the certification.

But in order for the strategy to have a prayer of success, he and his lawyers needed a win—somewhere. Once again, they looked south to Georgia, where the final certified tally by Raffensperger had him behind by 11,779 votes.

For weeks, the White House had been trying to get through to Raffensperger. "Mr. Secretary, Mark Meadows here. If you could give me a brief call at your convenience," the White House chief of staff texted the secretary of state on November 19. And again on December 5: "mr Secretary: Can you call the White House switchboard . . . Your voicemail is full." All told, the January 6 committee counted eighteen attempts by Trump and the White House to get through to the Georgia secretary of state in the weeks after the election. (Meadows, for his part, would only acknowledge initiating three such attempts.) But Raffensperger studiously ignored each and every one of them. He was being sued by the Trump campaign and knew well that anything he said could and likely would be used against him.

Finally, though, he relented. On the morning of January 2, Raffensperger did a Fox News interview during which host Neil Cavuto pressed him on the election results. Raffensperger went through the numbers in Georgia: Twenty thousand traditional Republican voters who had voted in the June GOP primary didn't show up on Election Day in November. Senator Perdue got nineteen thousand more votes in the metro regions of Atlanta and Athens (home of the University of Georgia) than Trump did. And overall, GOP congressional candidates got thirty-three thousand more votes than Trump.

In short, the evidence was clear. A not insignificant number of Republican voters in Georgia—enough to make the difference—had turned away from Trump, casting ballots for GOP candidates down-ballot but choosing Biden (or a third party or no candidate at all) for president. His numbers also pointed to the fundamental illogic of the Stop the Steal fanatics: Why would the Venezuelans or the "corrupt" Democrats or whoever was fraudulently stuffing or flipping ballots for Biden have only done so in the presidential race—and ignore critically important races that could have altered the balance of power in Congress?

Among those watching Raffensperger that morning was Trump. Not long after the interview, Fuchs got a call from a staffer. The president had called the secretary of state office's media line. He was looking for Raffensperger. Then Fuchs, who was in Florida visiting her grandparents, got a call from Meadows, who reiterated: The president wants to talk to the secretary.

Fuchs raced through the possibilities in her mind. This was now a direct appeal from the White House on behalf of the president, hard to blow off. But there were also pitfalls and huge risks, big ones. Fuchs made clear to Meadows there would be conditions on any phone call. This would not be a "one-on-one"—that was against office policy. Raffensperger's general counsel, Ryan Germany, had to be on the call, as well as senior staff. Meadows balked at one name Fuchs mentioned, Gabe Sterling. Fuchs really wanted him on. Sterling was the office pit bull, and Fuchs knew he would not hesitate to push back on any falsehood uttered by Trump. But it was clear the White House wanted nothing to do with him—not since Sterling's impassioned warning weeks earlier that Trump's inflammatory rhetoric about the election might end up getting somebody killed.

"Mr. Sterling does not need to be on that call," Meadows said sternly.

Sterling was her friend, but Fuchs consented.

Fuchs then notified Raffensperger, who was at first reluctant. But he agreed so long as Germany and Fuchs were also on the call. It was set up for 3:00 p.m.

Raffensperger drove home to Johns Creek, where he and his wife, Tricia, parked themselves in their kitchen to await the call. Germany was at home about to take his daughter on a bike ride when he was notified of the impending call. He quickly went upstairs, put his cell phone on speaker, and took out a miniature putting rug he had just gotten for Christmas to practice his putts while he waited for the president to lay out his case.

And Fuchs did what was arguably the single gutsiest and most consequential act of the entire post-election battle: She, more than anybody, was keenly aware of the dangers Raffensperger faced in talking to Trump, with the president's well-documented habit of inventing reality to suit his political needs. In the moment, Fuchs decided she would protect the boss. Without telling Raffensperger or Meadows, she taped the call.*

"Okay. All right, Mr. President, everyone is on the line," Meadows announced as it began. Then, "just so we all are aware," he called out everybody who was: Raffensperger, Fuchs, and Germany from the

---

* Fuchs has never talked publicly about her taping of the phone call; she learned, after the fact, that Florida where she was at the time is one of fifteen states that requires two-party consent for the taping of calls. A lawyer for Raffensperger's office asked the January 6 committee not to call her as a witness for reasons the committee's lawyers assumed were due to her potential legal exposure. The committee agreed. But when she was called before a Fulton County special grand jury convened by Fani Willis, she was granted immunity and confirmed the taping, according to three sources with direct knowledge of her testimony. Still, even if a Florida prosecutor chose to try to bring a case—as a first offense, it would be only a misdemeanor charge—Fuchs would have an effective defense: Florida law grants an exemption for law enforcement purposes. As enforcer of Georgia election laws, the secretary of state's office is a law enforcement agency.

secretary's office, and Trump lawyers Kurt Hilbert, Alex Kaufman, and Cleta Mitchell.

Trump thanked the secretary for taking the time, and got right to the bottom line: "I think it's pretty clear that we won. We won very substantially in Georgia. You even see it by rally size, frankly. We'd be getting 25,000–30,000 people a rally, and the competition would get less than 100 people. It never made sense."

The call lasted sixty-two minutes. Trump did nearly three-quarters of the talking, repeating the same points over and over. For nearly the first twenty minutes, he spoke completely uninterrupted, throwing out so many numbers and convoluted claims that Raffensperger and his team had a hard time keeping up. There were "a couple of hundred thousand of forged signatures" on absentee ballots in Fulton County, he asserted. Also: 50,000 voters who showed up to vote and were blocked from doing so, 18,325 voters who had no listed home address, close to 5,000 votes cast by dead people, 4,925 by out-of-state voters, and 904 who only listed a PO box.

"The bottom line is, when you add it all up, you know, 300,000 fake ballots," Trump said.

None of this was remotely true. Trump was offering a hodgepodge of concocted numbers and wild exaggerations: The total confirmed "dead" voters at that point had been not five thousand, but two—in both cases, a family member was found to have voted for a deceased person. (Raffensperger later found two more such cases, bringing the total number of dead voters in Georgia to four.) The idea that there had been 200,000 "forged" signatures on absentee ballots in Fulton County made no sense: The total number of absentee ballots in Fulton had been 148,319. None had been shown to have forged signatures.

As Trump's stream-of-consciousness spray of fantasy data continued, Raffensperger got antsy. If he didn't speak up soon and correct all this nonsense, he worried Trump's lawyers could depose him and say, *You never disputed what he said.* He had to speak up.

"We don't agree that you have won," he said politely but emphatically enough that he conveyed there was no room for negotiation. He tried to correct some of the president's mistakes, starting with the supposed two hundred thousand forged signatures in Fulton County. But Trump kept interrupting and deflecting, returning to his litany—the out-of-state voters, voters in vacant houses, the "corruption" of Dominion machines, his huge rallies—all of which added up to "many, many times" the 11,779 votes he was behind Biden in Georgia.

And realizing that Raffensperger was resisting, he started to ramp up the pressure, slightly at first.

"We have won this election in Georgia based on all of this," he said. "And there's nothing wrong with saying that, Brad."

Trump was planning a rally in Georgia the following Monday for Perdue and Loeffler—and, he said, he planned to be repeating all these numbers to the crowd. "The people of Georgia are angry, the people of the country are angry. And there's nothing wrong with saying that, you know, you've recalculated."

Recalculated? It was an odd term for Trump to use. How was Raffensperger supposed to recalculate? Whatever exactly Trump had just asked him to do, Raffensperger, now somewhat more forcefully, made clear there was nothing to recalculate.

"Well, Mr. President, the challenge that you have is—the data you have—is wrong."

After Raffensperger disputed Trump's numbers about dead voters—two, he said, not five thousand—Trump brought Cleta Mitchell into the conversation. "Well, Cleta, how do you respond to that?"

Mitchell, speaking for the first time, said the problem was that

Raffensperger's office had refused to turn over "certain information" about Georgia voters that could allow them to prove conclusively all the dead or out-of-state voters the president was talking about. It was the same question that Bryan Tyson, the election lawyer who had quit the Trump team, had raised nearly two months earlier when he was first directed by Mitchell to file lawsuits challenging the validity of votes purportedly cast by out-of-state or dead voters: How could they prove that the Joe Smith who moved away in 2018 or died in 2019 was the same Joe Smith who voted in 2020? The Trump campaign wanted personal information about those voters to make their case—data that Raffensperger wouldn't share with them. "We don't have the records you have," said Mitchell.

Fuchs had put herself on mute and hadn't said a word. But as she listened to this exchange with Mitchell, she was fit to be tied. *Oh my God*, she thought. *She wants us to give her the Social Security numbers of Georgia voters!* There was no way they could do that. That was privacy data protected by law.

Trump was soon off in another direction—one that he was fixated on: Ruby Freeman and the State Farm video. The African American volunteer election worker was, Trump said, a "professional vote scammer" and a "hustler."

"You know the Internet? You know what was trending on the Internet? 'Where's Ruby Freeman?' Because they thought she'd be in jail...It's crazy, it's crazy."

There were at least eighteen thousand—but probably fifty-six thousand—ballots that Freeman pulled out from "the suitcases" underneath the tables and then ran through the scanners, Trump claimed, all of them Biden votes. You can see it on "slow motion replay" on the video. "She stuffed the ballot boxes. They were stuffed like nobody has ever seen them stuffed before."

It was clear that the president was obsessed with Freeman, who had volunteered for the job to help out her daughter Shaye. Trump mentioned her by name eighteen times, calling her "totally corrupt."

"She's known all over the Internet, Brad," Trump said about Freeman. "She's known all over."

It was apparent to Raffensperger that Trump was getting much of his information from random postings by MAGA warriors on right-wing websites. Just weeks earlier, the GBI and FBI had discovered that a social media troll had created a fake account under Freeman's name in which she supposedly confessed to fraud, saying that she and her daughter had implemented a "plan in action" that guaranteed a Biden victory. The posting was a crude fabrication. But it went viral on far-right social media, riling up Trump supporters—and apparently, the president himself.

"Mr. President, the problem you have with social media, they—people can say anything," Raffensperger said.

"Oh, this isn't social media," Trump replied. "This is Trump media. It's not social media. It's really not. It's not social media. I don't care about social media. I couldn't care less. Social media is Big Tech. Big Tech is on your side, you know. "

Germany, Raffensperger's chief counsel, had been practicing his putts through much of the conversation. But he would at times put down the putter and rush over to the cell phone on his desk to correct the president. He emphasized that the office had investigated all the claims Trump was making.

"We had our law enforcement officers talk to everyone who was, who was there after that event came to light," Germany said after Trump and Mitchell talked about the "thousands and thousands" of Biden ballots that were run through the vote scanners at the State

Farm Arena on election night. "GBI was with them as well as FBI agents."

"Then they're incompetent," Trump retorted. "They're either dishonest or incompetent, okay?"

But Trump didn't want to be too tough on Germany. "I'm sure you're a good lawyer. You have a nice last name."

As the conversation meandered, Trump clearly realized he wasn't making any headway and started to ratchet up the pressure even more. At first, as is his wont, he tried ridicule. "They're going around playing you and laughing at you behind your back, Brad, whether you know it or not. They're laughing at you."

And then, a not so veiled threat: Given all the evidence of "corrupt" ballots, Trump told Raffensperger he could be in criminal jeopardy himself.

"It is more illegal for you than it is for them, because you know what they did and you're not reporting it," he said. "That's a criminal, that's a criminal offense. And you can't let that happen. That's a big risk to you and to Ryan, your lawyer."

Trump once again talked about the "shredding" of ballots "based on what I've heard" and made things even clearer: "You know, I mean, I'm notifying you that you're letting it happen." He noted that Raffensperger had said his office had found no criminality in the voting during his Fox News interview that morning. That was "very dangerous stuff," Trump said. "When you talk about no criminality, I think it's very dangerous for you to say that."

There was little question in Raffensperger's mind, at least at the time, what the president was doing here. Trump was "using the power of his position to threaten Ryan and me with prosecution if we don't do what he tells us to do," he wrote in his book, *Integrity Counts*.

Trump, getting increasingly frustrated, finally cut to the chase: "So look. All I want to do is this. I just want to find 11,780 votes, which is one more than we have, because we won the state."

The "recalculation" that Trump was looking for turned out to be quite specific: "Find" just one more vote than was needed to put him over the top.

And then: "So what are we going to do here, folks? I only need 11,000 votes. Fellas, I need 11,000 votes. Give me a break."

It may have been the most revealing line of all. It was as though Trump viewed the whole exercise as some sort of real estate negotiation. This was the world he knew best: Just cut him a small "break"— throw in a mere 11,780 votes—then they could all shake hands and seal the deal.

As the call approached the one-hour mark, Fuchs was thinking, *Is this going to last forever? How do I get these guys off this call?* She took it upon herself to shut it down.

"Need to end this call," she texted Meadows.

And then another one: "I don't think this will be productive much longer."

Meadows responded: "Ok." And then Fuchs: "Let's save the relationship."

Meadows did what he could to try to end things on an amicable note. He broke in and suggested maybe the lawyers on both sides could get together "expeditiously" and go over the disputed data— and once the Trump team got access to the secretary of state's personal data on Georgia voters they could "either validate or invalidate the claims that have been made."

Would Germany agree?

Not quite.

"I'm happy to have our lawyers sit down with Kurt [Hilbert] and the lawyers on that side and explain to him, hey, here's based on what we've looked at so far, here's how we know. This is wrong. This is wrong. This is wrong. This is wrong. This is wrong."

"So what you're saying Ryan . . . you really don't want to give access to the data. You just want to make another case on why the lawsuit is wrong?"

"I don't think we can give access to data that's protected by law. But we can sit down with them and say—

"But you're allowed to have a phony election?" said Trump. "You're allowed to have a phony election, right?"

"No, sir."

But somehow, most likely out of sheer exhaustion, the lawyers for the two parties agreed to have a follow-up conversation, although there seemed little reason to think it would lead anywhere.*

The next morning, Trump was the first to disclose the phone call. "I spoke to Secretary of State Brad Raffensperger yesterday about Fulton County and vote fraud in Georgia," he tweeted. "He was unwilling, or unable, to answer questions such as the 'ballots under table' scam, ballot destructions, out of state 'voters', dead voters, and more. He has no clue!"

Raffensperger decided to respond, also on Twitter: "Respectfully,

---

* Before getting off the call, Trump couldn't resist going after his favorite bogey-man in the whole Georgia saga. Even though it had nothing to do with anything they had talked about, Trump mentioned that Kemp would never have had a shot at either the primary or the general election when he was elected governor if it hadn't been for him. "He was dead, dead as a doornail," Trump said. "He never thought he had a shot at either one of them. What a schmuck I was. But that's the way it is. That's the way it is."

President Trump: What you're saying is not true. The truth will come out."

It didn't take long. Later that day, the tape of the phone call popped up in the inbox of Amy Gardner at the *Washington Post*. The story broke, with a link to the tape, at 9:59 p.m.

It was all the evidence Fani Willis needed to get started.

BOOK THREE

The State of Georgia v. Donald John Trump

CHAPTER NINE

The DA Speaks

"Well tonight, the person Donald Trump has to fear the most in the world is someone he has never heard of—Fani Willis."

If I hadn't heard that tape with my own ears, I couldn't believe a president of the United States would be doing that to a top election official in your state."

That was ABC News anchor George Stephanopoulos, expressing his incredulity at Trump's comments to Brad Raffensperger, when he questioned the Georgia secretary of state two days after the phone call on *Good Morning America*.

It was Raffensperger's first interview since the tape had gone viral. As always, he was calm and unruffled, sticking to what was by then a standard script: He and his investigators had been playing Whac-a-Mole with rumors about election fraud ever since Election Day and had "debunked" each and every one of Trump's allegations on the phone call.

"We believe truth matters," Raffensperger told Stephanopoulos, once the White House communications director for a president who had his own struggles with the truth.

But after brushing aside a question about whether he felt pressured during the call, Raffensperger—whether intentionally or not—dropped a small bomb into the conversation. Stephanopoulos had noted that a Democratic member of the Georgia Election Board had just called for Raffensperger himself to launch an investigation into the phone call. His office was a law enforcement agency with authority to police elections in the state. But since Trump's call had been with him—not to mention Trump's earlier phone call to his chief investigator, Frances Watson—Raffensperger opined "there might be a conflict of interest" for his office to conduct any investigation.

He then indicated he had picked up some inside intel. "I understand that the Fulton County district attorney wants to look at it," he said. "Maybe that's the appropriate venue."

Raffensperger had a point. He would be the prospective chief witness in any case that might result from the president's pressure campaign, making it untenable for his office to take the lead in getting to the bottom of what the White House was up to in Georgia. And by now, Willis had already gone through her first and most essential analysis of the phone call: She had established that because Raffensperger had been at his home in Johns Creek, just inside the Fulton County line, when he took the call, she had primary jurisdiction over what could be heard on the tape. She had not yet said anything publicly. But now, with Raffensperger's comments to Stephanopoulos, she effectively had no choice. She was about to get bombarded with press calls.

No sooner was the interview over than Jeff DiSantis's cell phone rang. It was Willis, desperately trying to reach him. DiSantis, who had

been Willis's campaign strategist, had agreed to be her chief spokesman at the DA's office. He hadn't even started working yet; his first
day on the job wouldn't be for a couple of days. But as a battle-tested
veteran of multiple campaigns, he had already emerged as Willis's all-
purpose political and crisis communications counselor.

"It was a Holy Shit call," said DiSantis. Willis hadn't actually
watched the interview but had immediately heard about it and realized she had been thrust into the middle of a national firestorm. Investigating Trump was not anything Willis had remotely thought about
when she had launched her campaign to replace Paul Howard as DA.
She had plenty else to deal with—a demoralized office and a depleted
staff swamped with backlogged cases amid a surge in violent crime.
This was the moment that Willis blurted out, with some exasperation, "This job is a shit magnet."

Still, after bemoaning what fate had brought her, Willis recognized she had to say something. DiSantis drafted a statement, making
no mention of Trump, but lifting a phrase from the historic motto
of *The New York Times* to describe how Willis would approach her
investigation—"without fear or favor." It was released later that day.

"Like many Americans, I have found the news reports about the
President's telephone call with the Georgia Secretary of State disturbing," Willis's statement read. "As I promised Fulton County voters last
year, as District Attorney, I will enforce the law without fear or favor.
Anyone who commits a felony violation of Georgia law in my jurisdiction will be held accountable."

By the evening, the story of the Fulton County investigation was
being reported by every major news outlet in the country, instantly
proclaimed by pundits as potentially the most serious legal matter
Trump would face upon leaving office. "Well tonight, the person

Donald Trump has to fear the most in the world is someone he has never heard of—Fani Willis," said Lawrence O'Donnell, the MSNBC host, leading off his show that night.

What neither O'Donnell nor Willis, nor anybody else, knew that night is that Trump and his allies were already engaged in yet more arm twisting, intimidation, scheming, and plots that would add considerably to their legal peril.

––––––––

A sense of looming danger hung over the Gold Dome all that week. Trump had called for his followers to assemble in Washington for a January 6 Stop the Steal rally at the Ellipse outside the White House ("Will be wild," he famously tweeted) while he ratcheted up the pressure on Pence to reject the duly certified Biden electors when the vice president presided over the formal counting of the votes in Congress. But there were plenty who stayed behind in Georgia to threaten state officials in one more desperate attempt to make them submit to Donald Trump's election lies. It was Vince Mooney's job to protect the Capitol—and make sure those threats came to nothing.

Mooney, balding and powerfully built with over twenty years in law enforcement, was the supervisor of the Dignitary Protection Unit of the Georgia State Patrol—the team assigned to provide security for the state's elected leaders. He had been monitoring the Trump protestors ever since Election Day, usually from his command post at the governor's mansion or in the state capital, where he kept a watchful eye on the video feed from a state patrol surveillance drone that hovered above. For good measure, Mooney had deployed a SWAT team of trained sharpshooters with long guns who were camped in a van with shaded windows just outside the Gold Dome.

But for all of his advance planning, Mooney was not quite prepared

for the volume of threats that poured in the first week in January. At
4:16 p.m. on January 4—not long after Willis had released her statement confirming her office's investigation of the president—a call
came into the radio room at Georgia Patrol headquarters that a bomb
was about to go off at Raffensperger's house in Johns Creek. Mooney
was immediately on the phone with the FBI, alerting them. Then, as
he was still on the phone with his bureau contact, a call came in on
his other phone. The same suspect behind the bomb threat was now
threatening to shoot Raffensperger and Stacey Abrams. It turned out
to be a false alarm, but at the time Mooney was unnerved. "All I can
say is that it was just crazy," he said. Never in his career had he experienced anything like this.

Even before this influx of new threats, Mooney already had one
potentially dangerous suspect on his radar. On November 21, the GBI
had alerted him that a Cobb County car wash owner named Cleveland Meredith Jr. was sharing tweets showing an arsenal of weapons
and saying "he was going down to the Capitol" to "shoot" Kemp
and Raffensperger. The GBI had him tracked down for a "knock and
talk"—a standard law enforcement technique that, besides sometimes
eliciting useful intelligence, had the added benefit of often deterring
suspects from going through with their plans. Confronted by an
agent, Meredith showed off an assault rifle and Glock handgun and
acknowledged openly carrying them to a pro-Trump protest at the
governor's mansion the day of his tweets—for his own protection,
he insisted. He also said he had worked for Trump's campaign after
he first announced for president in 2015. "Meredith noted that he is a
Patriot that is trying to get the truth out to the general public through
digital media," according to an internal GBI email summarizing the
knock and talk. What was most striking, though, was "the truth"
he wanted revealed to the world. "In approximately 2017, Meredith

discovered QAnon and has been trying to share the information he learned ever since," read the email. (Not bashful about his beliefs, he had once put up a giant billboard near his car wash saying simply #QANON.) It was one more example of the remarkable hold that the crazed conspiracy theories of the QAnon cult had on Trump world, inflaming passions and driving the actions of everybody from a lowly car wash owner to the president of the United States.

Meredith "denied having violent tendencies," according to the GBI summary, and since at that point he hadn't committed any crimes, he was free to go. Soon after, he decamped for Boulder, Colorado, where his ex-wife and children lived. But as authorities would later learn, on January 4, 2021, he loaded up his pickup truck and a trailer and headed to Washington, DC, for Trump's rally. He had packed a cache of guns, high-capacity magazines, and twenty-five hundred rounds of ammunition, including several hundred armor-piercing bullets. "Gonna collect...a ton of Traitors heads," he wrote in one text to a friend. In others, he wrote he was considering assassinating Speaker of the House Nancy Pelosi by "putting a bullet in her noggin on live TV." In due course, the texts would land Meredith—along with many others—in federal prison.

Two nights before Supervisor Mooney was dealing with the bomb threat in Atlanta, Trump had summoned the Justice Department's Rosen and Donoghue to the Oval Office for a three-hour-long, knock-down, drag-out meeting with Clark, the environmental lawyer he wanted to install as the new acting attorney general so he could send out the letter demanding that Georgia withdraw its certification of the Biden electors. Clark told the group that he would conduct "real investigations" that would uncover "widespread fraud." Rosen and

Donoghue confirmed that if the Department of Justice involved itself in the 2020 election in this way—and made bogus claims that there was reason to believe there had been "widespread fraud"—they would both promptly resign. And having canvassed the rest of the department's leadership earlier in the day, they continued, so would every other political appointee at Justice. And not just them, either. "What is that going to say about you, when we all walk out at the same time?" Donoghue, the deputy attorney general, said to the president. "And what happens if, within forty-eight hours, we have hundreds of resignations from your Justice Department because of your actions?"

Trump realized he was boxed in. If he went through with his plan to ditch Rosen and replace him with Clark, he was looking at a Saturday Night Massacre that would blow up in his face. "You're not going to get anything done," he finally told a dejected Clark.

But Trump couldn't take his mind off Georgia. If he couldn't fire Rosen, he would fire BJay Pak, the US attorney in Atlanta. At the direction of William Barr, Pak—a former Georgia GOP state legislator—had ordered the FBI to investigate Giuliani's claims about the supposed "smoking gun" State Farm video and reported back that it showed zero evidence of fraud. "No wonder nothing's been found in Atlanta, because the U.S. attorney there is a Never Trumper," Trump said about Pak. "How did this guy end up in my administration?" he said during the meeting with Rosen and Donoghue. Nobody interrupted to point out that Trump himself had appointed him. Trump wanted him gone—that day. Donoghue later passed along the message. He didn't need to. Pak was already planning to resign, and did so the next day.

After the meeting, Trump—with the clock ticking—seemed to shelve his obsession with Raffensperger, Kemp, and Pak, at least for the moment. He was focused instead on his last futile card—pressuring

Pence to reject the Biden electors in the battleground states and send the whole matter of electing a president back to Republican-controlled legislatures so they could replace the Biden electors with the fake Trump electors. (Or, in an alternative scenario dreamed up by the Trump lawyers, Pence could just reject the Biden electors outright and, under the Constitution, let the House of Representatives decide who should be president.*) The plan, still being pushed by Eastman, was fraught with danger—as some in the White House warned. One of them, deputy White House counsel Eric Herschmann, confronted Eastman about it in another contentious meeting on January 4. "Hold on," Herschmann told the constitutional law professor that day, according to his later testimony before the January 6 committee. "You're saying you believe the vice president, acting as President of the Senate, can be the sole decision maker as to who becomes the President of the United States? Are you out of your fucking mind? You're going to turn around and tell seventy-eight million-plus people in this country that your theory is this is how you're going to invalidate their votes. You're going to cause riots in the streets."

Eastman brushed him off. There have been times in the country's history of our country, he told Herschmann, that violence was used "to protect the republic."

In any case, Pence made it clear he would refuse to do any of this. Trump couldn't quite believe his own vice president would cross him. That night, Trump flew to Dalton, Georgia, for a last-minute rally for Loeffler and Perdue in the runoff scheduled for the next day. "I hope

---

* Under the Twelfth Amendment to the Constitution, if no candidate receives a majority of the electoral votes, the House chooses the president—with each state delegation awarded one vote. Since the GOP controlled a majority of state delegations to the House, the Eastman backup plan would have all but guaranteed a Trump victory.

Mike Pence comes through for us," he said in a speech in which he called the vice president "a great guy." Then he added, "Of course if he doesn't come through, I won't like him quite as much."

Trump summoned Pence to meet him the next day in the Oval Office. He derided him for being "naïve" and playing by "Marquis of Queensberry rules." He questioned his courage. Pence took offense. "I wouldn't be here if I didn't have courage," he replied. He would stick to his constitutional role—to count the votes, not decide which ones to count. Trump told him that, if he did that, he wouldn't be his friend anymore. Pence repaired to his office, exhausted, and, as he later wrote, folded his hands and bowed his head in prayer.

That night, at 9:52 p.m., Trump released a statement that he had just dictated to his aide Jason Miller—that he and the vice president were in "total agreement" that Pence had the authority under the Constitution to "decertify the results" and "send them back to the states for change." Pence could scarcely believe it. It was the exact opposite of what he had told Trump in the Oval Office hours earlier. Trump was living in a fantasy world.

"I had a feeling January 6, 2021 was going to be a very long day," Pence later wrote.

———

The chaotic and horrifying assault on the US Capitol that day will forever be remembered as one of the darkest moments in modern American history. At the rally on the Ellipse just before, Giuliani spoke and railed about the "crooked Dominion machines" and inflamed the crowd, shouting, "Let's have trial by combat!" Then Eastman got up and said the country's future as a "self-governing republic" was at stake if Pence didn't come through. Finally, Trump spoke for more than an hour. As the crowd chanted—"Fight for Trump! Fight for

Trump!"—he recycled his claims about stolen votes in Wisconsin, Michigan, and Georgia, citing—as one of his prime examples—the mythical "suitcases" of "fraudulent" ballots in Fulton County. He denounced Raffensperger ("I can't believe this guy is a Republican. He loves recording telephone conversations") and ridiculed Georgia's "pathetic" Brian Kemp ("who weighs 130 pounds"). In a last phone call with Pence that morning, Trump had taunted and insulted his vice president, telling him he was a "wimp" and a "pussy." Now speaking to the throng, he whipped them up into a frenzy. "If Mike Pence does the right thing, we win the election," he told the crowd. And if he does not, "then we're stuck with a president who lost the election... *We're just not going to let that happen.*" And then: "*When you catch somebody in a fraud, you're allowed to go by very different rules,*" he said. And: "*If you don't fight like hell, you're not going to have a country anymore.*" He exhorted the crowd of several thousand to join him on a march to the US Capitol. He did at one point say they should do so "peacefully"—a line written by his speechwriters. It may have saved him, at least at first, from criminal culpability for what happened next.

After the rally, the crowd started marching down Pennsylvania Avenue to the Capitol. More than two thousand of them would enter the Capitol, many storming past police barricades, assaulting police officers, smashing windows, and threatening the lives of lawmakers. One of the loudest and most aggressive was eighteen-year-old Bruno Cua from the upscale Atlanta suburb of Milton, a prime example of how even a clean-cut teenager from an idyllic middle-class family could get swept up by Trump's blizzard of disinformation. A religiously devout homeschooled son of two professionals (his father was an executive at a major hotel chain, his mother, a veterinarian), Cua had been consumed for weeks by the Stop the Steal movement, driving a giant Trump flag around his hometown in his pickup, honking his horn, and taunting Biden supporters. In the runup to January 6, he had posted a series of inflammatory comments on social media: "PEACEFUL PROTESTS ARENT GONNA MAKE THE CORRUPT #DEEPSTATE GO AWAY! They didn't hold signs in #1776, they shot and killed their oppressors!" he tweeted on December 21. And then the next day on Instagram: "we can storm the freaking senate/house... That's why I keep saying to bring guns. Holding signs is useless." At the Capitol, Cua wore a red MAGA hat and wielded a baton as he charged up the stairs and started down hallways, kicking and pounding on doors with his fists. "Hey! Where are the swamp rats hiding? This is what happens when you piss off patriots!" he shouted. After shoving a police officer, he burst into the Senate chamber, plopping himself down and leaning back in Pence's chair. "This is our house! This is our country!" he yelled.*

For three crucial hours—while US Capitol Police officers were trying to fend off this invading army like the last defenders at the Alamo—Trump refused pleas from his chief of staff, his daughter, his friends in Congress, and the media to call off the mob. His incitement of the riot and his manifest dereliction of duty while the Capitol was under attack soon led to Trump's second impeachment.

But as terrible as the events of that day were, they wouldn't deter

---

* More than two and a half years later, Cua was found guilty of two federal felonies for his actions that day. Pleading with the judge for mercy during his sentencing hearing, Cua said he was "mortified" and "ashamed" of his actions, adding: "I would do anything to go back and change what I did." His mother, choking up with tears, also made a plea for leniency for her son, expressing remorse that she had not watched more closely what he was posting on social media. But like her son, she had believed what Trump was saying. "I mean, I believed what I was hearing," she said. "So one of the things we've learned is this, the truly devastating power of words." Calling this a "tragic case," US judge Randolph Moss sentenced Cua to a year and one day in prison.

Trump's army in Georgia from their incessant scheming. In fact, the president's allies were about to pull off their most audacious act of all—the cyber heist of election machines and software in a tiny rural county two hundred miles southeast of Atlanta. It was a modern-day version of the Watergate break-in. Except in this case, the burglars were given the keys.

CHAPTER TEN

A Raid in Rural Georgia

"You guys should seize machines."

A little before 11:00 a.m. on January 7, a single-engine prop plane peeked over the horizon and started to gently bank toward the tiny airport in Douglas, Georgia, the county seat in rural Coffee County. On board were Scott Hall, an Atlanta-based bail bondsman with family ties to Trump's orbit (his brother-in-law David Bossie had been Trump's 2016 deputy campaign manager and was still a top adviser), and his sidekick, Alex Cruce, a data analyst. About thirty minutes later, four cyber forensics specialists equipped with the technical tools of their trade rolled into Douglas in a black BMW after the three-and-a-half-hour drive from Atlanta. They worked for Sullivan/Strickler, a computer tech firm that had been hired by the Tomotley crew in its frantic bid to gain access to Dominion voting machines.

Coordinating the two groups' arrival in Douglas was Cathy Latham, the chairwoman of the Coffee County Republican Party and a longtime public high school teacher. "Just landed," Hall texted at 11:08 a.m. on a group thread called Coffee_County_Forensics. "How far out are you," Latham texted Paul Maggio, leader of the Sullivan/ Strickler squad, which he'd dubbed S2. "We are in town waiting for Scott to let us know when to pull in," Maggio replied.

Latham stood waiting outside the drab, windowless Coffee County Elections and Registration building, a slightly tattered American flag flapping in the light breeze. The Sullivan/Strickler team arrived at 11:43 a.m. Latham greeted them and escorted them into the building. She introduced them to Misty Hampton, the county election supervisor; election board member Eric Chaney; and Ed Voyles, a former election board member who at the time had no official position. All were Republicans in the heavily pro-Trump county and all had bought into the election conspiracy theories that had taken root across the country.

The evening before, as the smell of tear gas and spent flash-bangs hung in the air at the US Capitol, a citadel of American democracy desecrated by a violent mob, the group had firmed up their plans for what they planned to do. "Scott Hall is on the phone with Cathy about wanting to copy our ballots from the general election like we talked about the other day," Hampton texted an election board member. "Ready to Roll," a member of the Sullivan/Strickler team texted that night.

Now, a few minutes before noon on January 7, the operation began. The Sullivan/Strickler team unloaded their forensics tools out of a large industrial-strength case—Dell laptops, external hard drives, USB sticks and cables—and went to work. The mission was nothing short of making complete forensic copies of all of the component parts of Coffee's voting system, the Dominion software that powered the voting, the ballot scanner that tabulated votes, and thumb drives and flash memory cards that contained every bit of data from past and present elections across the entire state of Georgia. For seven straight hours they were given free rein over the voting system by the same local GOP election officials charged with maintaining its integrity.

At one point, election supervisor Hampton brought in pizza for the group so they wouldn't need to stop their work.

The crime in progress was an astonishingly brazen breach of voting security. Election technology is designated "critical infrastructure" by the federal government, and of vital national security importance. Tampering with election equipment is a violation of Georgia criminal law, including statutes against computer trespassing and theft. Exposure of the data could put Georgia's entire election system at risk, potentially providing a road map for malign actors, foreign or domestic, to probe for vulnerabilities.

The operatives involved in this caper would later argue that they had gotten an "invitation" from the Coffee County election officials and were given "permission" to copy the Dominion software. It was an invitation that was questionable from the start. On New Year's Eve, Hampton had dashed off a breezy email to Preston Haliburton, a Georgia lawyer working with Rudy Giuliani, saying, "I do not see any problem assisting you with anything y'all need in accordance to Georgia law. Y'all are welcome to our office any time." The email was in response to a request from Halliburton seeking records about absentee ballots. It made no reference to election machine software, and if it had, the "invitation" would have been legally worthless—as Raffensperger's office had already made clear to all election officials in the state, including Hampton. "You may not produce any sensitive data that could harm election security," Chris Harvey, state elections director, wrote in the November 17, 2020, directive to election officials, which was obtained by the authors. "Copies of election software are *not* subject to public release and *cannot* be provided." Harvey had reason to be worried. Trump allies were filing open records requests for Dominion software in counties across the state and Harvey, citing Georgia election law, felt it important to remind them that such requests needed to be turned down. "I wanted to be very clear—nobody gets access to that equipment," he later said. "This is the line that was drawn." Now, in Coffee County, Trump's operatives had just crossed it.

Months later, the operation would leak into public view. And once it did, Fani Willis's investigators focused intently on the illicit activities in this far-flung rural county, an event they suspected—quite correctly—could lead directly to Trump's inner sanctum.

———————

The seeds of the Coffee County operation were planted just hours after the election. In another rural election office more than a thousand miles away in tiny Antrim County, in Northern Michigan, election officials had initially reported Biden ahead by thirty-two hundred votes. It was an unlikely outcome in the solidly Republican county—and turned out to be a mistake, the result of human error. In tabulating the results on election night, a harried county clerk had inadvertently put more than two thousand Trump votes in the Biden column on her spreadsheet—a mistake the clerk, to her chagrin, caught, confessed to, and fixed within a few days. But down in Georgia, Trump's lawyers, led by Giuliani, brushed off the idea that this was human error. They seized on the anomaly and used it to drive home their outlandish theories that Dominion machines were flipping votes. Giuliani would call the initial Antrim results "nothing short of mind-blowing" and implored Michigan officials "to halt any further approval of presidential electors until all of these machines have been seized for auditing and analysis."

Antrim was the start—and they believed the botched vote count in this tiny county, until then best known as the cherry capital of the world, gave them license to claim fraud everywhere and inspect Dominion machines across the country.

A driving force behind the frenetic efforts to gain access to the Dominion voting equipment and software was Trump himself. At the notorious December 18 Oval Office meeting, in Trump's presence, the Tomotley crew had raised the idea of accessing voting machines in Georgia, presenting him with a draft executive order that called on the US military to seize election machines—and specifically mentioning Coffee County.* The president was also focused on Coffee County, having raised the claims of voting irregularities three weeks earlier in his phone call to Attorney General Carr. "Look into it," Trump had told him. Although he didn't sign the executive order, Trump was obviously on board with the overall idea. "Why don't you guys seize machines?" the president implored Donoghue and Rosen during their December 27 conversation. "You guys should seize machines because there will be evidence."

When the president raised the idea of seizing voting machines, Rosen and Donoghue had swatted it away, exasperatedly pointing out that they had no legal or evidentiary basis to do so. What they did not know at the time was that Giuliani was already secretly working on an alternative plan to achieve the same goal.

On December 19, three weeks before the Coffee County raid, Giuliani appeared on *War Room*, Steve Bannon's podcast, and though nobody picked up on it at the time, he had previewed the whole Coffee County operation. It was a classic Rudy performance, by turns jovial and scathing. At one point he bantered with Bannon about how much fun

---

* In testimony before the January 6 committee, a White House official who attended the meeting, Derek Lyons, said: "I think the only state I specifically remember being discussed was Georgia."

it was hanging out with President Trump during the White House Christmas party the night before. "The president...is a heck of a lot of fun," the former New York mayor said with a grin. Then, when the conversation turned to Brian Kemp's continued refusal to order a special session of the state legislature, he laced into the Georgia governor as a "turncoat" and "traitor."

But amid the lighthearted talk and the recriminations toward balky Republicans, Giuliani hinted at a secret plan he and his crew had cooked up that he believed could be a game changer in the Peach State. "I think we're going to succeed in Georgia without him," Giuliani said, referring to Kemp. "We got a big project working in Georgia right now right around his back," Giuliani added cryptically. "He doesn't know what the heck is going on."

What Giuliani was hiding up his sleeve had started to come together days earlier at the Willard hotel, where the Trump coup plotters had set up their "war room."

The beaux-arts-style historic landmark, into which Abraham Lincoln was smuggled before his inauguration to avoid assassination attempts, served as another key command post for the plot to overturn the election. Giuliani and his chief "investigator," former New York City police commissioner Bernie Kerik, had just moved their operation there so they could be closer to the White House. Others who would later attend the strategy sessions at the Stop the Steal war room included Steve Bannon, Roger Stone, John Eastman, and Trump aide Jason Miller. It was at the Willard that Giuliani met a secret "whistleblower" from Georgia who, along with her Atlanta-based lawyer, had traveled to Washington—Cathy Latham, the GOP chair in Coffee County. Latham had been scheming with the rest of the group of local Republicans back in Douglas, Georgia, to put their tiny election office at the center of the Stop the Steal project. Although she had no authority over the country's election office, Latham used her position in the party to make sure the president's operatives got what they wanted most of all: access to Coffee County's Dominion voting machines.

It must have been an *aha* moment for Giuliani; it was now clear that the Trump team could bypass court authorization to gain access to the machines, which had been repeatedly denied by judges. Nor would they have to rely on a legally specious executive order or a reckless commando raid. They could get what they desperately wanted through "voluntary" means, accessing the sensitive voting information, in effect, by "invitation"—from Trump partisans with no authority to offer it.

The focus on Coffee County was improbable from the start: The far-off county was a Trump stronghold where he had captured 70 percent of the vote. What could have possibly gone wrong there? But after the state tipped in the post-election counting to Biden, Misty Hampton—the county election supervisor and a hard-core Trump supporter—was eager to use her position to expose what she suspected was statewide fraud. She made two videos purporting to show how easily an election supervisor could manipulate votes. "I think I want to vote for Biden," Hampton said in her South Georgia twang, in one of the videos. "Let's let Biden win this one," she added, clicking her mouse with apparent satisfaction. Of course, Hampton had no evidence this had actually happened. Unmentioned in the videos as well, there was a paper record of all of the electronic votes that could—and would—be used to verify the election results in every county in the state.

Nevertheless, the videos soon started to get traction. A few weeks later, in December, the Trump campaign included them in a lawsuit seeking to overturn the results of the election in Georgia. Moreover, the Coffee County evidence became prominent talking points for Giuliani and other Trump allies as they pushed for state legislatures around the country to call a special session and overturn the election, including the December 10 hearing before the Georgia General Assembly. At the hearing when Phil Waldron, the retired army colonel who was a key member of the election denial team, played clips from the videos, Giuliani's voice can be heard in the background excitedly saying, "This is really good stuff," adding, "We should try to get this on Newsmax, on OAN."

For their part, the Coffee County officials were excited to be foot soldiers in a Trump army determined to expose a massive fraud. They traded the latest conspiracy theories, including tweets from "Code Monkey," the Twitter handle of Ron Watkins, the QAnon luminary. In mid-December, Latham reached out to Robert Preston, the owner of a local trucking company who also ran an online news site called *Douglas Now*, to press him to expose the fraud by meeting with two Trump campaign workers who had traveled to Douglas. But what stood out most to Preston was how excited Latham was for Coffee County—and herself—to be in the middle of the Stop the Steal crusade. She humble-bragged to Preston that she'd given "Rudy" his number and that he should expect a call. (Giuliani never called.) "This was Cathy's moment," recalled one friend of Latham's, who talked to her at the time. "She loved the attention."

By New Year's Day, the operatives in Georgia preparing for the Coffee breach were in direct contact with Giuliani's team at the Willard in Washington. On the afternoon of January 1, a member of the Sullivan/Strickler squad, Jennifer Jackson, sent a message to the S2 team on Signal, the encrypted communications app. She'd forwarded a text message she'd received from Katherine Friess, a DC lobbyist and self-professed "election-integrity" lawyer who was working with Giuliani, Kerik, and the others out of the Willard. It read: "Hi! Just handed [sic] back in DC with the Mayor [Giuliani]. Huge things starting to come together! Most immediately, we were granted access—by written invitation!—to the Coffee County Systens [sic]. Yay!"

She appears to have been only one of many buzzing in Trump's orbit about what was about to happen in Coffee. On January 2, the same day as Trump's phone call to Raffensperger, Jeffrey Clark, the Justice attorney the president wanted to install as acting attorney general in order to upend the election results, had a sixty-three-minute phone call with Scott Hall, the Atlanta bail bondsman who was about to join the excursion to rural Georgia. As would soon become clear, the mercurial Hall had become Clark's chief informant in the Justice Department official's push to get sign-off on his draft letter urging the Georgia legislature to convene a special session to appoint new Trump electors to replace the legitimate ones for Biden.

In Hall, Clark had found the ideal partner. A beefy former marine, Hall liked to boast of his political influence, often dropping references to his family relationship to Bossie, a genuine Trump insider. But in the weeks after the election, a change came over him, according to Charles Shaw, a rival bail bondsman who served as president of the statewide association for the industry.* Shaw and Hall had known each other for years, serving together on the association's board. Shaw recalled that Hall had become obsessed with reversing Trump's defeat and was convinced that shadowy forces were trying to stop him from doing so. During executive board meetings of the bail bondsman association, Hall would suddenly burst into extended tirades about

---

* Shaw would soon resurface in the headlines as the bail bondsman for Trump's surrender at the Fulton County Jail.

the election. "And he would get into a diatribe about stolen elections and, you know, cell phones being hacked and computers being hacked and people having him under surveillance," said Shaw. "I mean it bordered on paranoia." At one dinner meeting of the association, Hall showed up and started talking about how he was forced to swap cars to escape his pursuers and even had cut off communications with his family. But one constant theme with Hall, Shaw said, was the nefarious manipulation of Dominion machines and how it had led to "election tampering and computer tampering and ballot box tampering. And I mean, it's so much that I kind of tuned it out because it was like somebody telling you, you know, the world's gonna fall out of the ground tomorrow."

Hall also believed that, in the end, he and the forces of righteousness would prevail. "He felt as though, yes, that Biden would not be sworn in," said Shaw, "that a judge or the military or someone would stop that."

But Hall was leaving nothing to chance. At one point, Shaw recalled, Hall let drop that he would be flying soon to "south Georgia" to what he cryptically referred to as "election stuff."

––––––––––

The "election stuff" in Coffee County dragged on into the evening on January 7. At 7:43 p.m., Maggio sent messages on the Signal encrypted communications app pronouncing the operation a success. "We just finished up at Coffee County and are on our way back to Atlanta. Everything went smoothly." Hall responded with "thank you" and American flag emojis. ("We scanned every freaking ballot," Hall later boasted in a recorded phone conversation with an election integrity activist.) The next day, Maggio sent a separate message to Sidney Powell, whose Defending the Republic nonprofit would fund the operation, nudging her about the payment. "We are consolidating all of the data collected and will be uploading it to our secure site for access by your team," he wrote. "Hopefully we can take care of payment today." He included an invoice for $26,200.

What Maggio, of course, did not indicate were the grave implications of their successful operation. According to Kevin Skoglund, a cybersecurity expert who analyzed the evidence for an election integrity group that sued the state over the issue, "The scope of their access and data collection was massive," yielding data from almost every component of Georgia's election system. Any hacker in his basement now "has the ability to get this software and analyze it and look for vulnerabilities."

Crucially, the stolen information was uploaded to a password-protected site giving widespread access to the pilfered data to at least ten people, including election deniers who were hellbent on spreading their disinformation to further the fraudulent claims that the 2020 election was stolen.

One of them was one of the more curious characters in Trump's Stop the Steal orbit. Conan Hayes was a QAnon-espousing professional surfer (he was a co-founder of the popular sports apparel brand RVCA) who tweeted under the handle @We_Have_Risen. He interacted regularly on Twitter with Ron Watkins and once claimed that Mike Flynn, an enthusiastic surfer himself, was showing his support for QAnon by tying his surfboard leash into a Q-shaped loop. Hayes's prolific tweeting about alleged voter fraud after the 2020 election gained him entrée into the Trump election truther crowd. Soon enough he was participating in the Antrim County forensic audit as an expert witness, as well as another audit in Mesa County, Colorado, though it was unclear whether he had any expertise on the subject.

In both places, as in Coffee County, Hayes obtained reams of highly sensitive voter data. And he was not exactly discreet with it.

At an August 11, 2021, cyber symposium in Sioux Falls, South Dakota, held by Mike Lindell, the MyPillow CEO and a promoter of baseless election-fraud conspiracy theories, forensic images of Dominion voting systems were shared by Hayes. They were discussed during a panel discussion moderated by none other than Ron Watkins, piped in remotely on a giant screen from his home in Japan.

The loop was complete. Dominion's proprietary voter software, seized covertly in rural Coffee County, had now ended up in the eager hands of the QAnon conspiracy cult.

Fani Willis knew nothing about the events in Coffee County as they were unfolding that month. But she was determined to let all the relevant players—and her constituents—know she meant business when it came to investigating Trump. On February 10, 2021—the day the Senate's second impeachment trial of Trump began—Willis sent out a stern letter to top Georgia officials, including Kemp, Duncan, Carr, and Raffensperger, directing them to preserve all documents and emails relating to the 2020 election, noting this was potential evidence in her probe. "Please remind your staff that it is a crime under Georgia law to destroy records created or received in the performance of government duty," she wrote. Calling the investigation a matter "of high priority," she noted that a new Fulton County grand jury would be convened in March "and this office will begin requesting grand jury subpoenas as necessary at that time."

The release of the letter—coming amid an impeachment trial that was certain to result in a Senate acquittal—ramped up hopes that Willis's investigation would be the one that could hold Trump accountable for his election lies. She was once again flooded with media requests and, at the suggestion of DiSantis, agreed to do one TV interview the next night with MSNBC's Rachel Maddow. It gave a national audience their first glimpse of Fani Willis and her no-nonsense, often brusque style.

Asked by Maddow if she planned to "depose" Trump, Willis corrected her. "First of all, in criminal law, we don't do depositions," she lectured the brainy Rhodes-Scholar-turned-TV-anchor. Maddow asked what impact the ongoing Senate impeachment trial would have on her inquiry. Willis replied, tersely, "Zero. None whatsoever."

But she did reveal something that should have been clear from the beginning. Asked if it had "crossed your mind" that there now might be concerns about her safety and that of her staff, Willis replied: "Oh, absolutely. Since we've opened this, we've gotten—my security has doubled. We've gotten a lot of comments. Interestingly enough, the comments are always racist, and it's really just a waste of time and foolishness...

"Some people think 'the nerve of me' to actually do my job," she added. "But I took an oath. I made a commitment to the citizens in my community, and I'm going to do my job."

It would take a lot longer than anybody expected.

CHAPTER ELEVEN

A Threat from Trump

"Hypothetically speaking, do you want a bodyguard following you around for the rest of your life?"

Good morning. Today, as many of you know, we are an office that is in crisis."

It was September 29, 2021, and Fani Willis, flanked by more than a dozen of her deputies—all of them, unlike the boss, wearing masks—had called a press conference to give the citizens of Fulton County an update on what she had been doing after seven months on the job.

It had been a trying time and Willis, looking weary and a bit haggard, did little to hide her exasperation. The workload she had inherited, she explained, was off the charts and genuinely frightening: a "historic backlog" of thousands of unindicted cases—suspected murderers and "vile" sex offenders among them, never charged for crimes investigators believed they had committed. Gang violence—such as that which had killed eight-year-old Secoriea Turner—was relentless and on the rise. In March, a crazed twenty-one-year-old gunman, under treatment for a sex addiction, went on a killing spree at spas in and around Atlanta, murdering eight people, six of them of Asian descent. Willis brought charges and announced she would seek the death penalty—a reminder of her willingness to buck the prevailing zeitgeist in her party on crime and punishment. The suspect in the spa shootings had bought the handgun he had used the morning of the massacre—easy to do in Georgia, where the Second Amendment reigns supreme and there is no waiting period on gun purchases.

"I make no secret about it that I feel like all of us are in a little bit of danger," she said. "We need to be very diligent about the way we move. There is something ugly going on in society."

At that point, Willis wasn't talking about the ugliness that surrounded the battle over the 2020 election results. She was referring to something deeper and for many Atlanta residents more pressing, but not wholly unrelated: a slow and steady erosion of civic authority, of respect for rules and the basic norms of civil behavior. Much of it, of course, had been aggravated by the school shutdowns and wholesale commercial disruptions and closures caused by Covid. It had all combined to lead to a surge in crime throughout Atlanta, even in tony Buckhead, which had once seemed immune to crime.

But as she was wrapping up, she got one last question about the investigation into the former president, Donald Trump, that she had announced just days after taking office. Where does that stand? a reporter asked. What was Willis's timeline?

"What I can tell you is there is an active, ongoing investigation," she said. "As I've told people, even when you're in a crime crisis, I do not have the right as District Attorney to look the other way on any crime that may have happened in my jurisdiction."

And then she reminded her audience why she had begun the investigation in the first place.

"And certainly if somebody did something as serious as interfere with somebody's right to vote,—which, you know as a woman, as a person of color, is a sacred right where people lost a lot of lives—we're going to invest in that."

As for her timing, Willis said, "We're going to do it until it's done. Until I'm comfortable. And should the facts and the law match up to a charge, the community should feel confident that this office will bring charges."

But the truth was that the Trump investigation was at that point stalled. True, Willis had dispatched investigators to interview some of the key players and collect some of the documents she had demanded be preserved in her letter back in February 2021. But she wasn't getting a ton of cooperation, starting with—somewhat to her surprise and frustration—Brad Raffensperger himself. He was the obvious central witness. But he made it clear from the start that if he was going to talk, he wanted a grand jury subpoena first.

This was a political move, pure and simple. Raffensperger was planning on running for reelection as secretary of state in 2022. It was already clear he was certain to be facing, in a GOP primary, a pro-Trump opponent who would hammer him over his refusal to go along with the ex-president's bogus fraud claims. Raffensperger had gotten a ton of favorable publicity in the national media for his uncompromising refusal to accede to the president's demands that he "find" the votes that would put Trump over the top in Georgia. But insisting on a subpoena to talk to Willis was for Raffensperger a modest political insurance policy: a way to make it clear to GOP primary voters he was not voluntarily cooperating with a Democratic DA's investigation aimed at criminally prosecuting the former Republican president.

But Willis wasn't anywhere close to presenting evidence to a grand jury for the Trump case. Before she did so, she wanted an experienced, top-notch prosecutor to oversee the probe—and she was having trouble finding one. She had reached out to Roy Barnes, the former Georgia Democratic governor and one of the state's premier lawyers, and asked him to serve as a senior adviser. He turned her down. So too did Gabe Banks, a well-respected Atlanta defense lawyer and former federal prosecutor who had once been a wide receiver for Vanderbilt's football team. Neither, it seemed, wanted to drop all their other cases and delve into a Trump investigation that would be all-consuming and result in them having to deal with the never-ending threats from the ex-president's cult-like followers. Barnes told the authors he didn't want to discuss his overture from Willis. But when pressed, he added: "Hypothetically speaking, do you want a bodyguard following you around for the rest of your life?"

In the end, Willis turned to Nathan Wade, a soft-spoken, part-time municipal judge in Marietta and solid member of the defense bar who had previously represented the Republican sheriff in Cobb County in an election dispute. (Wade, who rarely spoke publicly, was best known for snazzy attire that included an affinity for ascots.) Willis also retained as an office consultant John Floyd, the state's foremost expert on Georgia's RICO law who had tutored Willis on what a "beautiful tool" the statute was for prosecutors when she had used it in the Atlanta public school cheating case. It was an early signal of how Willis saw the case—as a wide-ranging racketeering conspiracy. It wasn't just the phone call to Raffensperger. It was the fake electors, the blatantly false testimony about the State Farm video, the pressure campaign on Kemp and state legislators to call a special session, the threats to Ruby Freeman, her daughter, and many others—all of them potential "predicate acts" by co-conspirators acting on behalf of a corrupt "enterprise"—the Trump campaign—with the single-minded goal of overthrowing the results of a democratic election.

But obtaining the witness testimony and documents she would need to do so was proving a far more complicated task than she first thought it would be. Willis could have turned to the Georgia Bureau of Investigation (GBI) to conduct the basic investigative work. But that was quickly ruled out: GBI ultimately reported to Kemp and a general assembly filled with Trump-friendly election deniers. Too risky, Willis concluded. Concerned about bogging down a regular grand jury—whose terms only lasted for two months—with a lengthy and complicated investigation it would be unable to finish, she used a more low-key if decidedly less effective tool for collecting evidence: On April 20, 2021, Willis had filed an open records request with the Georgia Secretary of State's Office seeking all "documents and other materials which might shed light on the propriety" of Trump's phone call to Raffensperger as well as any "related matters." She also asked for records about a separate call South Carolina senator Lindsey Graham had made to the secretary. An open records request was the same method any journalist, or for that matter any member of the public, might use to get information.

Raffensperger's office responded with no particular urgency. A few days later, the office reported that while it had identified responsive records, "additional time is needed" to process them, a staffer wrote back. The staffer estimated the office would need thirty business days to do so, adding helpfully, "We will waive any costs."

───────────

If Fani Willis at first had trouble finding a leader for her prosecution team, Trump early on found his first local lawyer to handle his defense—and it was not who anybody expected. Dwight Thomas wasn't a well-known partner at a fancy white-shoe law firm. He ran a small two-man firm with a thriving local practice of DUI, personal injury, and drug cases, as well as the occasional representation of local pols indicted for corruption. He was a somewhat colorful character, known for riding around the region on his trademark Harley-Davidson. And he had had his share of high-profile cases, including representing T.I., the rap star who had tried to pressure Willis to renounce her support from the police union, and GOP activist Mary Norwood during the 2020 campaign. In 2007, on the night he was due to perform at the Black Entertainment Television Hip Hop Awards, T.I. (a convicted felon who had served time on multiple drug charges) was arrested by federal agents for illegal possession of machine guns, silencers, and other firearms. Thomas, after much negotiation, got T.I. off with a one-year sentence—a resolution the lawyer hailed on his website as "the deal of the century," especially because "T.I. did not have to snitch on anyone."

But it was another old case of Thomas's that likely explained how he ended up with Trump as a client. In 2005, Thomas was the lawyer for Vernon Jones, then the Democratic CEO of DeKalb County, an Atlanta suburb. Jones had invited a young woman job seeker to his home for a party with roasted marshmallows, drinks, and dancing. While there, the woman said Jones had pinned her down and raped her. This triggered an investigation by the GBI and the DeKalb DA's Office. The story made the local news. Thomas vigorously denied the charges on behalf of his client and publicly floated an alternative narrative: that the young woman and another female friend of Jones at the party had engaged with Jones in a consensual ménage à trois. The phrase stuck, no charges against Jones were ever filed, and Thomas became colloquially known in the local defense bar as the ménage à trois guy.

By the time Willis was launching her probe, Jones, Thomas's client, had morphed into a MAGA Republican, earning him a spot speaking at the 2020 Republican National Convention, one of several African Americans to get such a nod. (Jones had once crowd-surfed at a Trump reelection rally.) He also had started boasting about his regular trips to Mar-a-Lago. It was widely assumed that it was Jones who had recommended Thomas, the lawyer who helped him beat the rape rap, to Trump. It also seemed logical that Trump and his advisers figured hiring a Black lawyer recommended by a Black supporter was the best way to deal with the pesky Black DA in Atlanta.

In late 2021, amid a flurry of media reports that Willis's probe might be about to move forward, Thomas called her out of the blue and asked for a meeting. Willis was amenable. Thomas's role as Trump's lawyer was not yet public. (It would not be revealed until seven months later, in a Yahoo News story by the authors of this book.) But Willis was reluctant to meet Thomas at her office. There was concern among her staff that some TV stakeout reporters might spot him arriving and start asking questions. So on December 17, 2021, Willis agreed to meet Thomas in a private conference room at a downtown InterContinental hotel. There was lots going on that day—the hotel lobby was crowded, making the venue a bit problematic. But Thomas had a specific assignment—he wanted to get a sense of where Willis was in her investigation of the former president. "What's going on? What's the status?" he asked. Thomas's approach was deliberately low-key—and, under the circumstances, prudent. He didn't come in guns blazing, blasting her entire investigation as a witch hunt or threatening to bury her in legal challenges. "He knew she didn't respond to dick swinging," said DiSantis, who attended the meeting. But Thomas did make a point of mentioning that he was headed down to Mar-a-Lago the next day to give his client an update on what he was facing in Georgia.

Willis was matter-of-fact: No, she was not on the verge of indicting the president. She was still assembling her team to conduct the probe. But she also made it crystal clear she wasn't messing around. "And so I assured them...that in the spring or so...I will be taking the next step," Willis recalled. That was, to seek a "special purpose grand jury" that could begin taking testimony under oath. This was the first time Willis was confirming she would go this route. Under Georgia law, special grand juries were unique creations and used relatively sparingly. They were reserved for complex investigations—cases where the evidence was multi-layered and diffuse and multiple defendants were involved. Special grand juries didn't have the power to issue indictments; only regular grand juries could do that. But they did have the authority to issue subpoenas, compel testimony, write reports on their findings, and make recommendations—all of which would be delivered to Willis for a final decision. (And they could also last longer than the two-month tenure of regular grand juries, making them well suited for sprawling investigations such as this one.) It would take some time to get this up and running. A special grand jury would be convened, she informed Thomas, sometime the following May. Willis's message was clear and unmistakable: Nothing was going to happen imminently. But the Trump case was moving forward.

The next day, December 18, Thomas flew to Mar-a-Lago to brief his client on the meeting with Willis. It didn't go well. Trump, already contemplating another run for the presidency, was infuriated he still had to deal with this. He blasted out a fiery statement on the web.

"All the Democrats want to do is put people in jail," he wrote. "They are vicious, violent, Radical Left thugs." He didn't mention Willis by name, but there was little doubt she was at the top of his list along with other African American prosecutors—New York's attorney general Letitia James and Manhattan district attorney Alvin

Bragg—who were conducting investigations into his conduct and he was convinced were out to get him.

While the Democrats were "letting thugs and murderers into our country—their DA's, AG's and Dem Law Enforcement are out of control," Trump stated.

———————

On January 20, 2022, one year to the day after Trump left office, Willis sent a letter to Christopher Brasher, the chief judge of the Fulton County Superior Court, formally requesting that a special grand jury be convened. The step was necessary, she wrote, given the "reasonable probability" that Georgia's 2020 election had been subject to "possible criminal disruptions."

Ten days later, Trump traveled to Conroe, Texas, for a boisterous second stop on his Save America Rally Tour (among the speakers: the ever-loyal Texas attorney general Ken Paxton and governor Greg Abbott). He upped the ante—and appeared to make ominous threats if Willis and the other prosecutors on his tail made the wrong move.

"If these radical, vicious, racist prosecutors do anything wrong or illegal, I hope we are going to have in this country the biggest protests we have ever had in Washington, D.C., in New York, in Atlanta and elsewhere, because our country and our elections are corrupt. They're corrupt," he said. Trump told the cheering crowd that he was the victim of "prosecutorial misconduct" by "vicious, horrible people" whom he called "mentally sick."

The call for "the biggest protests we have ever had" immediately raised the specter of another January 6. And far from remorse, Trump saw January 6 as he always pretended it was—a patriotic protest. "If I run and I win, we will treat those people from January 6 fairly," Trump said during the same rally. "We will treat them fairly. And if it requires pardons, we will give them pardons, because they are being treated so unfairly."

The rhetoric—the attacks on the prosecutors as "corrupt" and the talk of pardons for the January 6 rioters—made it abundantly clear not only that Trump was unchastened by the violence that had come as a result of his election lies, but also that he had no intention of curbing his incendiary rhetoric. Willis responded the next morning with a letter to the special agent in charge of the FBI in Atlanta. Citing the "alarming" comments by the former president at the Texas rally, she asked the bureau to conduct a "risk assessment" and provide "resources to include intelligence and federal agents" to protect the Fulton County Courthouse where her office was located.

"We must work together to keep the public safe and ensure that we do not have a tragedy in Atlanta similar to what happened at the United States Capitol on January 6, 2021," Willis wrote.

She also did something else that never became public. She directed that the members of her "election team" conducting the investigation, as well as other key personnel, including her spokesman DiSantis, wear bulletproof vests. Some months later, she also directed that her senior staff working on the case receive key fobs attached to their phones with buttons to push that alerted the Fulton County Sheriff's Office if they felt threatened or in danger. Willis was gearing up for a battle—and her investigators, as well as she, were getting ready with flak jackets and what were informally referred to as panic buttons.

———

As Trump was making his threats and Willis was trying to protect her staff, archivists in Washington were reviewing fifteen boxes of government documents that Trump had taken with him when he left the White House. National Archive officials had been asking for the material for over a year after noticing that certain well-publicized records known to have been in Trump's possession—a letter President Obama had left for him and his "love letter" correspondence with North Korean dictator Kim Jong Il—were missing. Where were they? But as the archivists started poring through the material in Trump's boxes, they got an even bigger surprise: They found 197 documents with classified information, including thirty that were marked TOP SECRET or above. The discovery raised obvious questions: How did they get there? Why had Trump kept them? And most of all, were there other classified documents still in his possession?

On February 9, barely a week and a half after Trump made his threats at the Texas rally, the archives referred the matter to the Justice Department for criminal investigation. Unbeknownst to Trump, his legal problems were only growing—and, in this case, the jeopardy had nothing to do with his attempts to steal an election. It was entirely for conduct after he left the White House.

CHAPTER TWELVE

A Very Special Grand Juror

"How can you plead the Fifth to your own Twitter?"

It is one of the basic tenets of the American legal system: Ultimately, rendering justice rests not just on the work of lawyers, prosecutors, and judges, but also on the judgment of ordinary citizens asked to perform their civic duty by serving as jurors. So it was for Fani Willis's investigation into election interference in Georgia. After Willis got approval to convene a special grand jury, twenty-three Fulton County residents were sworn in to start issuing subpoenas and hearing testimony in May 2022.

One of them was Emily Kohrs, an irrepressible, chirpy twenty-nine-year-old who had just left her job as a candle maker for a New Age mystical candle shop in Alpharetta, twenty-six miles north of Atlanta. ("We have something every modern-day spiritual babe would love," the shop advertised on its website.) The day she and more than two dozen others were administered their oath, Kohrs jumped to her feet and excitedly asked, "Can I do it?" when the presiding judge, Robert McBurney, asked for volunteers to serve as jury foreperson. "I wasn't employed, so I figured it made perfect sense," Kohrs recalled. Nobody else expressed the least bit of interest—so she got the job. Kohrs was thrilled. "It's the coolest thing I've ever done," she said.

While Washington pundits and cable commentators speculated endlessly about the possible direction of Willis's probe, Kohrs brought an unusual set of pristine eyes to the inquiry. She had gone to college "for about two minutes," and had never voted in her life—not for president or any other office. By her own account, she had only a minimal interest in American politics, having more or less completely tuned out during the 2016 election when, she explained, she would watch some of Trump's speeches and then Alec Baldwin's impersonations on *Saturday Night Live*. "I couldn't tell which one was real and which one was the comedy actor," said Kohrs. None of it seemed to make any sense to her.

Kohrs would later become a mini-celebrity after she gave a round of interviews* once the grand jury's work was done, giggling, rolling her eyes, and teasing her interrogators about whether Trump would get indicted, all of which led to Kohrs being spoofed herself in a *Saturday Night Live* skit. And she unquestionably brought a measure of goofiness to the serious business at hand. At one point, she got into a vigorous debate with the deputy foreperson—a lawyer—over whether it was appropriate for her to wear a Santa Claus hat to the questioning of South Carolina senator Lindsey Graham during his

---

* The fact that Kohrs gave interviews at all highlights the significant differences between federal and state procedures when it comes to grand juries. In the federal system, anything that goes on inside grand juries is considered secret—and prosecutors as well as jurors can't talk about it. But Judge McBurney made clear that Georgia special grand juries operate under different rules. After the special grand jury completed its work in December 2022, he ruled that jurors like Kohrs were free to talk about their own impressions of the various witnesses and evidence presented, though they were directed not to discuss the grand jury's "deliberations."

testimony two days before Thanksgiving. (The debate, she insisted, centered on whether this was too early in the season to wear a Santa hat. She asked the senator what he thought—and, laughing, Graham told her it was not too early at all.) Kohrs "brought a well-needed spirit of lightness" to the otherwise somber proceedings, said the deputy foreperson, who asked not to be identified by name.

But Kohrs could also be an aggressive questioner. Frustrated by White House chief of staff Mark Meadows's invocation of his Fifth Amendment rights to every question, Kohrs whipped out her iPhone. "Do you have a Twitter?" she asked him. Meadows pled the Fifth, as he did to every question asked. Kohrs called it up on her phone and confronted him with it. "I'm sorry. This is your Twitter. How can you plead the Fifth to your own Twitter?" she asked indignantly. She then turned to an item in his Wikipedia entry about his involvement in a film about the discovery of rare dinosaur bones by homeschooled creationists in Colorado that purported to prove the biblical account of Noah's Flood. Are you going to deny what's in your own Wikipedia entry? Kohrs asked him. Meadows once again took the Fifth.

Kohrs, it turned out, was a formidable presence in the special grand jury's inquiry. She swore in all the witnesses and sat squarely in front of them during the questioning by prosecutors. In between doodling and drawing sketches of the witnesses, and occasionally slipping them wrapped pieces of candy during emotional moments, she was often the most aggressive questioner, confronting the witnesses—as her grilling of Meadows showed—when they seemed slippery. And for all her flighty demeanor, she had a razor-sharp memory that allowed her to recount with verbatim accuracy exact exchanges from the grand jury questioning months after they had taken place. One of her fellow grand jurors would later say she was in awe of Kohrs's "near photo-graphic" recall.

Perhaps most important, her reactions to the testimony proved to be one yardstick by which Willis and her team measured the impact of the parade of more than seventy-five witnesses they brought into the grand jury room. Early on in the proceedings, the prosecutors played the full sixty-two-minute tape of Trump's phone call with Raffensperger. The recording was the single piece of damning evidence that had launched the investigation. But as Kohrs listened, she wasn't quite sure what to make of it. When Trump told Raffensperger to "find" votes, was he actually telling the secretary of state to commit fraud, to concoct votes that didn't exist? Or was it more ambiguous than that? Maybe he actually believed there were legitimate Trump votes to be found. Maybe, she wondered, he was suffering from a "mental disorder" and couldn't tell the difference anyway. It was a crucial issue and Kohrs at first wasn't sure. "It's not like watching somebody break a window—that's clearly a crime," she said. "The question was what constitutes election interference?"

Intently watching Kohrs and the other grand jurors inside the grand jury room that day was Willis, no stranger to the art of reading jurors' reactions. The puzzlement of some of the jurors like Kohrs appears to have influenced her. "The phone call is good," Willis told Nathan Wade, the chief of her election interference team as they assessed the matter in her office. "But it's not enough."

And Raffensperger didn't help all that much. As a witness, he proved a little more circumspect than some of the grand jurors or Willis's prosecutors would have liked. At the time of his testimony, Raffensperger was in the midst of a primary battle to hold on to his job as secretary of state, running against a pro-Trump, election-denying challenger, Congressman Jody Hice. Just as he had insisted on a subpoena before agreeing to testify in the first place, inside the grand jury room he seemed intent on avoiding any comments that might leak out and inflame the hard-core Trump base, some of whose votes he might still need in the general election.

So when Raffensperger was pressed by the deputy foreperson about how he reacted on the phone call when Trump had told him he could be committing a "criminal offense" if he and his counsel Ryan Germany didn't reverse the results of the election, the cagey secretary of state ducked the question and refused to give a straight answer. The deputy foreperson, with his legal training, was frustrated. It sure sounded like a direct threat to him, yet Raffensperger wouldn't say so.

It was left to Wade, the chief of Willis's team, to do cleanup. He got out Raffensperger's book, *Integrity Counts*, which had been published the previous November. He turned to page 191, where the secretary had quoted Trump's line about a "criminal offense" as well as Raffensperger's reaction to the threat, putting the passage up on an audiovisual screen: "Now President Trump is using the power of his position to threaten Ryan and me with prosecution if we don't do what he tells us to do," Raffensperger had written in his book.

You write that? Wade asked him.

Yes, I did, Raffensperger replied.

And you stand by what you wrote?

Yes, I do, Raffensperger said.

As time went on, the full dimensions of the election plot started to come more sharply into focus and Trump's unwavering persistence with his claims of election fraud by the Democrats started to sound increasingly hollow to the grand jurors. The president, it seemed, would believe whatever he wanted to believe and nobody could tell him any different—as was clear on November 22, 2022, when Graham showed up in the grand jury room.

There may have been nobody in public life who had a more tortured, head-spinning relationship with Trump than South Carolina's senior senator. Graham's best friend and mentor in the Senate had been John McCain, the self-styled maverick who relished bucking his own party and whose heroism in service to his country Trump consistently mocked. Graham had run for president against Trump in 2016, denouncing him at times in blistering terms as a "jack-ass," "race-baiting bigot," and "kook." But Graham, for reasons nobody could quite explain, also seemed to have an insatiable need for approval. After Trump's election, he embraced him wholeheartedly, slavishly defended him, and became a regular partner of the president on the links in Bedminster and West Palm Beach. ("When we play golf, it's fun," he once told a reporter.)

Back in July, Graham had gotten a subpoena from Willis to testify about two phone calls he had made to Raffensperger in the days after the election. Graham, acting on Trump's behalf—"I just wanted to tell Trump I did my due diligence," he explained to a reporter—questioned the Georgia secretary of state on the procedures for reexamining absentee ballots and, as Raffensperger remembered it, wanted to know whether, if there were enough signatures that didn't match, the results in some counties could be tossed—a scenario that could pave the way for Trump to be declared the winner. Although it was never revealed publicly, joining him on one of the calls was Larry Ellison, the billionaire co-founder of Oracle, who appeared to be pitching the idea that software—presumably developed by Oracle itself—could be used to identify mismatches that could then be used to challenge the election results in court.

Upon receipt of the subpoena, Graham held a press conference and breathed defiance, vowing to fight the subpoena in the courts and "go as far as we need to."

"This weaponization of the law needs to stop," Graham said, otherwise any "county prosecutor" could come after members of Congress for simply doing their jobs. Graham hired Donald McGahn, Trump's former White House counsel, to challenge the subpoena on the grounds that as a senator—and at the time chairman of the Senate Judiciary Committee—he was merely engaged in legislative "fact finding." Therefore, it was argued, anything the senator said to Raffensperger was covered by the "speech and debate clause" of the US Constitution, giving him "absolute immunity" from testifying. But the courts didn't buy the senator's claim. Graham and McGahn did indeed fight it all the way up to the Supreme Court, which ruled against them. Graham was ordered to testify, although he could challenge certain questions that squarely involved his legislative work, as opposed to those in which he was simply carrying the president's water in an election dispute.

His four-month legal battle over, once inside the grand jury room, Graham was affable and ingratiating. And then, without the slightest hesitation, he "threw Trump under the bus," said one source familiar with his testimony. Under questioning from Don Wakeford, one of Willis's prosecutors, Graham accepted that there was no legitimacy to Trump's claims that the presidential election of 2020 had been rigged. He testified that Trump had been repeatedly informed that his claims of fraud had been investigated and debunked—and yet he clung to the idea that he had been robbed anyway. "If you told Trump that Martians came and stole the election, he'd probably believe you," Graham told the grand jury.

Graham even suggested that Trump himself was a cheater—at least at golf. Asked by one of the grand jurors who won their frequent golf games, Graham replied, "You never win when you're playing Mr. Trump and his caddy," the apparent suggestion being the caddy dropped hidden balls to the president's advantage.

As striking as his testimony was, there was an even more remarkable scene when Graham wrapped it up. The grand jury room was on the third floor of the district attorney's office and, as he emerged, Graham spotted Willis in the office's "Ruby Bridges hallway" (which Willis had named for the African American schoolgirl from New Orleans who in 1960 was the first to integrate an elementary school in the South). Willis, as she usually did for high-profile witnesses, went up to thank the senator for appearing. "That was so cathartic. I feel so much better," he told her. Then, to the astonishment of onlookers, Graham hugged her. Willis's reaction: "She was like, 'Whatever, dude,'" said one of those who witnessed the strange encounter.

By this point, Willis's team—and the prosecutors—were benefiting from a secret collaboration that proved an invaluable boost to the investigation: The January 6 committee had quietly agreed to give Willis's prosecutors access to just about everything they had gathered related to Georgia in their sprawling investigation. How that came about is one of the untold stories of both the committee's and Willis's probes.

Throughout the early months of 2022, Willis's prosecutors had tried to contact the January 6 committee, leaving multiple messages in an effort to get access to the panel's evidence, including transcripts of its behind-closed-doors depositions. Nobody returned their calls. Then, in early March, Mike Hill, the senior investigator on Willis's team and a former military intelligence officer, finally got through to the committee's chief counsel, Timothy Heaphy, an affable but dogged veteran federal prosecutor. The Willis team figured the committee had already uncovered reams of important evidence that could be crucial to the case in Georgia. Now, as Willis's office was getting ready to impanel its special-purpose grand jury, they were salivating over the chance to get their hands on the committee's evidence.

That was easier said than done. The committee had already stiff-armed Justice Department prosecutors who had asked for their witness transcripts and other supporting evidence. By then, DOJ had numerous active cases stemming from the assault on the Capitol, including ones against ringleaders Stewart Rhodes, founder of the Oath Keepers, and Enrique Tarrio of the Proud Boys, both of whom would be charged with seditious conspiracy. And department lawyers took an expansive view of their obligation to turn over their evidence to the defense under federal rules governing the discovery phase that takes place before any trial. This meant if the committee shared its material with Justice, the lawyers for the January 6 rioters would get to see transcripts of its prized depositions. The last thing the congressional sleuths wanted was for their evidence to be turned over to the very people they were still investigating.

But there was another problem, potentially much stickier: The members of the committee, especially Liz Cheney, the hard-nosed, politically savvy Republican vice chair, were loath to have any other investigation steal the panel's thunder. They wanted to "hold back our crown jewels so the hearings would make more of a splash," as a committee source would later put it. For Cheney, who was appalled by Trump, the January 6 probe was a critical forum for holding him accountable for his assault on American democracy. But it was also a platform for her to resuscitate her political career after she had been effectively excommunicated by the House Republican Conference and was fighting for her political life back home in Wyoming. The committee's upcoming hearings, if they made a big enough splash, could conceivably mortally wound Trump—and even potentially provide a springboard for a Cheney presidential run, something she was quietly contemplating.

When Heaphy spoke to Hill, he was noncommittal about the investigator's request. The truth was that Heaphy wanted to help the Fulton County team; he figured that given Willis was still months away from bringing any charges, it was unlikely that she would be forced to turn over any evidence before the panel finished its hearings. But Heaphy also knew that he'd have to convince Cheney, perhaps the most tough-minded and skeptical lawyer on the committee, to get on board.

So he came up with a proposal he hoped would do the trick. The Fulton County team would be given access to the evidence, but only in a circumscribed "in-camera" session, an allusion to the private meetings judges hold in their chambers to review sensitive evidence. The Atlanta investigators would receive oral "proffers," or accounts, of the witness testimony from Heaphy and another staffer; they would be allowed to review the accompanying exhibits, which committee staff had assembled into thick binders. But nothing left the room.

So in one of his regular weekly Zoom meetings with Bennie Thompson, the Mississippi Democrat and committee chairman, and Cheney, Thompson's Republican counterpart Heaphy made his pitch. Thompson, physically imposing but, generally speaking, easygoing, signed onto the plan. Cheney was far more suspicious—"cagey and cautious" in Heaphy's words. She fixed a hard stare and began peppering the chief counsel with questions: What if Willis indicted sooner than expected and they were required to turn over evidence to the defense? What if the hard-earned information they'd gathered over the past year leaked to the press? Cheney didn't want any disclosures that would interfere with the integrity of their investigation, and she certainly didn't want anything that risked diminishing the impact of the flashy televised hearings they were preparing for the summer. Still, in the end, Heaphy was able to persuade Cheney that the benefits outweighed the risks and she approved his proposal.

That spring, as the committee was feverishly planning its extravaganza hearings, a group from Willis's team—Nathan Wade, Mike Hill, and two of her top prosecutors, Don Wakeford and Will Wooten—flew to Washington and avidly reviewed the very material the panel had refused to share with the Justice Department. The bonanza of evidence included interviews with Raffensperger, Gabe Sterling, Cassidy Hutchinson, Richard Donoghue, and David Shafer, the ringleader of the fake elector scheme in Georgia. When they returned to Atlanta, Willis's team was excited. The committee's trove of evidence opened their eyes to a much broader conspiracy than they had previously understood—and the best nuggets and witnesses from the panel's probe would soon be shared with the special grand jury.

But even as Willis's team started getting their hands on the committee's damning evidence, there was an embarrassing stumble—thanks to Willis herself. In June, she had hosted a campaign fundraiser for Charlie Bailey, her former colleague who had pushed her to run for DA in the first place and was now running for lieutenant governor. Bailey had just emerged from the Democratic primary in second place, well behind his opponent, Kwanza Hall, a fixture of Atlanta politics who enjoyed high name recognition. Bailey would have to face off against Hall in less than a month, "an all-hands-on-deck-moment" as he would later refer to it. That meant he needed to raise money—and fast. Fani stepped up and offered her support just when Bailey needed it most. The decision would blow up in her face. The problem was that the Republican in the race was Burt Jones, the state senator and Trump booster who had been one of the so-called fake electors being investigated by Willis's office.

The fundraiser was a modest affair held in the parking lot of an organic grocery store with a rock band playing in the background on a makeshift stage. There were no speeches, fewer than twenty people were in attendance, and a paltry sum of money was raised. Willis had contributed more money to Bailey herself, $2,500, than was collected at the fundraiser. But the optics of the DA lending her name to a political event for a friend whose Republican opponent would be squarely in her crosshairs was catnip for her critics. Indeed, Jones's lawyer jumped on the issue and filed a motion to disqualify her from the probe entirely, citing her attendance as evidence of a conflict of interest and political bias. Just weeks earlier, Willis's prosecutors had sent target letters to all sixteen of the so-called fake electors—Jones among them—notifying them they were at risk of indictment. McBurney, the presiding judge, agreed that Willis's sponsorship of a fundraiser for Jones's opponent was troubling. "It's a 'What are you thinking' moment," he said about Willis's participation in the fundraiser during a court hearing on the issue. "The optics are horrific." The judge declined to disqualify Willis from the entire case, but did rule that— even as Willis pursued the fake electors—the probe of Jones's role should be handed over to another prosecutor in a different jurisdiction. Although the carve-out for Jones would have little impact on the investigation itself, it was an unforced error that would play out in the PR wars, providing Trump and his allies with fresh fodder to portray the DA as a committed partisan.

But the real story was inside the grand jury room, where the fresh evidence from the January 6 committee caused the jurors to start reexamining the case and understanding the specific episodes in Georgia in a broader context. Over the summer, they had typed up a brief "interim" report that was largely noncommittal, concluding only that the issue of election interference in Georgia needed further investigation. But as they started to hear directly from some of the key January 6 witnesses—Pat Cipollone, Trump's White House counsel; Cassidy Hutchinson, the staff aide to Meadows; and others—the scales started to drop from their eyes.

"A lot of it was talking to people on a national scale," said Emily Kohrs. Regarded in isolation, it may have been possible to think when listening to the tape of the Raffensperger call that "maybe Donald Trump genuinely believed there was election fraud," she said. Indeed, Kohrs said, when the grand jury proceedings began, "I was willing to believe Donald Trump was just misguided and things got out of hand...But when you get to the national level and you talk to those who dealt with him every day—they're telling him, again and again and again that this wasn't a thing."

The FBI had investigated the State Farm video and found no wrongdoing on the part of election workers. All of Trump's own Justice Department and Homeland Security officials had rejected his claims as nonsense.* So, too, did Cipollone, the White House counsel.

---

* Chris Krebs, the director of the Department of Homeland Security's Cybersecurity and Infrastructure Security Agency, had concluded that the 2020 presidential election was "the most secure in American history" and called the president's claims "technically incoherent." After he did so, Trump fired him.

Fresh off her testimony before the January 6 committee, Meadows's
top aide Cassidy Hutchinson described the endless series of preposter-
ous conspiracy theories—the election had been hacked by military
satellites in Italy; Chinese communists had hacked the election using
wireless thermostats—that her boss pressed national security officials
to check out at Trump's behest. Hutchinson explained that "these
were theories that the president talked about and was giving credence
to," Kohrs recalled. Trump would get emails from Mike Flynn, among
others, print them out, and take them to Meadows, directing him to
follow up. As she related all this, Hutchinson was as diplomatic as she
could be when talking about the president. "I never heard anybody so
politely call their boss a maniac," Kohrs said.

"At some point, reasonable doubt becomes unreasonable," Kohrs
continued. "It was, like, 'Dude, the FBI told you that you were
wrong' . . . His own campaign told him he was wrong. Either he genuinely believed it—which is like almost at the level of psychosis at this
point, okay?—or he was just lying."

There were also new details and testimony about events that
hadn't gotten much if any notice by the January 6 committee, starting with the escapade in Coffee County. The idea that Trump's political operatives would fly to the rural county in South Georgia to gain
access to sensitive Dominion machine software was an eye-opener.
Not only that, they were granted access to the machines, and the
proprietary data purchased with Georgia state funds, by local Coffee County election officials, who were die-hard Trumpers. It was a
clear violation of the directive Chris Harvey, the elections director
in Raffensperger's office, had sent to every local election official in
November. "Nobody who authorized it had any authority to autho-
rize anything, right?" said Kohrs of the Coffee County raid. Just as
startling was the defiant testimony of Scott Hall, the bail bondsman

and Dave Bossie's brother-in-law, who had chartered the plane from Atlanta to conduct the operation. What he did, he told the panel, was required by the oath he took when he joined the marines—to "protect the United States from threats foreign and domestic." Kohrs found Hall's testimony mind boggling. That's what you were doing in Coffee County? Defending the country?

By the fall, the grand jury started organizing its evidence into indictable buckets. One was the Raffensperger phone call. Another was the blatantly false testimony by Giuliani and others about the State Farm video. Coffee County became one more bucket. Yet another was the creepy operation to intimidate Ruby Freeman.

For all the shocking evidence of political skullduggery laid out before the grand jury, on a purely human level it was the victimization of everyday citizens like Freeman simply doing their civic duty that Kohrs and her fellow jurors found the most disturbing. "Lady Ruby" Freeman and her daughter Shaye had been through the wringer ever since Giuliani and Jacki Pick accused them before the Georgia legislative committee of pulling out "suitcases" of fake Biden ballots and fraudulently stuffing them through the scanners at the State Farm Arena on election night. Trump himself had relentlessly targeted the two women: He had played snippets of the State Farm video at a December 5 rally in Valdosta, Georgia, proclaiming that it showed a "crime" committed by "Democrat workers." Then he called Freeman a "professional vote scammer" and "hustler" in his phone call with Raffensperger, referring to her eighteen times. As right-wing websites like the Gateway Pundit spread the claims far and wide, and portrayed the two African American women as fraudsters, the president's allies taunted her mercilessly. They repeatedly sent pizzas to her house that she had never ordered, with the deliverymen demanding immediate payment. There were crude racial overtones to these pranks: The pizzas had hamburger toppings, an allusion—lead counsel Nathan Wade explained to the grand jurors—to the hair of African Americans. Freeman was also bombarded with threats on social media that she was about to be arrested.

On the morning of December 15, a red sedan drove up into Freeman's driveway in a section of town known as East Point. The driver, a pro-MAGA pastor from Illinois named Steve Lee, got out and banged on the door, insisting he was there to help Freeman and needed to talk. Alarmed, Freeman called the police. Lee concluded that Freeman wouldn't talk to him because he was white, so he reached out to the Trump campaign, specifically to Harrison William Floyd, executive director of Black Voices for Trump, which operated out of campaign headquarters. That led to yet a second attempt to intimidate Freeman.

At about 8:30 p.m. on January 4—two days before the official Electoral College count in Congress—a woman named Trevian Kutti showed up at Freeman's home. Kutti was a Chicago-based publicist who had worked for Kanye West and R. Kelly, and was active in Black Voices for Trump. She had been dispatched by Floyd and was driven to Freeman's house by a man named Garrison Douglas, a Georgia leader of Black Voices for Trump who served as a spokesman for the state Republican Party.

The mission of all these unwanted visitors: to convince Freeman to turn herself in and confess to her supposed crimes. When Kutti knocked on the door, Freeman—like she did with Lee—hid in her house and called the cops. When a Cobb County police officer showed up, Kutti told the officer that "she was a crisis manager and was sent from a high-profile individual," according to a Cobb County police report. Freeman "was in danger and had forty-eight hours to speak with her...unknown subjects were going to be at Ms. Freeman's residence...it was due to the election." Kutti did not identify the "high-profile individual" who sent her nor who the "unknown subjects" were that were about to show up at her door.

The officer's body cam video of Kutti's visit was played to the grand jury. Kohrs found the whole thing "sketchy as shit."

"All right, she represents herself as some mysterious, powerful organization, which she never names," she said. "She won't tell the police what she's talking about. She won't tell anyone what she's talking about. And she goes to freakin' East Point to find a woman she's never met, never spoken to and who doesn't know who she is. Okay, to tell this woman that terrible things are gonna happen in the next like forty-eight hours if you don't tell us the truth."

The police officer somehow persuaded Freeman and Kutti to come to the police station and talk. Once there, Kutti stepped up the pressure. If Freeman didn't admit to the fraud, "she would go to jail," she said. She then called Floyd, the Black Voices for Trump chief, who on speakerphone proceeded to push Freeman further. She needed to confess. They would get her immunity if she did. Freeman stood her ground.

But her visitors were right that she would face consequences for doing so. The next day, January 5, a troop of Trump protestors—some of them with signs and waving flags—showed up once again on Freeman's doorstep, telling neighbors they were "upset with Ruby Freeman." By then, Freeman—at the recommendation of the FBI—had already fled her home. She wouldn't return for two months. She was, she told the grand jury, living in fear.

To be sure, Kohrs said there was a "gaping hole" in the story. Kutti ducked persistent efforts by Willis's prosecutors to serve her with a subpoena—and the grand jury never heard from Floyd or Lee, either, leaving the panel without a clear account of who directed the plot to intimidate Freeman at her own house. But there was a damning money trail that tied directly back to the Trump campaign. That fact was never presented to the special grand jury, but the authors discovered it buried in federal campaign records: Floyd, who was a central figure in the effort, was no volunteer or freelancer. He was on the Trump campaign payroll, receiving $136,236 in thirty-two payments during the 2020 election cycle. Phone records obtained by Willis's investigators showed that Floyd was also in frequent contact with all the principals involved in the operation to intimidate Freeman, placing or receiving fifteen calls on January 4 and 5 with the pastor Lee, the publicist Kutti, a Trump lawyer named Robert Cheeley, and David Shafer, the chairman of the Georgia Republican Party. (Shafer would later tell the authors he didn't recall talking to Floyd during this period.) Also showing up in the phone records for this period was the ubiquitous Scott Hall, who had seven calls on January 5 with Cheeley—in several cases, shortly before or after Cheeley called Floyd or Kutti. The phone records show that the contacts went on late into the night, with a conference call at 11:35 p.m. on the fifth among Hall, Cheeley, and Kutti.

In short, the core facts were clear: Ruby Freeman, a woman who had volunteered to help count election ballots and, according to the FBI, had done nothing wrong, had been terrorized by the president's operatives and supporters, subjected to months of harassment and intimidation, and ultimately driven from her home. It had begun with the falsehoods by Giuliani, Trump's chief lawyer, at the December 3, 2020, legislative hearing. And it culminated at Freeman's front door, with threats she was about to be arrested, conveyed by a coterie of operatives with clear ties to Donald Trump's campaign.

The very real danger that witnesses like Freeman experienced was what disturbed the grand jurors the most. It came up time and again during the proceedings. The testimony at times would get emotional. Both Freeman and Moss wept as they described the threats they had faced. (After listening to them, one of the grand jurors bawled in her car as she left the courthouse.) A top Dominion executive, Eric Coomer, the company's director for product development and security, broke down as he described how he was falsely accused of being an Antifa activist who rigged the election, resulting in a stream of death threats and the doxxing of the address of his elderly father. Gabriel Sterling choked up as he described the Dominion tech worker who was inundated with social media threats—including the GIF with the undulating noose outside the young man's home.

And when Tricia Raffensperger took the stand, she was asked about the horrific sexualized text messages she got on her cell phone after her husband was targeted by the president and his allies. As she did so, recalled Kohrs, the quiet and dignified wife of Georgia's secretary of state started to cry. She was invited to take a break in a side room and offered tissues. Then, after composing herself, she returned, determined to tell her story.

In early January 2023, the grand jurors wrapped up their secret report. It was drafted on a laptop provided by prosecutors; the deputy foreperson created the format, sketched out the first few paragraphs on his personal laptop, and transferred it with a thumb drive onto the DA team's laptop. Then, with the contents up on a screen, the special grand jurors collaborated on the wording, with Kohrs, with lightning-fast fingers, typing it up. It had one overarching conclusion, voted unanimously: "No widespread fraud took place in the Georgia 2020 presidential election that could result in overturning the election." After hearing seven months of evidence, the special grand jurors rejected the entire premise of Trump's post-election fantasy in Georgia.

The report was then submitted to Robert McBurney, the Fulton County judge who presided over the grand jury. Immediately, media organizations went to court for its public release. But in a court hearing later that month, Willis urged that it be kept under wraps, at least for the time being. "Decisions are imminent," she told McBurney in her characteristically grave and lawyerly tone. "The state understands the media's inquiry and the world's interest. But we have to be mindful of protecting future defendants' rights."

Her comments that day would raise expectations that her big indictment might be only weeks away. But behind the scenes, known only to the handful of people investigating Trump and his confederates, there were indications the team was stumbling through the complexities of the case and not yet ready for prime time.

CHAPTER THIRTEEN

A True Bill

"We all have to live by a certain standard of rules.
And if you violate them, you catch a charge.
It's not sexy. I'm sorry, it's just not."

Fani Willis can be a demanding boss, as any of the prosecutors who work for her will attest. She's an acknowledged "preparation freak" who has zero patience for perfunctory efforts—and does not hold back when her team falls short of expectations. In early February 2023, the prosecutors on her team investigating Donald Trump and his cohorts found themselves on the wrong end of a full-blown Willis eruption.

It wasn't pretty.

With the special grand jury report complete, the team had filed into her office to present a PowerPoint of the charges they had contemplated bringing against Trump and his confederates. But as Willis listened, she was underwhelmed. One of the prosecutors, Will Wooten, was making the presentation, taking the defendants one by one and describing their alleged crimes. Cutting Wooten off, Willis impatiently began firing questions.

"What document is going to prove that fact?" she demanded. "What testimony? How many pieces of evidence you got to say that?"

Wooten and his colleagues were vague—too vague for Willis. "No, y'all aren't even close," she told them. "This is fucking terrible. Get the fuck out here." Then she briskly walked out of the meeting herself, leaving her election team in a daze. DiSantis, her communications chief who witnessed the scene, tried to break up the tension. You just got the Fani treatment, he told them, intending it as a joke.

But not that much of a joke. The truth was, Willis had a habit of sharply questioning her deputies, focusing with laser-like intensity on potential holes in the cases they were proposing to bring. She had done it on the eve of one of her big RICO cases against Atlanta gangs, mercilessly grilling one of her lead prosecutors, telling him his proposed indictment didn't cut it; the humiliated prosecutor quit soon thereafter to take a job as an assistant DA in a neighboring county. Willis wasn't the least bit apologetic about her exacting standards—to the contrary, it was something she was quite proud of.

When she became DA, Willis had implemented a major overhaul of the office's procedures for bringing indictments. Before then in Fulton County, "Police officers would fax in a statement. It would be a couple of paragraphs long, and from those statements, indictments would be drafted...it was unethical," she said in a 2023 podcast interview that focused on her gang cases. Willis shook up the process, demanding that her lawyers and investigators do all the work necessary to take a case to trial *before* they brought an indictment, not after. It's what *she* did when she was a line prosecutor. "Get the 911 tape, read the full police report, get drugs tested. If you don't have the drug lab [tests] back, you can't indict," she told her staff. More than a few cases, as a result, would be dropped. But since her reforms, said Willis, "when we bring indictments, I'm comfortable with bringing them because the work has been done."

The prosecutors on the Trump case came back a week after she had reamed them out. But—as Willis related it—there had been only small improvements, nothing to write home about. "I told them we went from an F to a C," Willis said about her follow-up grade for her team of deputies. Then she paused and lowered the grade: "C minus." It was another window into the "Fani treatment." "We don't get awards for participation around here," she explained during an interview with the authors shortly after the meeting, displaying obvious disdain for bosses who coddle their employees. "I'm not from that generation."

The upbraiding of her deputies in the Trump case was not a signal that Willis had doubts about the underlying strength of the case against Trump. It was much more about her all-consuming obsession with preparation—a passion that dates back to her days staying late into the night at the Emory Law School library preparing for the Frederick Douglass National Moot Court contest. Given the enormous stakes, she wanted every possible lead run down and every potential hole plugged. And, as would also soon become clear, there was more investigating she wanted her team to do.

Notwithstanding her comment in late January to McBurney that decisions were "imminent," Willis also made clear to the authors in an interview in February 2023 that she wasn't going to be stampeded into bringing indictments.

"I'm not going to let anybody rush me—not you, not McBurney, not anyone," she said. "We're going to do things right."

By this time, Trump had found a new top lawyer in Atlanta to take over from Dwight Thomas (the ménage à trois guy), one who was fittingly flamboyant for a case that had the potential to become the most publicized and controversial in Georgia history.

Drew Findling, with his trademark sunglasses, slicked-back hair, and Gucci sneakers, had become famous for defending Atlanta rap stars accused of dealing drugs, gunrunning, and other crimes. And he was no one to be toyed with. Willis's longtime colleague in the DA's office, Clint Rucker, described him as a white version of Johnnie Cochran, the famed Los Angeles attorney who got OJ Simpson off. ("If it doesn't fit, you must acquit.") Politically, Findling couldn't have been further from Trump; a liberal Democrat and former president of the National Association of Criminal Defense Lawyers, he had been withering in his criticism of the forty-fifth president, at one point during Trump's presidency referring to the "stench hovering over POTUS." He'd lashed out at Trump as "racist, cruel, sick, unforgivable and un-American" when he stood by his condemnation of the Central Park Five, a group of young Black men who had been wrongfully convicted of rape in a notorious case during Trump's heyday as the toast of the city's tabloids in the late 1980s. Among Findling's legal heroes were Supreme Court justices Thurgood Marshall and Ruth Bader Ginsburg; colorful paintings of the liberal icons hung on the wall of his Buckhead office. He was also an engaging character. As The New York Times noted in a 2018 profile, well before he had been retained by Trump, Findling was gregarious and "disarmingly casual," asking those he met to forswear formalities. "Dude, call me Drew," he would say.

But Findling could be just as combative as Willis, and it didn't take long for their sparring to start. When Findling first surfaced as Trump's lawyer in the summer of 2022, Willis had told him his client was welcome to come in and voluntarily testify to the special grand jury. Trump, to no one's surprise, didn't take her up on the offer. Willis ultimately decided not to subpoena the former president, concluding it would just lead to months of legal challenges that would slow down her probe. But now, with the special grand jury report complete, Willis gave Findling a heads-up and suggested he join her at the upcoming hearing before Judge McBurney over whether the report should be made public. Having read its damning contents, Willis suggested that the president's high-powered new attorney might want to join her in urging McBurney not to release the report. "You may want to consider entering on behalf of your client," Willis told him. "Trust me, it's in your client's interest. You don't want this coming out. You don't want it on the street." But Findling turned her down. "We're not going to appear," he told her.

On the eve of McBurney's hearing, Findling put out a statement that infuriated Willis. Trump "was never subpoenaed nor asked to come in voluntarily by this [special] grand jury or anyone in the Fulton County District Attorney's office," he said. Findling then used this only half-true claim (Trump was in fact never subpoenaed, but according to Willis's account had been invited to testify) to argue that his client must be in the clear. "Therefore, we can assume that the grand jury did their job and looked at the facts and the law, as we have, and concluded there were no violations of the law by President Trump," he said in a statement joined by his co-counsel Jennifer Little, a veteran former prosecutor.

Willis was in her office when she saw Findling's statement, and she went ballistic. "This is just fucking bullshit," Willis snapped at DiSantis. "Can you believe this?" Nathan Wade was on speakerphone. "This is so unprofessional," he chimed in. Wade said he was surprised that Findling would pull a stunt like this.

"That's exactly who he is," said Willis. "I'm not surprised." (Findling did not respond to an email request for comment about this incident.)

But in the end, it wouldn't matter much. Trump, who had a habit of firing lawyers whenever he didn't get the results he wanted, would in due course ditch Findling, too—and he would do it when the high-profile litigator least expected it.

———

The special grand jury was not empowered to issue indictments. It could only investigate and make recommendations for Willis to consider. When the special grand jurors handed in their report to Judge McBurney in January, they recommended that thirty-nine people be indicted, starting with Donald Trump, for his phone call to Brad Raffensperger. The vote to indict the former president was 21–1, on the felony count of attempting to influence a witness's testimony with "threats" or "intimidation." A woman who was the sole Trump supporter on the special grand jury was the only dissenter. The grand jurors had also thrown in multiple other counts against Trump, including one for making "false, fictitious or fraudulent" statements to a government agency (for his comments to Raffensperger during the phone call) and another for criminal solicitation of election fraud.

The grand jurors recommended indicting Giuliani over his false testimony about the State Farm video by a vote of 19–0. Also unanimous were the votes to indict others who had testified before the Georgia Senate committee at the same December 3 legislative session—Jacki Pick, Robert Cheeley, Ray Smith, John Eastman, and

Scott Hall. For good measure, the special grand jurors even voted to indict William Ligon, the state senator who presided over the hearing.

The votes were also unanimous in recommending indictments of Sidney Powell, Scott Hall, Cathy Latham, and Misty Hampton for the Coffee County caper. For Shafer, Eastman, Kenneth Chesebro, and Mark Meadows and their roles in the fake electors scheme, the votes were 20–1.

But inside the grand jury room, there had also been disputes, sometimes pointed ones. Two grand jurors had voted against indicting most of the lower-level fake Trump electors in Georgia, concluding— according to the panel's report—that they were only doing "what they were led to understand was their civic duty." The grand jurors, by a vote of 17–4, recommended indicting former senator Perdue and, by a vote of 14–6, former senator Loeffler for their roles in the conspiracy. (It had been Perdue and Loeffler's post-election statement that Raffensperger should resign that triggered the onslaught of threats to the secretary of state and his wife.) Among the dissenters on indicting Perdue and Loeffler was the deputy foreperson, the one lawyer on the panel. In a footnote, he concluded that while the two senators' actions constituted "pandering to their political base," they did not constitute crimes.

The dissents were a red flag for Willis. The standard for grand juries is "probable cause" that the crime had been committed, and a simple majority vote by the grand jurors was sufficient to indict. But the standard for conviction at trial was of course much higher— beyond a reasonable doubt by a unanimous jury. The revelation that there were four special grand jury members who voted against indicting Perdue and six against charging Loeffler was a pretty good sign that conviction at trial would be extremely difficult, if not impossible.

So Willis and her team started narrowing down the list of thirty-nine proposed defendants and weaving the evidence into a grander indictment under Georgia's RICO statute. As they did so, more potential defendants got dropped from the list—state senator Ligon, Lindsey Graham, Michael Flynn—on the grounds that the evidence against them was less than clear-cut. Even Lin Wood, the QAnon-obsessed lawyer who had hosted the Trump strike force at his Tomotley plantation, got scratched. The special grand jury had voted to recommend indicting him 19–1, but Willis's prosecutors rejected it, apparently concluding Wood, his questionable mental stability notwithstanding, might work better as a witness to the events at Tomotley.

Among the closer calls was over Cleta Mitchell, the conservative lawyer whom Mark Meadows had dispatched to Atlanta in the days after the election to gin up lawsuits challenging the election. She had been on Trump's phone call with Raffensperger—though she'd said relatively little—pressing the Georgia secretary of state at one point to turn over protected personal data on state voters that could allow Trump's litigators to somehow prove that out-of-state, underage, and dead voters had cast illegal ballots.

Did Mitchell's comments, and her earlier role in spearheading the filing of bogus lawsuits, make her a co-conspirator in the larger racketeering scheme? The team went back and forth on the question. Ultimately, Mitchell was dropped from the list. Willis—in interviews for this book—declined to discuss any of the individual defendants or prospective defendants. But she confirmed that some of them required multiple reviews, prompting debates within her office. Were there some defendants whom her deputies wanted her to indict but whom she crossed from the list? "The DA was more conservative than the team," she said, referring to herself.

In refining the case, Willis and her deputies weren't just relying on the special grand jury report. For months, they had been taking aggressive steps to marshal the evidence against their top targets. They had reached out to witnesses and subpoenaed documents that had never been presented to the special grand jury. They tracked down Dave Hancock, the former security chief at Tomotley, who provided a road map to the plotting and scheming, bolstered by his voluminous cache of emails, texts, and other documents. He helped strengthen the case against Sidney Powell, a regular presence at Lin Wood's plantation, where she incessantly sought "evidence" that she imagined would back up her nonsensical claims about Dominion machines—a quest that ultimately led to the Coffee County raid. Willis's deputies "drilled down hard on Powell," Hancock said. "They came back to her over and over again."

In July, Willis's deputies also took another critical step that wasn't public at the time: They subpoenaed Microsoft for the contents of the personal email accounts of Kenneth Chesebro, the primary architect of the fake elector scheme. A sealed affidavit from one of the Willis investigators—revealed much later in a court filing—cited Chesebro's frequent communications with Eastman and Giuliani about the scheme and the plan to use alternate pro-Trump electors in Georgia as a basis for Pence to reject the officially certified electors for Biden on January 6. In one significant passage, Willis's investigator quoted from one of Chesebro's memos during this period as evidence that potentially reflected Chesebro's consciousness of guilt—meaning that he understood that his elaborate plan for the fake electors was legally problematic given that Georgia law clearly specified that presidential electors went to the winner of the popular vote. "Voting by an alternate slate of electors," Chesebro had written, "... is somewhat dicey in Georgia."

As they reviewed the charges in regular meetings in Willis's office, another sensitive issue they had to grapple with was the likelihood that some of the defendants would seek to have their cases removed to federal court on the grounds that they were acting under "the color of law" in their roles as US government officials. It was a tricky legal issue. The courts had long held that if federal employees had a plausible claim to be acting in an official capacity, it was up to federal courts—not the states—to determine their fate. Motions to remove state indictments against US government employees to federal court were often granted, usually when it involved federal law enforcement agents—even state police officers who served on federal task forces—charged by state prosecutors with acting illegally or violating a suspect's civil rights.

But did the relatively low standard for removal—acting plausibly under the color of law—apply to the conduct of Trump and his confederates? It was assumed that Trump would seek removal, as would at least two key defendants—Meadows, the White House chief of staff, and Jeff Clark, the acting Justice Department civil division chief who had drafted the letter seeking a special session of the Georgia legislature to overturn the election results. But Willis's team believed there was more than enough evidence to portray both men's actions as nakedly political, aimed at furthering the interests of Trump and his campaign, and not the interests of the US government.

Clark, as the acting civil division chief, had no responsibility for investigating claims of electoral fraud. His election meddling, on its face, had nothing to do with his job at the Justice Department. When in late December, Clark first pressed Justice officials to sign off on his letter to Georgia lawmakers alleging that electoral "irregularities" had cast the outcome of the election in doubt, Acting Attorney General Rosen and Deputy Attorney General Richard Donoghue—both utterly contemptuous of the civil division lawyer—had instructed him in a December 27 meeting to call the US attorney in Atlanta, BJay Pak. He, not Clark, was the relevant Justice Department official in charge of investigating any electoral wrongdoing in Georgia. And Pak had investigated, overseeing the FBI probe into Giuliani's false testimony about the State Farm video and concluding that the claims of fraud were groundless.

In a "very heated" meeting at Justice on January 2, Donoghue demanded, "Did you call BJ Pak?" as he had been instructed to do just a few days earlier. Clark acknowledged he had not. But to the astonishment of the two top officials at the Justice Department, Clark told them he had talked to another source whom he believed had crucial information about election fraud in Georgia. Donoghue, in his notes on the meeting, described Clark's source as "the largest bail bondsman in Georgia" who had conducted "surveillance at a warehouse." Clark had had his sixty-three-minute phone call that very day with the bail bondsman, Scott Hall, the obsessed Trump acolyte who was serving as a self-appointed private investigator for the Stop the Steal movement and became a key player in the Coffee County raid. In short, Clark had been freelancing, tapping a member of Trump's political army to end-run official channels, not exactly acting under "the color of law."

And as for Meadows, Willis's team believed it could also prove that the White House chief of staff had strayed far from his official duties and was acting primarily as Trump's political agent. There was his decision to deploy Cleta Mitchell to file suits on behalf of the Trump campaign, his surprise visit to observe the Cobb County audit, and his role in setting up and participating in the phone call to Raffensperger. But the Fulton County prosecutors had discovered something even more powerful: an email thread showing that Meadows, as the top official in the White House, had worked with Trump campaign

officials to orchestrate the fake electors scheme dreamed up by Eastman and Giuliani to allow the president to cling to power. It was an
email thread they would soon use to devastating effect.

———————

By the summer of 2023, the case started to take shape, with Meadows
and Clark squarely on the list of defendants, along with seventeen others, including Trump, Giuliani, Eastman, and Shafer, the chairman of
the Georgia Republican Party. Willis started preparing to present her
entire case to a regular grand jury, one that, unlike the special grand
jury, could actually return "true bills" of indictments. Two such regular grand juries would be sitting for a two-month term starting in July.

———————

As she did so, Willis and her prosecutors were hearing footsteps—
from the Justice Department.

Ever since early 2021, federal prosecutors in Washington had been
bringing hundreds of cases against the January 6 rioters, including
charges for seditious conspiracy against leaders of the Oath Keepers
and Proud Boys who had earlier showed up for the Stop the Steal protests at the Gold Dome in Atlanta. But department officials, starting
with the innately cautious Attorney General Merrick Garland, were
reluctant to target Trump himself absent compelling evidence that
directly tied him to the violence at the Capitol. In the spring of 2022,
a senior Justice official, a top member of Garland's team, spent the
Easter holiday with family members who besieged him with questions about the department's failure to go after Trump for his election lies and the January 6 attack. The official had one response—and
it reflected the prevailing thinking among many at main Justice at
the time. The way to stop Trump was through the ballot box, not

criminal charges. If you don't like him, don't vote for him, the official told his family members.

But by the summer, the House January 6 committee had begun its hearings—the first one in prime time—detailing Trump's appalling refusal to call off the mob for 187 minutes while the Capitol was under attack and lawmakers were fleeing for their lives. The panel followed up with more bombshell testimony—from Raffensperger and Rusty Bowers, the Speaker of the Arizona House—about the calls from Trump demanding that they alter the vote counts, from Ruby Freeman and Shaye Moss about the barrage of threats they had faced, from top Justice Department officials like Jeff Rosen and Donoghue about Trump's attempts to install Clark as attorney general.

Garland began to pepper his staff with questions: Did we know about this? Have we interviewed these witnesses? In some cases, they had, but in many others they had to sheepishly acknowledge that the committee was ahead of them. Garland was not pleased. The department was forced into the embarrassing position of asking the committee to turn over its interview transcripts—interviews FBI officials and federal prosecutors soon began to realize they should have done themselves. Although there was no public announcement of the shift, Garland had effectively authorized his prosecutors to begin focusing on Trump's post-election conduct in addition to the already well-publicized department probe into the classified documents discovered at Mar-a-Lago.

On November 15, 2022, in a speech at Mar-a-Lago, Trump announced he would once again run for president—to unseat Garland's boss, President Biden. The AG's hand was now forced. Three days later, he appointed a former chief of the Justice Department's public integrity section, Jack Smith, as special counsel, a guarantee that the probes of the former president would be done with at least some degree of independence from day-to-day interference by political appointees (although, even under department regulations, Garland retained ultimate authority over the investigations). Smith's brief: to conduct the ongoing probes into the Mar-a-Lago documents as well as efforts to overturn the results of the 2020 election. "I will ensure that the Special Counsel receives the resources to conduct this work quickly and completely," Garland said in a brief Justice Department press conference in which he took no questions.

With a special counsel now on the case, it was now an open question: Who would indict Trump first? To the surprise of many, Alvin Bragg, the Manhattan district attorney, was first out of the block, indicting Trump on New York State felony charges over five-year-old allegations relating to hush-money payments to Stormy Daniels to cover up an alleged sexual dalliance—a case widely criticized by commentators on both sides of the aisle as lacking in gravitas as well as sound legal footing. Bragg's premise, although never clearly articulated, was that the payments to Daniels constituted an election law violation because they were intended to influence the outcome of the 2016 campaign. Yet Garland's Justice Department prosecutors—who enforce violations of federal election law—had the same evidence as Bragg and never thought the case was worth bringing.

In June 2023, Smith brought his first case, charging Trump with forty felony counts for willful retention of classified documents at Mar-a-Lago and obstructing the federal investigation into the matter. Then in August, Smith—after aggressively issuing subpoenas to Pence, Meadows, Jared Kushner, and Ivanka Trump, among others—indicted Trump over his post-election conduct on four conspiracy counts, focusing on the plot to gin up fake electors and to pressure Pence to reject the Biden electors from battleground states on January 6.

But Smith's election indictment was narrowly crafted—with no co-defendants—in an apparent effort to move the case targeting Trump along quickly, and take it to trial before the 2024 presidential election. Willis had staked out a much broader and more expansive case, writing a racketeering indictment that was designed to tell the full story of what had happened after the 2020 election. Her proposed draft detailed a conspiracy stretching from the wee hours of the morning on election night—when Trump himself had publicly proclaimed the election to be "a fraud on the American public" and declared that he actually had won—until September 2022 when, according to the charges, Cathy Latham had perjured herself before the special grand jury about her role in the Coffee County raid and lawyer Bob Cheeley had falsely denied advance knowledge of the fake elector meeting.

The indictment was crafted under Georgia's RICO law, identifying the entire effort as a multi-layered "criminal enterprise" in which Trump and his co-defendants acted for the common purpose of subverting the legitimate results of an American election and restoring the president to power. The use of RICO was often controversial, especially under Georgia's version, which allowed prosecutors more leeway than the federal law to connect a wide number of defendants and portray them as part of the same conspiracy even if they didn't know one another. But it was the same "beautiful tool" Willis had deployed nearly a decade earlier when she and Clint Rucker had indicted and convicted public school teachers for doctoring the test scores of their students. In that case—the first major triumph in her career—the "criminal enterprise" had been the Atlanta public school system; the top-ranking conspirator was the school system's superintendent. Now it was an alleged criminal enterprise, national in scope but most of all targeting actions throughout the state of Georgia. And it was headed, not by a local school official, but by the man who had been president of the United States.

As Willis was getting ready at long last to move forward with her case, the threat level around the Fulton County Courthouse spiked dramatically. It was not a surprise. In March, Trump had held a giant rally in Waco, Texas. The venue itself, and the timing, seemed ominous. The rally was being held during a month that marked the thirtieth anniversary of the siege of the Branch Davidian compound in Waco that had culminated with the deaths of eighty members of the religious cult led by David Koresh and four federal law enforcement agents. Trump's rally began with a display on a giant video of a choir of January 6 defendants singing the national anthem. Then he riled up the crowd about the prosecutors closing in on him. "The thugs and criminals who are corrupting our justice system will be defeated, discredited and totally disgraced," he proclaimed. The crowd screamed its approval, waving signs that read WITCH HUNT.

Unbeknownst to the roaring rally-goers, Willis had dispatched two of her investigators—white men posing as MAGA warriors—to the Waco event to gauge the threat level. The undercover investigators returned to Atlanta with a hair-raising report. It portrayed the crowd as consisting of hard-core fanatics who could not be reasoned with—and could well engage in violence.

In late July, Willis sent a letter to Atlanta-area law enforcement officials advising them to "stay alert" and "make decisions that keep your staff safe" as she moved to present her case to the regular grand jury. (To underscore the severity of the threat, Willis had attached to her letter excerpts from some of the threats that had come in to her and her staff—obscene letters and emails with the ugliest of racist messages. Many of them were rife with racial epithets and threats of sexual violence. "I am sending [these messages] to you in case you are unclear on what I and my staff have come accustomed to over the last 2½ years," she wrote. "I guess I am sending this as a reminder that you should stay alert over the month of August and stay safe." She ordered anyone whose work was not essential to the Trump case to work from home.)

In truth, the messages in Willis's letter only scratched the surface. As the indictment drew near, the DA's office received intelligence reports that members of the Proud Boys were headed to Atlanta. There was talk on social media about assassinating Willis herself. Then came the threats from the digitally altered voice that mentioned not only the DA's home address but the names and addresses of her daughters as well. Willis had gotten that call in an SUV while she was on the way with Wade to meet a witness in the case. But the same caller also rang Willis on her cell phone while she was at the office– repeatedly–and, after she put those calls on speaker, her assistants recorded them, including repulsive utterances that sounded like he was simulating masturbation. "We need a dumb ass n***er like you to hang and we're gonna come see you soon," he said in one of the taped calls. At times, Willis engaged with the caller to keep him on the line in hopes of allowing investigators to learn enough to track him down. When the caller said she was a "puppet for the white man," she asked him, "What white man is she a puppet for?"

"The white man, Mr. Biden," he replied. "Just a Black puppet for Mr. White Biden."

In this season of threats and hate, that was only one of multiple abusive calls to Willis. "You will get what's coming to you, bitch," said another caller to the DA whose voice mail message was recorded by her office. "The best thing you can do is pack your bags and leave this country–because when Trump does get back in power..." His voice trailed off and the caller laughed. "You'll get yours," he said, completing his thought. "Justice will prevail."

A regular talking point of Willis's was that the Trump case had no more inherent worth than the other significant criminal cases that were the bread and butter of her office—the murders, the sexual assaults, the gang violence. These were the cases that were wreaking havoc on the lives of the people in her community, crime victims and their families whom she would often meet with to provide comfort and assurances that her prosecutors and investigators were seeking justice on their behalf. Willis wasn't naive; she understood that the investigation of a former president for seeking to undermine the democratic rights of Georgians was gravely important and, by several orders of magnitude, different from any investigation ever undertaken by her office. But with mild annoyance, she'd still sometimes complain about the media's obsession with the elections investigation to the exclusion of the rest of the vital work her office was doing. Trump "was just a man…a human being like every other human being," she told the authors in an interview. "We all have to live by a certain standard of rules," she went on. "And if you violate them, you catch a charge. It's not sexy. I'm sorry, it's just not."

In fact, Willis was getting nervous. In late July, an elderly woman who had once worked in the DA's office as a secretary under Paul Howard reached out to Willis with an unusual message. God, the lady said, had instructed her to fast and pray with Willis for seven days before going forward with her "big announcement." Willis, a practicing Catholic who described herself as "very spiritual," had not gone to church much during this period; she didn't want to be a distraction to Sunday churchgoers or disrupt their services with her security needs. But she already had a habit of communing with God before big decisions. And she was familiar with the Christian practice of spiritual fasting as a way of finding focus and clarity. She decided to follow the woman's advice. "I don't play with old black ladies who talk to God," she said.

A week before the grand jury was expected to hand up the indictment, Willis began a liquid fast, limiting herself to smoothies, broth, and juice. Each day she'd print out a Bible verse and tape it to the wall near her desk. In between meetings, Willis would read the verses, sometimes quietly to herself, often marking lines that had particular resonance for her. "I'm highlighting, making notes, I had them all stuck on my wall and my wall was a mess," she said. The verses were calming, given the stress. "So I wasn't eating. And I'm starving. My nerves were bad because I knew what we were about to do."

Some of the verses that hit home the most spoke of receiving "protection" from God. "I actually think that is what God wanted me to hear at that time," she said. "Like, I'm not going to let anything happen to you."

Someone else who wanted to make sure nothing happened to her was her father, John Floyd. The Black-Panther-turned-civil-rights-lawyer, now eighty-one, was extremely close to his daughter and, according to Willis, called her ten times a day. "He's my dad, but he is obsessed with security," Willis said. "He wants security with me when I go to the bathroom, he wants them there every second of the day. It's gonna kill the man because he's really, really worried that something's gonna happen."

On Monday, August 14, the area around the Fulton County Courthouse looked like an armed camp. Streets were blocked off from traffic; plastic orange barriers and steel crowd-control barricades formed a well-fortified perimeter around the beaux-arts-style building. Dozens of sheriff's deputies were keeping guard outside the courthouse, while others circled the area in unmarked cars. Bomb-sniffing dogs were deployed to detect the possible presence of a car or truck bomb, while snipers with long guns prowled the rooftops looking for threats.

By early afternoon, reporters had crowded into Judge McBurney's courtroom waiting for news of the charges. In the absence of actual news, some of the journalists had filled out their pre-written indictment stories with B-matter, while the cable TV reporters filled the airtime with whatever meager scraps they could gather, padded with breathless speculation. The real action was taking place in secret a couple hundred feet away, where Nathan Wade and his deputies continued to present evidence to the regular grand jury, which met in a large conference room just steps away from the DA's office on the third floor of the courthouse.

While it was widely believed that the grand jury's work was pro forma—they would, like most grand juries, likely rubber-stamp whatever prosecutors recommended—Willis's team was not taking anything for granted. Nathan Wade and the others spent hours in the grand jury room carefully going over the evidence, patiently answering the jurors' questions and presenting the witnesses the grand jurors wanted to hear from. Among those who testified that day were some of the prosecution's most important, including Brad Raffensperger and Gabriel Sterling, as well as state senator Jen Jordan and former representative Bee Nguyen, Democrats who had been at the December hearings where Giuliani had spread his lies about Ruby Freeman and Shaye Moss. At about eight o'clock that evening, the grand jurors asked the prosecutors to leave the room, indicating they wanted to talk by themselves. Were they going to vote? Did they want to hear more evidence, come back the next day for further deliberations? The prosecutors had no idea, and it made them edgy.

Willis's Bible verse of the day had come from James 1:4, and it seemed appropriate enough: "Let patience have its perfect work, that you may be perfect and complete." Her stomach was churning. She paced alone back and forth between her office and the conference room. "What are these people gonna do?" she kept asking herself, referring to the grand jurors who held the fate of her case—and her reputation—in their hands.

At 8:30 p.m., the grand jurors sounded a buzzer, summoning the prosecutors. Wade, Wooten, and the other members of the team filed back into the conference room—and they got the news that had been waiting for: It was a "true bill," signed by the foreperson of the grand jury—*The State of Georgia v. Donald John Trump*. A wave of relief came over the team.

Willis was waiting anxiously in the anteroom outside her office for the news. The grand jury had adopted every charge that Willis's team had proposed, for all nineteen co-conspirators. Willis walked into her office and collapsed on the couch. She brought her hands to her face as her eyes welled with tears.

DiSantis, who was in the room, attributed Willis's emotions to a combination of relief and absorbing the gravity of the moment. "It was relief," he said, "but it was also like, *holy shit.*" Willis later added another explanation. She was well aware of the doubts people would have about her—a Black, female local DA few had ever heard of taking on a former president of the United States. Now she could start putting those doubts to rest. "I'm a damn good lawyer," she'd thought to herself at the time.

———

Soon enough, the DA had to collect herself. In two hours, she would hold a high-stakes press conference with reporters from around the world. DiSantis had already written the speech, and the decision had been made that she would read it rather than speak extemporaneously.

Locally Willis was known for her zingers and combative retorts. But the moment called for a more sober, just-the-facts delivery, and she was committed to keeping her emotions in check. So when she stepped up to the podium at the Fulton County Government Center building just before midnight, surrounded by the entire election investigation team, Willis and every member of her team were wearing tiny American flags next to their Fulton County lapel pins. The DA spoke deliberately, enunciating each word clearly: "Today...a Fulton County grand jury returned a true bill of indictment charging nineteen individuals with violations of Georgia law arising from a criminal conspiracy to overturn the results of the 2020 election in this state." Willis went on to lay out the charges, detailing the forty-seven felony counts in the ninety-seven-page indictment. She listed the full names of every defendant, starting with Donald John Trump. Her voice grew a little louder and her words even more pronounced when she invoked her beloved RICO law: It was a conspiracy that had one overriding "illegal goal," she said: to allow "Donald J. Trump to seize the presidential term of office beginning on January 20." Those words—"to seize the presidential term of office"—had been chosen deliberately.

After finishing her prepared remarks, Willis addressed a few questions from the assembled reporters. Her answers were perfunctory. Yes, she hoped to schedule the trial in the next six months, but that would be up to a judge. No, she wouldn't discuss whether she'd had any communications with special counsel Smith. (In fact, she hadn't.) Another subject she wasn't going to discuss was the imminent threats that had been pouring into her office, one of them—which the press knew nothing about—the posting on a MAGA website that *the best time to shoot her is when she's leaving the building.* That alarming post dictated what happened next.

As the team filtered out of the room, Willis made a beeline to a back office where she had a change of clothing pre-positioned. In about ninety seconds, she had removed her black business suit, pumps, and a pearl necklace and put on sweats, a T-shirt, sneakers, and a baseball cap. The other members of the team also changed into casual clothes. Earlier in the day the team had gone through a dry run and had the plan down to clockwork. Nearby, an investigator on the staff, Willis's designated body double, was wearing a black business suit, a string of large pearls, high heels, and a black bob wig, the same attire Willis had been wearing during the press conference. The only accessory she added that set her apart from the way Fani Willis had appeared moments before was a weighty bulletproof vest.

With careful choreography, the body double, accompanied by a number of men posing as her deputies, moved in one direction and headed down the front stairs of the building, a diversionary operation designed to confuse any would-be assassins they feared might be lying in wait. Willis and her team moved in the opposite direction, slipping out the back stairs. The body double and her team left in official black SUVs. Willis and the rest of the election team sped off in several unmarked sedans and were driven to an Atlanta hotel where they would stay for the next few days, under tight security.

Willis arrived around 1:30 a.m. There was nothing she wanted more than to be back home rather than in a nondescript hotel suite protected by armed guards. She felt "physically sick" from exhaustion, but also a bit wired from the intensity of the day. She flipped on the TV, and the news was replaying her press conference. She watched with a critical eye, and she liked what she saw. "I did good today," Willis thought to herself.

The Mug Shot

"You can tell that he'd been practicing that for months."

If there is a consistent theme to Donald Trump's politics and character, it is his remarkable ability to portray himself as a victim. It is quite a trick for a rich man who became president to constantly complain that he is somehow being treated unfairly. But no matter what would be revealed about him—his strange affinity for Russian dictator Vladimir Putin, his eagerness to use the powers of his office to exact revenge and punish his political foes, his crude insults and sexual aggressions toward multiple women, his hoarding of classified documents at his Mar-a-Lago estate—the forty-fifth president would respond the same way. His conduct was always flawless (or "perfect" as he often said). It was his "radical" and "deranged" enemies who were persecuting him with bogus charges that amounted to a "witch hunt."

This victimhood counter-narrative would have seemed impossible to sell in the aftermath of Trump's unprecedented scheming to stay in power following the 2020 election and the resulting assault on the US Capitol. At the time, even Republican leaders had condemned his conduct. "The mob was fed lies," said Senate minority leader Mitch McConnell about the January 6 riot. "The president bears responsibility for [the] attack," added House minority leader Kevin McCarthy. After he was impeached by the House for a second time, fifty-seven senators, including seven Republicans, voted to convict him. What may have saved him was the fact that he had already left office by the time the vote took place, raising a novel question as to whether it was constitutionally permissible for the Senate to try an ex-president. At least that was the main excuse Republicans like McConnell gave for not joining the clear majority of their colleagues who wanted to permanently banish Donald Trump from ever holding high office again.

Yet the more prosecutors, congressional investigators, and the press tried to hold him accountable for his myriad transgressions of norms and laws, the more Trump was able to turn it to his advantage. "Every time they give me a fake indictment, I go up in the polls," he said. It was Trump's peculiar genius that he was able to whip up his base and convince them that his courtroom fights for survival were really their fights. "In the end, they're not coming after me," he told his faithful at rallies and on social media. "They're coming after you—and I'm just standing in their way."

With messages like that, Trump seemed to be turning his legal troubles to his advantage. By the summer of 2023, he appeared on a glide path to recapture the Republican nomination. And so it was that after Fani Willis's damning RICO indictment—Trump's fourth of the year—the former president once again found a way to profit and boost his campaign to return to the presidency.

Late on the afternoon of August 24, 2023, the former president flew into Atlanta on his private jet and, accompanied by an entourage of

Secret Service agents, drove in a motorcade through the streets of the city, winding his way through historically Black neighborhoods—past Morehouse College, Martin Luther King Jr.'s alma mater, and down a street named for Joseph Lowery, the Atlanta-based minister who founded the Southern Christian Leadership Conference. In what *The Washington Post* described as a "carnival atmosphere," many residents stood outside, snapping cell phone pictures, jeering and taunting him. Another group, smaller but boisterous, cheered.

Trump's ultimate destination was the Fulton County Jail. It was here he would formally surrender and be booked as a criminal defendant. The setting might well have been lifted from the pages of a novel by Victor Hugo.

Just five weeks earlier, the Justice Department had announced a civil rights investigation of the jail, portraying it as an overcrowded and filth-infested disaster area with "credible" allegations it was "teeming with insects, rampant violence resulting in death and injuries and officers using excessive force," as the US attorney in Atlanta, Ryan K. Buchanan, had put it. The probe was launched after the well-publicized death of an inmate named Lashawn Thompson, who had been arrested for vagrancy and had a history of mental illness, whose body was found crawling with lice and bedbugs while in the jail's psychiatric wing. He was among sixty inmates who had died at the jail since 2009.

Trump was spared any exposure to the jail's horrors. He was brought in through a special antiseptic central intake room—well separated from the more than three thousand inmates—where he was greeted somewhat surprisingly by an accommodating Fulton County sheriff Pat Labat. "Mr. Trump, how are you?" said the sheriff as he welcomed the defendant to his facility with a handshake. "We're going to try to move this process along." Then Labat outlined the process—some forms that needed to be filled out, fingerprints, and a mug shot.

There had been much discussion in the weeks leading up to Trump's booking about whether he would be required to have his mug shot taken. In his three previous bookings on criminal charges—in New York for the hush-money payout, in Florida for concealing classified documents, in Washington, DC, over the election—there had been no mug shot. Labat had initially taken a hard line on the issue, insisting that Trump would get one in his jail. Then he appeared to waver. Fani Willis bucked him up, sending the sheriff a letter reminding him that the law in Georgia required a mug shot for any defendant facing the serious felonies for which Trump was being indicted. Besides, she told the sheriff, "If you don't mugshot him, you're going to need to explain to our constituents why you mugshot their nephews and not the president of the United States. He needs to be treated like everybody else."

The process moved quickly, with Trump barely saying a word. Then he posed for the picture, eyebrows furrowed with an angry scowl on his face. Charles Shaw, the bail bondsman hired by Trump's lawyers to guarantee his $200,000 bond, watched the scene through a glass window with some amusement. "You can tell that he'd been practicing that for months," he said. "I've never seen anyone look quite so . . ."—and then he struggled for the right word—"defiant."

Labat later gave an interview to CNN in which he said, "It was heartbreaking to see someone of that stature and who represents our country in that fashion having to go through this." It was not at all clear Trump saw it that way. Within hours of the iconic photo's release, his campaign blasted out the image for a fundraising appeal, plastering the scowl on coffee mugs, bumper stickers, and T-shirts that it sold on its online store, raking in more than $7 million in the first two days.

If the mug shot—and Trump's effort to exploit it for campaign cash— had not been a surprise, there was an unexpected last-minute twist to his appearance at the Fulton County Jail. The arrangement for the booking had been made by Trump's "billion-dollar lawyer" in Georgia, the flamboyant Drew Findling. It was Findling who hired Shaw to serve as the former president's bail bondsman. But on the morning of the booking, Findling—somewhat sheepishly—informed Shaw that he had been fired. "He was completely surprised," said Shaw. "He had no idea it was forthcoming. I think he was probably disappointed."

To be sure, Trump had a well-documented history of shaking up his legal team, a practice that, whether calculated or not, injected chaos into his courtroom battles, sometimes turning them into spectacles. Some of his attorneys would get fired, others would quit amid fierce infighting over strategy and wrangling over how to placate the temperamental client. (No one, it seemed, ever quite measured up to Trump's original lawyer and mentor, the notorious Roy Cohn.) And soon enough, there was a report that Findling had clashed with Trump's pugnacious internal consigliere, Boris Epshteyn, over his refusal to launch a "scorched earth" strategy of harsh attacks on Willis or mount a vigorous defense of Trump's election lies by trying to argue that everything he had said to Raffensperger was on the money. (Findling declined to comment to the authors, and the precise circumstances of his departure remain a mystery.)

When Trump showed up for his booking at the jail, he was accompanied by new counsel, another high-priced local lawyer, Steve Sadow. A prominent member of the Georgia defense bar, partial to ostrich cowboy boots though not as flashy as Findling, Sadow had represented many of the same sorts of clients as his predecessor—including the rappers Gunna and T.I. (whom Trump's original Georgia lawyer, Dwight Thomas, had also represented). Perhaps Sadow's most celebrated case had been two decades earlier when he defended the Gold Club, an Atlanta strip club with alleged ties to the Gambino crime family, whose owner, Steve Kaplan, was accused of paying dancers to have sex with famous athletes to boost the establishment's profile. Sadow pled his client out, landing Kaplan a sixteen-month prison sentence and a $5 million fine, but allowing him to keep the bulk of his $50 million fortune, an arrangement Sadow called "a very good deal for all concerned." Still, it turned him into a critic of the RICO law that had been used to prosecute his client. "It's been overused," he told *The Atlanta Journal-Constitution* in 2021. "There's just no limit to it."

The indictment in mid-August set off a flurry of legal motions and maneuverings that provided the first tests of Willis's case. Most of those motions wound up before the Fulton County Superior Court judge assigned to preside over the trial, Scott McAfee, a thirty-four-year-old member of the conservative Federalist Society who had been appointed to the bench by Kemp. Given the Georgia governor's bitter clashes with Trump, it was not at all clear whether McAfee's pedigree would hurt or help Trump. In initial court hearings, McAfee struck most observers as a calm, reasonable, and strikingly evenhanded jurist, mostly shooting down motions brought by defense lawyers but also brushing back Willis's team on their request to go immediately to trial. But the first significant challenge to the DA's case actually came from elsewhere—just a few blocks away from the Fulton County courthouse, in US District Court for the Northern District of Georgia. It was in that court, before US District Court judge Steven Jones—the same African American Obama appointee who had shot down all of Stacey Abrams's claims of voter suppression—where Trump's White House chief of staff Mark Meadows had showed up on August 28 to argue that his case should be removed from state court jurisdiction and tried in federal court, on the grounds that everything he had done on behalf of the president had been part of his "official" duties as White House chief of staff.

The hearing began with a revealing snapshot of how the American legal system usually works for the powerful and privileged. As he walked in, the silver-haired Meadows was flanked by no fewer than seven lawyers—an army of impeccably tailored litigators, six of them from the white-shoe law firm of McGuireWoods. The team was led by one of the firm's senior partners, George Terwilliger, an éminence grise of the Washington, DC, bar who served as deputy attorney general under President George H. W. Bush and before that as a US attorney in Vermont. It was the kind of legal defense that few can afford. A federal public defender in the audience noted that when he appears in the same courthouse on behalf of one of his less fortunate clients, all he's usually got is a paralegal and, if he's lucky, the occasional investigator.

Much was riding on the hearing. At this point, Trump was also widely expected to file a similar motion for removal to federal court, and if Jones ruled for Meadows, the former president's lawyers would certainly have an easier time of it. Since this was a conspiracy case, in which all the defendants were allegedly linked in the same racketeering enterprise, a favorable ruling for Meadows could mean that all the defendants would have to be tried in federal court. If so, it would expand the potential jury pool to include additional counties north of Fulton, where more conservative pro-Trump voters lived. (Another consequence: If the case were removed to federal court, it would mean that, as with those brought by Justice Department special counsel Jack

Smith in Florida and Washington, DC, there would be no cameras in the courtroom. If Willis's case remained in a Georgia court, however, under state rules, all the proceedings, including the trial, could be televised, allowing the entire country to watch.)

It was shaping up as a genuine legal showdown; reporters lined up for hours early that morning to secure a seat in the crowded courtroom. Yet despite the considerable legal firepower marshaled on Meadows's behalf, things did not go well for the former White House chief of staff.

In an unusually risky move, given that his client was facing multiple criminal charges, Terwilliger decided to put Meadows on the stand. "I don't know that I did anything that was outside my scope as chief of staff," Meadows testified. Under Terwilliger's gentle questioning, he then proceeded to admit under oath many of the acts ascribed to him in the indictment. Yes, Meadows acknowledged, he had set up a meeting for Michigan and Pennsylvania legislators to come to the White House so Trump could pressure them to change the election results in their states. And yes, he had arranged for the notorious phone call to Raffensperger where the president urged him to "find" the necessary votes to flip the results of the election in Georgia. But all this was well within his job duties, he insisted. "It was not uncommon for me to set up phone calls for the president," he said. Meadows then proceeded to put a novel twist on his efforts to assist the president's efforts to overturn the election. What he was really trying to do, he testified, was bring a quick resolution to the election disputes so he could "land the plane."

What did he mean by land the plane? Terwilliger asked him.

"We had to do the transfer of power," Meadows explained, emphasizing several times that he wanted it to be a "peaceful" transfer that included working with the "transition team" to arrange national security briefings for "president-elect" Biden. It was a striking argument that went by so fast hardly anybody in the press corps caught it at first: Meadows was implicitly rejecting Trump's entire claim that he had rightfully won the election.

Meadows was ingratiating to Judge Jones, his only real audience, quickly correcting himself to say "Your Honor" after first mistakenly referring to him as "sir." He portrayed himself throughout as a humble besieged public servant simply trying to manage a volatile boss. Everybody in the world had been calling him, trying to bend the president's ear. "There were times I felt my phone number was blasted over every bathroom wall in America," he said. It was his job to be the president's "gatekeeper"—and that was a "challenge" when it came to Trump.

For cross-examination of this high-level witness, Willis had hired a new member of her team, Anna Cross, a former protégée who had worked closely with her at the DA's office under Paul Howard. A polished litigator, Cross confronted Meadows with sharp, staccato questions.

Please explain, she demanded, how each of the steps he took on behalf of the president had constituted "official" duties or otherwise advanced legitimate interests of the government of the United States. What was the official business when he showed up to watch the Cobb County audit?

Meadows insisted it was to ensure an accurate vote count for the signature audit, and that was a federal interest.

Did he coordinate his visit with anybody from the Department of Justice, the Department of Homeland Security, or any other federal agency? Cross asked. When he arranged the phone call to Raffensperger, why was it that he only reached out to Trump campaign lawyers to be on the call? Did he reach out to anybody from the Department of Justice to be on the call? Did he reach out to anybody from the White House counsel's office? Cross's point was clear. Despite a federal law, the Hatch Act, that bars all government employees—including a White House chief of staff—from engaging in campaign activity, Meadows was advancing the interests of Trump's campaign and the personal political interests of the president, not those of the federal government.

What about Meadows's December 27 email to Jordan Fuchs in Raffensperger's office asking if a signature audit in Fulton County could be sped up and be completed before January 6 "if the Trump campaign assists financially"?

"Why are you as the Chief of Staff making a financial offer to the Georgia Secretary of State's office on behalf of the Trump campaign?"

He hadn't exactly been making a financial offer, Meadows insisted. He was only seeking to determine if there was a "financial resource issue" so he could "advise the President of the United States."

Then Cross sprung her Perry Mason trap. What about the fake electors scheme in Georgia and other battleground states—the plan concocted by Trump's personal and campaign lawyers to provide the grounds for Pence to reject the Biden electors on January 6? Did he have any role in coordinating the electors? Cross asked.

"No, I did not," Meadows said.

"No role at all?" Cross asked, archly.

"As chief of staff, I did not coordinate those efforts," Meadows repeated.

"May I approach the witness," Cross asked the judge, who gave his approval. "Your Honor, at this time, we move State's Exhibit Number 1 into evidence."

It was an email thread Meadows had initiated with Jason Miller, one of Trump's chief campaign strategists—about the fake elector scheme that he had just testified he had nothing to do with.

At 4:11 p.m. on December 6, 2020, Meadows had sent Miller a copy of one of Chesebro's memos about anointing the alternative Trump electors.

"Let's have a discussion about this tomorrow," Meadows wrote to Miller.

Miller had quickly replied that he had just done background calls "on this very subject" with several journalists and commentators.

"We just need to have someone *coordinating* the electors for states," Meadows wrote back. Cross had him read the email to the judge.

She sat down, the witness impeached.

The following week, Judge Jones rejected Meadows's motion. "The Court concludes that Meadows has not met even the 'quite low' threshold for removal," the judge wrote. "The evidence adduced at the hearing establishes that the actions at the heart of the State's charges against Meadows were taken on behalf of the Trump campaign with an ultimate goal of affecting state election activities and procedures."

Although Meadows's legal team immediately filed an appeal with the Eleventh Circuit Court of Appeals, Sadow, Trump's new lawyer, likely saw the handwriting on the wall. On September 28, he notified Judge McAfee that the former president would not seek to remove his case to federal court. The next day, Judge Jones rejected a separate motion for removal filed by Jeff Clark, the Justice Department lawyer, and Shafer, the Georgia Republican chair who had presided over the fake elector meeting.

Willis had prevailed in her first big courtroom battle of the case. Unless Jones was overturned, always a possibility, Fani Willis's RICO indictment would be tried in state court in Georgia, vindicating her right as a local prosecutor to take on an American president.

The ultimate question raised by Willis's indictment is whether someone as powerful as a former president of the United States can be held accountable at all. Despite multiple scandals and an impeachment, more than seventy-four million Americans had voted for him in 2020—47 percent of the electorate—making the election a lot closer than most pundits expected. After his fourth indictment, the polls showed him competitive with, if not beating, President Biden in a hypothetical 2024 rematch. Historians and political scientists will struggle for years to explain the mystical hold Trump seems to have on his voters. But unquestionably, a big part of it is his cunning ability to capitalize on the distrust that many of them have—in some cases for entirely legitimate reasons—for the ex-president's many targets: the FBI, the Justice Department, the courts, and the press, which was labeled from the outset of his presidency the "enemy of the people." In this sense, Trump's vicious rhetoric and egregious violations of long-standing norms of political behavior really did matter. By tearing down institutions that are central to the civic order and democratic discourse, Trump had effectively helped to create a political free-fire zone where verifiable facts didn't matter and wild conspiracy theories such as those that he and his confederates promoted about the 2020 election flourished as never before.

American justice is predicated on rules of evidence and facts, and to function, it relies in part on ancient notions of shame and contrition as a measure of accountability. That's the ideal, anyway. But Donald Trump's shamelessness is his superpower. How does the American justice system account for a criminal defendant who shows contempt for the rule of law, refuses accountability, and maintains that *all* claims about his conduct are hoaxes, fake news, and witch hunts? Trump had demonstrated something at once very powerful and profoundly troubling—that in American politics, if you are brazen enough, the truth doesn't matter.

Fani Willis came from a very different world. She had been raised by her father, an ex–Black Panther and political activist. But her professional career as a prosecutor was governed by what happened inside courtrooms, arenas where verifiable evidence mattered and juries and judges had the final word. It was a world in which Willis racked up many triumphs—putting away murderers and rapists, convicting Atlanta schoolteachers for doctoring test scores. But Willis's sprawling ninety-seven-page indictment of Trump and his cohorts would be not only her biggest test, but—along with the two federal cases brought by Justice Department special counsel Jack Smith—one of the biggest tests ever for the American system of justice.

In early court hearings, Willis's deputy Nathan Wade told Judge McAfee that trying the Georgia case would take four months and require testimony from more than one hundred witnesses—a formidable and unwieldy undertaking that would tax court resources and possibly the patience of jurors. Willis had hoped to try all nineteen defendants together. But her plans quickly hit a snag: Two of the alleged co-conspirators, Kenneth Chesebro and Sidney Powell, invoked their rights to a speedy trial, a strategy that would force the DA's team to reveal a significant amount of its evidence long before Trump and the rest of the defendants file into court for the main event.

But within weeks, there were strong signs that Willis's strategy was working. One huge advantage of using RICO was that its heavy penalty—a five-year mandatory minimum sentence upon conviction—tended to cause defendants to flip to spare themselves the prospect of time in a Georgia penitentiary. It's what happened in Willis's school cheating case when a parade of teachers cut deals and testified for the prosecution. So, too, in the Trump case. Scott Hall, the bail bondsman who had chartered the plane for the Coffee County raid, was the first to flip, pleading guilty to five misdemeanors and agreeing to cooperate. In mid-October came an even bigger breakthrough. Willis's team was rushing to prepare for the upcoming Powell-Chesebro case, holding mock trials, honing arguments, practicing delivery. Then, on the eve of trial, Powell's lawyer reached out: She was ready to cave as well. It was Powell who had unleashed "the Kraken," vowing to "blow up" Georgia with fantastical claims about Venezuelan socialists flipping Trump votes to Biden. It was also Powell who had pushed the idea of "hunting license" pardons for Trump operatives to criminally break into election offices and who later bankrolled the Coffee County raid. And perhaps most important, as this book has demonstrated, although she was never formally a member of the president's legal team, Powell had a direct line to Trump throughout the post-election disputes, talking to him by phone from Tomotley and Atlanta and meeting with him in the Oval Office, where the president briefly agreed to name her his "special counsel" to investigate voter fraud. But on October 19, a day before jury selection was to begin in her trial, she showed up in Judge McAfee's courtroom and essentially admitted it was all a lie. The evening before, in a conference room across the street from the District Attorney's office, she sat for a videotaped "proffer," answering questions from Wade and Willis's other deputies in a session that lasted up to four hours. The next morning in Judge McAfee's courtroom, she entered a guilty plea to six misdemeanors involving conspiracy to interfere with election duties in exchange for no prison time and a promise to truthfully testify for the District Attorney's office in future proceedings. She also agreed to write a letter of apology to the citizens of Georgia. "Are you pleading guilty today because you agree there is a sufficient factual basis that support a plea of guilty?" McAfee asked her in open court. "I do," she responded softly, a tone markedly different from her cocksure demeanor when she was standing side by side with Rudy Giuliani making baseless claims that the election had been stolen from Donald Trump.

And the very next day, Kenneth Chesebro—the Larry-Tribe-protégé-turned-MAGA-consigliere—pled guilty to a felony for conspiracy to file false documents related to the fake elector scheme. As with Powell, the deal allowed Chesebro to avoid prison (as well as a lengthy trial in a Fulton County courtroom). It also spared Willis's team having to rush into a speedy trial and risk giving Trump's defense lawyers an advance preview of their case. Chesebro—while perhaps not as well known as Powell—was every bit as important a player in the racketeering conspiracy: He had led the legal effort in the fake election strategy designed to give Pence a basis to block certifying Biden's victory on January 6. Just like Powell before him, Chesebro had also sat for an extensive video proffer with Willis's prosecutors, providing testimony that Willis's office was said to be particularly pleased with.

The next week, a fourth defendant, Jenna Ellis, pled guilty as well. Ellis, a lawyer, had appeared along with Giuliani, Eastman, and others at the December 3 legislative hearing to press state senators to convene a special session and appoint Trump electors, and she had then tweeted out the falsehoods about Ruby Freeman and Shaye Moss, writing "SHOCKING...VIDEO EVIDENCE FRAUD!!." Choking back tears, Ellis read a statement to Judge McAfee in which she apologized for her conduct and acknowledged "I failed to do my due diligence," adding: "If I knew then what I know now, I would have declined to represent Donald Trump in these post-election challenges. I look on this whole experience with deep remorse."*

In rapid-fire fashion, four co-conspirators in the plot to overturn an American election—Hall, Powell, Chesebro, and Ellis—had thrown in the towel and agreed to cooperate in the case against Donald Trump. Exactly what they had said about Trump and others in their video-taped proffers was not immediately clear, and a few naysayers noted that the deals they had struck—probation with no jail time—were exceedingly lenient. Indeed, soon after her admission in court, Powell started posting or retweeting posts on social media that seemed to suggest she had not fully abandoned her denialism about the 2020 election results—actions that potentially jeopardized her probation-only plea deal. Still, the plea deals and videotaped proffers were the first major breaks in the investigations into Trump's post-election conduct. And it did not go unnoticed in the legal world: It was Fani Willis in Fulton County, Georgia, not Jack Smith, the Justice Department special counsel in Washington, who made it happen. It seemed a vindication of Willis's decision to aggressively indict the entire election conspiracy under RICO.

And beyond her considerable skills as a prosecutor, Willis possesses another set of qualities that makes her a uniquely formidable adversary for Trump, perhaps more than any of his other inquisitors. She has a combativeness and an instinct for the jugular that even

---

* In November 2023, ABC News reported that Ellis had told prosecutors about a conversation she had with Trump's social media aide Dan Scavino at a White House Christmas Party in December 2021. After Ellis apologized for the failure of the Supreme Court lawsuit to block Biden's election, she said, Scavino told her "in a kind of excited tone, 'Well, we don't care . . . The boss is not going to leave under any circumstances. We are just going to stay in power.'"

Trump would have to grudgingly admire. "I was always that girl with that mouth," she told the authors in an interview for this book.

Those qualities were very much on display when, ten days after the indictment, Willis received a letter from Ohio representative Jim Jordan, chairman of the House Judiciary Committee, demanding answers to a series of questions about whether her case was "politically motivated." Other prosecutors might have opted to ignore the letter and tune out the political noise, limiting their comments to dry court filings. Not Willis. She fired back with a scathing letter, skewering Jordan with constitutional arguments about interfering with a state criminal investigation and ridiculing him for his "misinformed" understanding of the charges against Trump. "Allow me the opportunity to provide a brief tutorial on criminal conspiracy law," Willis wrote with calculated condescension. And then, twisting the knife, Willis suggested Jordan buy a legal tome on racketeering laws written by John Floyd, her RICO adviser and a key member of her prosecution team (not to be confused with her father of the same name). "As a non-member of the bar," she wrote, "you can purchase a copy for two-hundred forty-nine dollars." Left unsaid was that Jordan, who had carefully cultivated a reputation as one of the Republican Party's most aggressive interrogators, had gone to law school but never passed the bar exam.

The letter was vintage Willis and demonstrated a major part of her appeal. But it sent a larger message that the Fulton County district attorney was determined to stand up to Trump and his allies. A former colleague at the DA's office and now a House member in the Georgia General Assembly, Tanya Miller, may have put it best. She saw in the DA's response a fierce determination that resonated in Atlanta's Black community. Nine years ago, Miller had quit the Fulton County DA's Office after refusing to prosecute the controversial school cheating case that wound up on Willis's desk. But whatever doubts she may have once had about her former colleague's handling of that case, Miller today sees Willis as a powerful symbol for her community.

"If there is a culture of Black women, it's that we don't like a bully," she said. "Don't beat up on the little guy. Don't take advantage of your power. If it's not fair for everybody, it's not fair for anybody. And we know that deep down in the marrow. We've been talking about it and talking about it—'We can't believe [Trump] did this and we can't believe he did that, how does he get away with this and how does he get away with that?' And here is this Black woman throwing down the gauntlet and saying, 'You know, actually he's not going to get away with it... It's just really a source of pride for a lot of Black women, and within my circle everyone is just talking about how we can support her. What does she need? What can we do?'

"Democracy means something to us. It's a real thing. We fought and bled for it, the right to vote and to participate in democracy and have our voices heard. And we view Fani as an extension of that legacy."

There is no way to know, of course, what Fani Willis's ultimate legacy will be. She, like the Justice Department's Jack Smith, will have to secure convictions, and even if they do, the verdicts could well be tied up with appeals that drag on for years. But Willis's indictment itself demonstrates an extraordinary feature of the American system: Even a locally elected county prosecutor can seek to hold a president accountable. And in this case, that prosecutor has her own superpower. As Fani Willis had said, "When I walk into a courtroom, I'm always underestimated, which can be a powerful thing."

That's something Donald Trump never saw coming.

ACKNOWLEDGMENTS

All books present challenges, and this one had more than its share. We were writing about a criminal case that is very much ongoing, with no way of knowing how it will all turn out in the end. But Gail Ross, who deserves her own wing in the book agent Hall of Fame, saw the potential from the outset in telling the story of a gutsy local prosecutor willing to take on a powerful ex-president. So, too, did the ever-gracious Sean Desmond, who bought the idea over lunch with the authors and championed it through its early stages. His departure from Twelve Books for another publishing house left us bereft and, for a time, worried about who we would turn to for advice as we sought to bring things to a conclusion. But the incomparable Mark Warren stepped into the breach as editor, offering shrewd suggestions and wise counsel as to how to improve the manuscript. We owe him a huge debt of gratitude. And a special shout-out to Gail's assistant, Cameron Dames, for always being on hand to set up our never-ending Zoom sessions.

We also want to thank our publisher Ben Sevier and the wonderful team at Twelve Books—including our publicist Megan Perritt-Jacobson, production director Bob Castillo, director of non-fiction Colin Dickerman, editorial assistant Ian Dorset, legal counsel Jennifer McArdle, and jacket designer Jim Datz—for their quick turnaround of the manuscript, creative design, legal review, and crash edit, all of which, amazingly, made *Find Me the Votes* a reality.

There was no shortage of folks who provided valuable insights that helped us understand the events of 2020. Among them: Greg Bluestein, George Chidi, Charles Bailey, Pallavi Purkayastha, Chris Huttman, Brian Robinson, Bryan Tyson, Heath Garrett, Joan Carr, Clint Rucker and Shaunya Chavis, Dave Hancock, Chris Smith, Jason Carter, Marilyn Marks, Norm Eisen, Mark Whitaker, and Jonathan Alter. And as should be clear from the book, we benefited from the access and time afforded us by Fani Willis, Jeff DiSantis, Brad and Tricia Raffensperger, Jordan Fuchs, Chris Carr, Geoff Duncan, and John Porter—as well as many others who shared their recollections on a confidential basis.

We also want to acknowledge several books that informed our reporting and thinking for this story: *Where Peachtree Meets Sweet Auburn: A Saga of Race and Family* by Gary M. Pomerantz, *The Temple Bombing* by Melissa Fay Greene, *Flipped: How Georgia Turned Purple and Broke the Monopoly on Republican Power* by Greg Bluestein, *The Steal: The Attempt to Overturn the 2020 Election and the People Who Stopped It* by Mark Bowden and Matthew Teague, *Giuliani: The Rise And Tragic Fall of America's Mayor* by Andrew Kirtzman, *So Help Me God* by Mike Pence, *None of the Above: The Untold Story of the Atlanta Public Schools Cheating Scandal, Corporate Greed, and the Criminalization of Educators* by Shani Robinson and Anna Simonton, *The Condemnation of Little B: New Age Racism in America* by Elaine Brown, and *Race & the Shaping of Twentieth-Century Atlanta* by Ronald H. Bayor.

Numerous colleagues, friends, and family members read parts or all of the manuscript as the project evolved, providing useful feedback and much-needed encouragement. Jeff Bartholet, our former *Newsweek* colleague and a fine editor, was particularly helpful. We'd also like to thank our former colleagues at Yahoo News who provided valuable editorial guidance and support along the way. They include: Lauren Johnston, Jon Ward, Colin Campbell, Alex Nazaryan, David Knowles, Crystal Hill, Jerry Adler, and Sharon Weinberger.

During most of the time we worked on *Find Me the Votes*, we also cohosted a podcast for Yahoo News called *Skullduggery*. Focused on the scandals, controversies, and, well, skullduggery that are permanent parts of today's political landscape, the show featured the Trump election plot in Georgia as regular fodder. Many of the guests we had on were invaluable sources of information and analysis as we worked on the book in parallel, and we thank them for their contributions. But we especially want to thank the two other essential members of our *Skullduggery* team, the razor-sharp Victoria Bassetti, who is the only actual lawyer among us, and Mark Seman, our producer extraordinaire who gets all the credit for making us sound good despite ourselves. And a big shout-out to Holly Peterson, who began promoting our book long before we had anything to show for ourselves. Your salons are sanctuaries for intelligent and civil conversations about the difficult issues of the day.

We also want to give a special thank-you to Trent Gegax and Samara Minkin and their lovely daughters, Stella and Hattie, who generously invited us to stay with them in their beautiful home during multiple reporting trips to Atlanta. Their warm hospitality, particularly during the final, frenetic weeks of this project, was just what we needed.

From Michael Isikoff

I'm enormously fortunate to have a large loving and endlessly entertaining extended family that helped keep me going through a long and challenging project. Starting with the Akers side, there are the fantastic Akers sisters and their significant others—Maggie Akers and the late Honorable Todd Campbell, Grace Akers and Maria Price, and Charlotte Akers and Dale King. Here's to many more weeks at Bald Head—along with Ashley, Harper, Hudson, Joel, Seth, and Holt!

And on the Isikoff side, there is the all-star Falby clan: My sister Nancy Isikoff and her husband Bruce Falby, Dan Falby and his wife Cici Cyr, baby Zinnia, Anna Falby, and Jake Falby. There is little we look forward to more than our annual visits to the Falby New Hampshire compound and—thanks to the laughs, great food, awesome Squam Lake boat rides, and limitless supply of Pabst Blue Ribbons—it's a tradition we plan to continue in perpetuity (and well after Donald Trump has faded from the scene).

On the home front, I don't have enough thanks to go around—to Winky, for her hilarious leaps across the house; to Sunny, for accompanying me on long walks in the woods during which I tried to figure out what we should write in the next chapter; and of course to Zach. He's now, amazingly, the tallest one in our family—a strapping, good-natured teenager and first-class first baseman whose tenacity and fortitude in bouncing back from multiple sports injuries is an inspiration to one and all. And as before he played an important role: His persistent question—are you done with your book yet?—prodded Klaidman and I to actually finish!

And speaking of inspirations, there is my awesome wife, the journalist Mary Ann Akers. Her wit, dedication, hard work, and passion for the truth make her a role model for her colleagues—and for that matter anybody interested in the greater cause of journalism in a truth-challenged world. But there is no end to her many talents, including her jaw-dropping ability to recite from memory the entire lyrics to the Charlie Daniels song that should make the perfect soundtrack for this book if it ever makes it to the big screen. I love you, babe. You are the best!

From Daniel Klaidman

As Isikoff said, book writing is challenging, full of ups and downs, and often lonely—even when doing it with a co-author as collaborative and fun as Mike. So it would be unimaginable doing it without the support and encouragement of family and friends. I want to start, as always, with my parents, Kitty and Steve Klaidman, whose deep interest in this project and willingness to *always* let me tell them about every twist and turn in the reporting and writing provided great sustenance. Steve taught me how to write and Kitty made me appreciate how important the human dimension is in storytelling. My sister, Elyse, read parts of the book along the way and bucked up my confidence at key moments of vulnerability. I was always aware of her husband, Elyakim, and terrific sons, Liam and Itai, cheering Isikoff and me on from the sidelines. The love and support of my amazing in-laws was invaluable. Thank you, Carole (bubbe) and Alan, Gerry and Carol, and all the children and grandchildren—Sherri, David, and Jack; Adam, Mirna, Hector, and Bina; Michael, Sarah, Elliott, Cameron; and Scott. I couldn't hope for a more loving and fun extended family. A special thank-you to Steve and Becky Lewis and their irrepressible kids, Danny and Lorelei. Friday-night dinners with Steve's bracingly cold martinis and juicy steaks and Becky's incredible graciousness were all the incentive I needed to get my writing done at the end of each week. Jen and Sam Goldberg are extraordinary friends. My daily trips to the gym with Sam kept me sane, and all I ever had to do for a sympathetic ear was walk two doors over and find Jen. Emmy, Sydney, and Maddie (aka the Goldberg Girls) always put a smile on my face. The Lewises and the Goldbergs are my rocks. And of course, thank you, Bella and Shayna, my extraordinary girlies, whose love, support, consideration, and gentle teasing have sustained me every single day. I love you so, so much.

In memory of Monica.

NOTES ON REPORTING AND SOURCES

This book is based in large part on original research by the authors, including interviews with Fulton County district attorney Fani Willis and members of her team, as well as scores of others involved in the disputes over the 2020 election. These included principals in the secretary of state's office, the Fulton County election office, the Trump campaign, the Georgia General Assembly, and lawyers who represented all sides in cases challenging the results. In some cases, sources asked to speak on a confidential basis, without their names being disclosed, in order to talk about politically sensitive matters more freely. We have honored those requests and duly noted them, both in the text and in the notes below.

The authors also obtained exclusive access to thousands of emails, text messages, audiotapes, and other material that illuminated the events at Lin Wood's Tomotley plantation. Marilyn Marks, executive director of the Coalition for Good Governance, pointed us to multiple documents that emerged in a lawsuit brought by her group that shed light on the events in Coffee County. The final report of the January 6 committee, as well as thousands of pages of depositions its investigators conducted, were an invaluable resource. So too was the original reporting done by numerous news organizations, most notably, *The Atlanta Journal-Constitution*, *The Washington Post*, *The New York Times*, Lawfare, Axios, ProPublica, Frontline/PBS, and George Chidi's Substack feed and his iHeart radio podcast. We have reconstructed meetings and conversations described in these pages based on firsthand accounts of the participants. What follows is a chapter-by-chapter guide to our sourcing.

Prologue: The Body Double

The accounts of the threatening phone call from the digitally altered voice and the use of a body double to throw off potential assassins is based on interviews by the authors with Fulton County DA Fani Willis and her aide Jeff DiSantis.

Chapter 1: Badass

The account of Willis's visit to the Fulton County DA's office, her initial reaction to the Raffensperger phone call, and her view of Trump's pressure campaign as a voting rights case is based on interviews she gave the authors.

John Floyd related his life story, including his experiences in the civil rights movement and with the Black Panthers, in an interview with the authors.

For the *Los Angeles Times* story on Floyd's co-founding of the Black Panther Political Party, see "Black Nationalist Political Party to Be Established in California," *Los Angeles Times*, February 20, 1967, 103.

His comments about his relationship with Angela Davis in the oral history interview for the Black Power Archives at the Tom & Ethel Bradley Center at California State University, can be found at https://www.csun.edu/bradley-center /black-power-archives-oral-history-project.

For more on Willis's trips to DC Superior Court with her father, see "Meet Fani Willis, Georgia DA who could bring charges against Trump," *USA Today*, February 14, 2022.

The comments of Rebecca Christian Smith and Felicia Stewart are from interviews with the authors.

For an account of Merrick Garland's role in the Oklahoma bombing prosecution, see "Merrick Garland at the Helm," *Legal Times*, May 8, 1995.

For Howard Schmuckler's conviction on federal fraud charges, see "Mortgage Rescue Business Owner Sentenced to 90 Months for Fraud," Washington

Field Office, FBI, press release, June 25, 2012, https://archives.fbi.gov/archives /washingtondc/press-releases/2012/mortgage-rescue-business-owner-sentenced -to-90-months-for-fraud.

Alvin Kendall's comments on Willis, interview with authors. For an account of Willis's arguments in the school cheating case, and "holding forth like a fire-and-brimstone preacher," see Shani Robinson and Anna Simonton, *None of the Above: The Untold Story of the Atlanta Public Schools Cheating Scandal, Corporate Greed, and the Criminalization of Educators* (Beacon Press, 2019), 148–150. For Willis's comments to Sharon Reed on the school cheating case, see "Exclusive: Sharon Reed Goes One-on-One with Fani Willis," Atlanta Voice, YouTube, July 17, 2020, at 19:15, https://www.youtube.com/watch?v=AtVspEqjt9c&t=1155s.

Chapter 2: The Law-and-Order Candidate

For the *Atlanta Journal-Constitution* story about the complaints against Paul Howard lodged by Tisa Grimes, see Christian Boone, "Administrator Alleges DA Paul Howard Sexually Harassed Her," *Atlanta Journal-Constitution*, December 26, 2019, https://www.ajc.com/news/crime—law/administrator-alleges-paul -howard-sexually-harassed-her/LbsYvyiyUWgbCJxW1xQexO. The *AJC* story about Cathy Carter can be found here: Christian Boone, "Former Records Clerk Alleges Sexual Harassment by Fulton DA," *Atlanta Journal-Constitution*, March 5, 2020, https://www.ajc.com/news/crime—law/former-records-clerk -alleges-sexual-harassment-fulton/sQVx07rU4K00UQmoE2HVQP.

The comments of Fani Willis, Charlie Bailey, Bill Edwards, Clint Rucker, Shaunya Chavis, Daphne Jordan, and Fred Hicks, interview with authors. Jeremy Harris, Willis's campaign manager, provided a detailed account of Willis's meeting with T.I. and the George Soros vetter in an interview with the authors.

The text messages between Fani Willis and Daphne Jordan and her husband, Walter, were provided to the authors by Jordan.

Chapter 3: Chaos in Atlanta

For the protests in Minneapolis and other cities, see " 'Absolute Chaos' in Minneapolis as Protests Grow across U.S.," *New York Times*, May 29, 2020, https://www .nytimes.com/2020/05/29/us/floyd-protests-usa.html.

For Mayor Bottoms's first plea for calm in Atlanta, see " 'Absolute Chaos' in Minneapolis as Protests Grow across U.S.," *New York Times*, May 29, 2020, https://

www.nytimes.com/2020/05/29/us/floyd-protests-usa.html; Richard Fausset and Michael Levenson, "Atlanta Protesters Clash with Police as Mayor Warns 'You Are Disgracing Our City,'" *New York Times*, May 29, 2020, https://www .nytimes.com/2020/05/29/us/atlanta-protest-cnn-george-floyd.html; and Victoria Albert, "Atlanta Mayor Makes Impassioned Plea to Calm Violence: 'If You Care about This City, Then Go Home,'" CBS News, May 29, 2020, https:// www.cbsnews.com/news/atlanta-mayor-makes-impassioned-plea-to-calm -george-floyd-violence-if-you-care-about-this-city-then-go-home.

George Chidi provided his account of his confrontation at the site of the burned-out Wendy's in an interview with the authors.

For the special prosecutor's decision not to charge the two police officers in the shooting of Rayshard Brooks because he believed they had a reasonable basis to use force against Brooks, see Shaddi Abusaid, Alexis Stevens, Henri Hollis, and Asia Simone Burns, "No Charges against Atlanta Officers in Fatal Shooting of Rayshard Brooks," *Atlanta Journal-Constitution*, updated August 23, 2022, https:// www.ajc.com/news/crime/breaking-no-charges-for-apd-officers-in-fatal -shooting-of-rayshard-brooks/KDDYTQKCCNF6HMH2ZRVHFKJEK4.

For the murder of Secoriea Turner, see Emilie Ikeda, "Police Identify 8-Year-Old Girl Killed in Atlanta 4th of July Shooting," Fox 5 Atlanta, July 5, 2020, https://www.fox5atlanta.com/news/police-identify-8-year-old-girl-killed-in -atlanta-4th-of-july-shooting.

For Mayor Bottoms's emotional press conference following the murder of Secoriea Turner, see J. Scott Trubey, Joshua Sharpe, and Asia Simone Burns, "Atlanta Mayor Bottoms Calls on Violence to Stop after 8-Year-Old's Death," *Atlanta Journal-Constitution*, July 5, 2020, https://www.ajc.com/news/crime—law/atlanta-mayor -bottoms-shooting-year-old-enough-enough/ewb45h1m1KcuIMJFRxpkOI.

Turner's parents shared details about the murder and their meeting with Fani Willis in an interview with the authors.

For Willis's press conference announcing the indictment of two members of the Bloods in Turner's murder, see "Watch Live: Fulton County D.A. Discusses the Secoriea Turner Case," Atlanta News First, Facebook, August 13, 2021, https://www .facebook.com/AtlantaNewsFirst/videos/173834954816172.

For Drew Findling's comments—"it's completely fucking racist"—see "Attorney Drew Findling: Young Thug, Gunna's Case a 'Racist Reach'; Where's Tarantino RICO?" TMZ, June 3, 2022, https://www.tmz.com/2022/06/03/attorney -drew-findling-young-thug-gunna-ysl-rico-racist-tarantino.

Chapter 4: A Confederate in the Attic

The comments by Chester Doles and details of his past with the Ku Klux Klan, the neo-Nazi National Alliance, and the Charlottesville rally came from an interview with Doles by the authors.

For Doles's role in leading the Hammerskins rally in 2015, and his comment "its victory or Valhalla," see Vegas Tenold, *Everything You Love Will Burn: Inside the Rebirth of White Nationalism in America* (Nation Books, 2018), 197–198.

For a full account of the 1912 lynching and subsequent expulsion of Blacks from Forsyth County, Georgia, see Patrick Phillips, *Blood at the Root: A Racial Cleansing in America* (W. W. Norton, 2016).

Raffensperger wrote about the substance abuse of his son in his book, *Integrity Counts* (Forefront Books, 2021), 32–45. Tricia Raffensperger shared the detail about waiting outside the Atlanta crack house in an interview with the authors.

Bryon Tyson shared details about his experience at the Trump campaign, his confrontations with Cleta Mitchell over the filing of lawsuits, his decision to withdraw from representing the president, and the scene with Lin Wood on the speakerphone at GOP headquarters in an interview with the authors.

One of Tyson's co-counsels who left during this period, Stefan Passantino, later returned as a Trump-allied lawyer and was accused by one of his clients, Cassidy Hutchinson, the former top aide to White House chief of staff Mark Meadows, of coaching her to give the January 6 committee misleading testimony in order to protect the former president. Passantino denied the charges and said he represented Hutchinson "honorably" and "ethically." "Exclusive: Trump's former White House ethics lawyer told Cassidy Hutchinson to give misleading testimony to January 6 committee, sources say," by Katelyn Polantz, Pamela Brown, Jamie Gangel, and Jeremy Herb, CNN, December 21, 2022.

For Judge Steven Jones's ruling in the lawsuit brought by Fair Fight Action, the political organization founded by Stacey Abrams, see Maya King, "Federal Judge Rules against Fair Fight Action in Georgia Voting Lawsuit," *New York Times*, September 30, 2022, https://www.nytimes.com/2022/09/30/us/politics/voting-lawsuit-georgia.html.

Cleta Mitchell's email to John Eastman seeking a memo about state legislators being able to designate electors on their own can be found here: https://www.govinfo.gov/content/pkg/GPO-J6-DOC-Chapman006671/pdf/GPO-J6-DOC-Chapman006671.pdf.

For Robert Sinners's testimony about the Buckhead meetings, see Select Committee to Investigate the January 6th Attack on the U.S. Capitol, U.S. House of Representatives, Washington, D.C., "Interview of: Robert Sinners," June 15, 2022, 48–50, https://january6th-benniethompson.house.gov/sites/democrats .january6th.house.gov/files/20220615_Robert%20Sinners.pdf.

For Trump Jr.'s press conference and his vow to be "watching this nonsense," see Molly Curley, " 'We're Going to Fight': Trump Jr. Speaks in Atlanta as Count Continues," WSAV.com, November 5, 2020, https://www.wsav.com/news/your -local-election-hq/trump-campaign-to-hold-press-conference-in-atlanta.

David Shafer described the concerns among Georgia Republicans about displeasing Trump in an interview with the authors.

Tricia Raffensperger shared the text messages she received in an interview with the authors. She and her husband also described the harassment of their late son's wife and the break-in at her home in an interview.

Chapter 5: The Targeting of Innocents

The account of Ralph Jones's childhood in Collier Heights, Atlanta, comes from the authors' interview with Jones. Accounts of the threats against Jones are based on office emails and voice mails obtained by the authors from an open records request to the Fulton County Registration and Elections Board. Additional details came from interviews with Jones and with Richard Baron, former Fulton County election director.

This in-depth Reuters series disclosed the first major details about the harassment of Georgia election workers, including Jones, Freeman, and Moss: "Campaign of Fear: The Trump World's Assault on U.S. Election Workers," Reuters, https://www.reuters.com/investigates/section/campaign-of-fear.

For "He was always falling shitfaced": Andrew Kirtzman, *Giuliani: The Rise and Tragic Fall of America's Mayor* (Simon & Schuster, 2022), 239.

For accounts of the Clark-Giuliani conversation, see Kirtzman, *Giuliani*, 370; Mike Pence, *So Help Me God* (Simon & Schuster, 2022), 431; Select Committee to Investigate the January 6th Attack on the U.S. Capitol, U.S. House of Representatives, Washington, D.C., "Interview of: Justin Clark," May 17, 2022, https:// s3.documentcloud.org/documents/23531669/20220517_justin-clark.pdf.

For Justin Clark's account, see deposition to January 6 committee, "Interview of: Justin Clark."

Powell's email from the woman with "visions" of vote flipping was entered into evidence in Dominion's lawsuit against Fox News and can be read here: https://www.washingtonpost.com/documents/ac73ed35-fccd-45df-bc49 -4e1a8cd4b37d.pdf.

Giuliani's and Pick's testimony before the Georgia Senate committee can be found here: "Second Georgia Senate Election Hearing," 11 Alive, YouTube, December 3, 2020, https://www.youtube.com/watch?v=hRCXUNOwOjw.

The conclusions of the Georgia secretary of state's investigation into the State Farm video—conducted with agents of the GBI and FBI—are in an internal report obtained by the authors.

Georgia senator Elena Parent's "Alice in Wonderland" comments can be found in the video of the December 3 hearing: "Second Georgia Senate Election Hearing," 11 Alive, YouTube, December 3, 2020, at 6:11:26, https://www.youtube .com/watch?v=hRCXUNOwOjw&t=22286s. Parent's account of her encounter with a Covid-infected Giuliani at the hearing comes from an interview she gave to the authors.

The story of Ruby Freeman's mother instilling in her a reverence for voting can be found here: Lucien Bruggeman and Marjorie McAfee, "Mother-Daughter Election Workers Describe How They Lived through Trump-Backed Accusations of Conspiracy," ABC News, November 3, 2022, https://abcnews.go.com /US/mother-daughter-election-workers-describe-lived-trump-backed/story?id =92500318.

The independent review of the Fulton County Registration and Elections Board's handling of the 2020 primary vote can be found here: "State Election Board Report: Post-Election Executive Summary," January 12, 2021, https://www.document cloud.org/documents/20484973-fulton-county-state-election-board-report.

Chapter 6: The QAnon Commission

For Lin Wood's response to a voter asking for guidance on how to respond to friends who said Trump's claims about the election being stolen were "crazy conspiracy theories," see Greg Bluestein, *Flipped: How Georgia Turned Purple and Broke the Monopoly on Republican Power* (Viking, 2022), 50.

QAnon's messaging about secret tunnels beneath Central Park can be found at "Fact Check: 35,000 'Malnourished' and 'Caged' Children Were Not Recently Rescued from Tunnels by U.S. Military," Reuters, June 15, 2020, https://

www.reuters.com/article/uk-factcheck-children-rescued-tunnels/fact-check
-35000-malnourished-and-caged-children-were-not-recently-rescued-from
-tunnels-by-u-s-military-idUSKBN23M2EL; and David Schmidt, "'Won't Somebody Please Think of the Children?'" *Brooklyn Rail*, December 2020–January
2021, https://brooklynrail.org/2020/12/field-notes/Wont-somebody-please-think
-of-the-children. Also, see Will Sommer, *Trust the Plan: The Rise of QAnon and the
Conspiracy That Unhinged America* (HarperCollins, 2023), 1–4.

For Trump's comments on QAnon, see Shannon Pettypiece, "Trump on QAnon
Conspiracy Theory: 'Is That Supposed to Be a Bad Thing?'" NBC News, August
19, 2020, https://www.nbcnews.com/politics/white-house/trump-qanon-conspiracy
-theory-suppose-be-bad-thing-n1237358.

For Trump's retweets of QAnon accounts, see Tina Nguyen, "Trump Isn't Secretly
Winking at QAnon. He's Retweeting Its Followers," *Politico*, July 12, 2020,
https://www.politico.com/news/2020/07/12/trump-tweeting-qanon-followers
-357238; Alex Kaplan, "Trump Has Repeatedly Amplified QAnon Twitter
Accounts. The FBI Has Linked the Conspiracy Theory to Domestic Terror,"
Media Matters for America, August 1, 2019, https://www.mediamatters.org
/twitter/fbi-calls-qanon-domestic-terror-threat-trump-has-amplified-qanon
-supporters-twitter-more-20.

Details from Lin Wood's former law partners' lawsuit against him can be found here:
https://s3.documentcloud.org/documents/7220637/AMENDED-COMPLAINT.pdf.

Details of Wood doxxing his son Matthew can be found here: David Edwards, "'I
Do Not Regret It': Pro-Trump Attorney Lin Wood Cites 'Jesus' after 'Doxxing'
His Own Son on Telegram," Raw Story, January 31, 2021, https://www.rawstory
.com/lin-wood-telegram; and on his Telegram account.

Wood's claims about tech entrepreneurs Zuckerberg, Musk, Thiel, his children,
and the CIA comes from an audio recording of Wood obtained by the authors.

For Trump's retweet of OAN interview with Ron Watkins, see Rachel E. Green-
span, "Trump Tweeted a False Claim about Rigged Voting Machines after
a Network Known for Airing Conspiracy Theories Did the Same," *Insider*,
November 12, 2020, https://www.insider.com/trump-tweets-out-fake-voting
-claim-right-after-oan-segment-2020-11.

The detailed account of the activities at Lin Wood's Tomotley plantation were provided to the authors in multiple interviews by Dave Hancock, a private security
expert who worked for Wood and lived on the estate for several months during
2020. Additional information came from thousands of emails and texts between

the Tomotley participants provided to the authors by Hancock. The account of the altercation between Wood and Hancock was provided by Hancock and was backed up by an October 21, 2020, Beaufort County, South Carolina, police report: https://www.documentcloud.org/documents/21754972-bcso-report -altercation-lin-wood-plantation-with-david-hancock.

An account of Michael Flynn's role at Lin Wood's Tomotley estate can be found in Robert Draper, "Michael Flynn Is Still at War," *New York Times Magazine*, February 4, 2022, https://www.nytimes.com/2022/02/04/magazine/michael-flynn -2020-election.html.

Russell Ramsland's views on the vulnerability of Dominion voting machines in 2018 can be found here: Emma Brown, Aaron C. Davis, Jon Swaine, and Josh Dawsey, "The Making of a Myth," *Washington Post*, May 9, 2021, https://www .washingtonpost.com/investigations/interactive/2021/trump-election-fraud -texas-businessman-ramsland-asog.

The description of the meeting at the Westin Hotel where "hunting licenses" to protect operatives who seized voting machines was discussed is based on accounts from Michael Trimarco and Chris Smith in interviews with the authors.

For details on the criminal charges against Ryan Dark White, see Will Sommer, "Lin Wood's Fave QAnon Oracle Hopes for Trump Pardon," *Daily Beast*, January 5, 2021, https://www.thedailybeast.com/lin-woods-fave-qanon-oracle-hopes -for-trump-pardon-after-pain-pill-scheme.

The email from Andrew Whitney referencing a "hunting license that provides the top cover for ops," dated November 21, was obtained by the authors.

For Powell and Wood viewing the Salazar video as the "holy grail," see Doug Bock Clark, Alexandra Berzon, and Kirsten Berg, "Building the 'Big Lie': Inside the Creation of Trump's Stolen Election Myth," ProPublica, April 26, 2022, https:// www.propublica.org/article/big-lie-trump-stolen-election-inside-creation.

Sidney Powell's phone call to Ezra Cohen was first reported by ABC's Jonathan Karl in his book, *Betrayal: The Final Act of the Trump Show* (Dutton, 2021); see pages 168–175. See also Will Steakin, "Trump Allies Pressed Defense Department to Help Overturn Election, New Book Says," ABC News, November 16, 2021, https://abcnews.go.com/US/trump-allies-pressed-defense-department -overturn-election-book/story?id=81182008.

Chris Miller confirmed the phone call he got from Mark Meadows about "Italygate" and his follow-up conversations with Lt. General Scott Berrier, the director of the Defense Intelligence Agency, in an interview with the authors.

Powell's November 21, 2020, interview previewing her so-called Kraken lawsuit in Georgia can be found at "Sidney Powell: It will be BIBLICAL," Newsmax, You-Tube, November 21, 2020. https://www.youtube.com/watch?v=Y68pEknYyCM.

For Watkins's denial about being Q, see Jacob Rosen, Aaron Navarro, Dan Patterson, and Adam Brewster, "QAnon Promoter Ron Watkins Is Running for Congress in Arizona," CBS News, October 15, 2021, https://www.cbsnews.com/news/qanon-promoter-ron-watkins-is-running-for-congress-in-arizona.

For his claims about being the new Rosa Parks of a modern digital civil rights movement, see Jessica Wang, "Suspected QAnon leader, Ron Watkins[,] Spotted in Sydney, Australia, Father Confirms Move," News.com.au, August 11, 2022, https://www.news.com.au/technology/online/internet/suspected-qanon-leader-ron-watkins-spotted-in-sydney-australia-father-confirms-move/news-story/f911c9ce7e70c0159f12381bf5a6cc39.

For Gabriel Sterling's remarks at his December 1 press conference, see "Georgia Election Official Gabriel Sterling: 'Someone's Going to Get Killed' Transcript," Rev, December 1, 2020, https://www.rev.com/blog/transcripts/georgia-election-official-gabriel-sterling-someones-going-to-get-killed-transcript.

Chapter 7: The Republican Stone Wall

The account of Johnny Isakson's meeting with President Trump at the White House is based on interviews with three of the participants: Joan Carr, John Isakson, and Heath Garrett.

Chris Carr related his phone call from President Trump and the messages he received from Texas attorney general Ken Paxton in an interview with the authors.

For the Kemp-Duncan statement rejecting calls for a special session, see "Gov. Kemp, Lt. Gov. Duncan Issue Statement on Request for Special Session of General Assembly," Office of Governor Brian P. Kemp, press release, December 6, 2020, https://madmimi.com/p/50e7a11?pact=1301484-161142215-11561983238-b09ac0db7ff3f3c8bd594d6a33e7f63d0cf4c135.

For Kenneth Chesebro's political evolution, see Cam E. Kettles and Neil H. Shah, "'The Architect of the Whole Plan': Harvard Law Graduate Ken Chesebro's Path to Jan. 6," *Harvard Crimson*, September 8, 2023, https://www.thecrimson.com/article/2023/9/8/chesebro-jan-6-harvard-law-school-graduate-feature.

For analysis of the Hawaii vote and Nixon's choice of the Kennedy electors over him, see Michael L. Rosin and Jason Harrow, "How to Decide a Very Close Election for Presidential Electors: Part 2," *Take Care* (blog), October 23, 2020, https://

takecareblog.com/blog/how-to-decide-a-very-close-election-for-presidential
-electors-part-2.

The certificates signed by the Georgia fake electors proclaiming themselves as the "duly elected and qualified electors of the President and Vice President of the United States from the state of Georgia " can be found here: https://www .archives.gov/files/foia/ga-full.pdf.

The certificates signed by fake electors from the six other states can be seen here: "American Oversight Obtains Seven Phony Certificates of Pro-Trump Electors," American Oversight, March 2, 2021, https://www.americanoversight.org /american-oversight-obtains-seven-phony-certificates-of-pro-trump-electors.

For the weaknesses in the Trump campaign lawsuit filed in the days before the December 14 fake elector meeting, see David Wickert, "Georgia Rebuts Trump's Voter Fraud Claims in Court," *Atlanta Journal-Constitution*, updated December 18, 2020, https://www.ajc.com/politics/election/georgia-rips-trumps -voter-fraud-claims-in-court/P6TI4J3CKVDQZMNVG66Q2GBQCE.

Chapter 8: The "Perfect" Phone Call from Hell

Excerpts of the Trump phone call to Watson and her account of being "shocked" can be heard here: Mark Winne, "New Recording Reveals Trump Called Georgia Investigator Leading Signature Match Audit," WSB-TV, March 11, 2021, https://www.wsbtv.com/news/local/new-recording-reveals-trump-called -georgia-investigator-leading-signature-match-audit/WEIRQJXKOJFVDG BGATBZOAMSPA.

Lin Woods's attack on Jordan Fuchs for having been a "witch" was reported in Mark Bowden and Matthew Teague, *The Steal: The Attempt to Overturn the 2020 Election and the People Who Stopped It* (Atlantic Monthly Press, 2022), 71–73.

For Fuchs's response on Twitter to Wood, see Jordan M. Fuchs, "Have you ever met a man with a tiny man ego? How do you manage little man syndrome? Asking for a friend," Twitter, December 16, 2020, https://twitter.com/jordyfuchs /status/1339382525647597571.

For Eastman's email to Trump lawyers about a future DA or US attorney investigating them, see Kyle Cheney, Josh Gerstein, and Nicholas Wu, "Trump Lawyers Saw Justice Thomas as 'Only Chance' to Stop 2020 Election Certification," *Politico*, November 2, 2022, https://www.politico.com/news/2022/11/02 /trump-lawyers-saw-justice-thomas-as-only-chance-to-stop-2020-election -certification-00064592.

There have been multiple media accounts of the December 18, 2020, meeting at the White House, the most notable being Jonathan Swan and Zachary Basu, "Inside the Craziest Meeting of the Trump Presidency," *Axios*, February 2, 2021. For Patrick Byrne's readiness to "bury [his] knuckles" in Pat Cipollone's throat, see Patrick Byrne, *The Deep Rig: How Election Fraud Cost Donald J. Trump the White House, by a Man Who Did Not Vote for Him* (Deep Capture, 2021). For Giuliani's reference to White House lawyers as a "bunch of pussies," see Cameron Joseph, "Giuliani Called Trump Lawyers 'a Bunch of Pussies' in 'Screaming' White House Meeting," *Vice*, July 12, 2022, https://www.vice.com/en/article/xgyxmk/rudy-giuliani-screamed-at-trump-lawyers.

Raffensperger's most detailed account of the phone call and his reaction to Trump's comments can be found in his book, *Integrity Counts*, pages 164–204.

Ryan Germany shared his recollection of the phone call in an interview with the authors.

Chapter 9: The DA Speaks

For child murders in Atlanta, see "Fulton County Has More Than 20 Child Homicides Still Being Prosecuted; These Are the Victims," 11 Alive, January 27, 2022, https://www.11alive.com/article/news/crime/fulton-county-atlanta-22-child-homicide-cases/85-fba5e428-7c54-4458-a9b8-1c4216545425.

Vince Moody's monitoring of threats at the Gold Dome and his concerns about Cleveland Meredith are based on an interview with the authors.

For the January 3, 2021, meeting at the White House with Jeff Rosen and Richard Donoghue, and threats of a mass resignation at the Justice Department if the Clark letter was signed, see *Final Report: Select Committee to Investigate the January 6th Attack on the United States Capitol, December 22, 2022*, 117th Congress, Second Session, House Report 117-663, pp. 398–402, https://www.govinfo.gov/content/pkg/GPO-J6-REPORT/pdf/GPO-J6-REPORT.pdf.

The January 4 confrontation between Eric Herschmann and John Eastman in which Herschmann warned about "riots in the streets" was recounted in the White House lawyer's testimony to the January 6 committee and can be seen here: "Former WH Lawyer to Former Trump Lawyer: 'You're Going to Cause Riots in the Streets,'" ABC News, Facebook, June 16, 2022, https://www.facebook.com/watch/?v=757538358607962.

An abbreviated version of the conversation can also be found in paragraph 94 of the second Justice Department indictment of Donald Trump. See Charlie Savage and Adam Goldman, "The Trump Jan. 6 Indictment, Annotated," *New York Times*, August 1, 2023, https://www.nytimes.com/interactive/2023/08/01/us /politics/trump-jan-6-indictment-2020-election-annotated.html.

Chapter 10: A Raid in Rural Georgia

The account of the Coffee County elections office raid was largely drawn from court filings in *Donna Curling et al. v. Brad Raffensperger*, including the declaration of Kevin Skoglund as well as surveillance footage of the operation introduced in the case. The lawsuit, brought by a group of voters and the Coalition for Good Governance, alleged that officials in Georgia had not done enough to ensure the security of the state's elections. https://coaltionforgoodgovernance .sharefile.com/share/view/s6f2a57537bb54543b85242dafaac0652.

For more on the Coffee County raid, see these detailed accounts: Jose Pagliery, "Texts Reveal GOP Mission to Breach Voting Machine in Georgia," *Daily Beast*, June 4, 2022, https://www.thedailybeast.com/how-a-coffee-county-gop-chair -coordinated-a-voting-machine-breach; Emma Brown and Jon Swaine, "Inside the Secretive Effort by Trump Allies to Access Voting Machines," *Washington Post*, October 28, 2022, https://www.washingtonpost.com/investigations/2022 /10/28/coffee-county-georgia-voting-trump.

For the email from Missy Hampton to Preston Halliburton saying "Y'all are welcome to our office any time," see a court filing by Sidney Powell's lawyers here: https://ga-fultoncountysuperiorcourt2.civicplus.com/DocumentCenter /View/2261/POWELLS-GENERAL-DEMURRER-AND-MOTION-TO -DISMISS-COUNTS-1-AND-32-37-9-27-23.

Chris Harvey's memo stating that election software was not subject to public release was in a November 17, 2020, "Official Election Memo" obtained by the authors. His comment that "nobody gets access to that equipment" was in an interview with the authors.

For the role of Misty Hampton and her video, see Emma Brown and Amy Gardner, "Georgia County under Scrutiny after Claim of Post-Election Breach," *Washington Post*, May 13, 2022, https://www.washingtonpost.com/investigations /2022/05/13/coffee-county-misty-hampton-election; and Doug Richards, "Coffee County Attention Started with YouTube Video," 11 Alive, September 29, 2022, https://www.11alive.com/article/news/politics/elections/coffee -county-youtube-election-dominion-vote/85-14b18082-6f80-4657-8e37 -b27e0d892735.

For more on the Trump campaign's efforts to gain access to Dominion voting machines in Antrim County, Michigan, see Jon Swaine, Aaron C. Davis, Amy Gardner, and Emma Brown, "Files Copied from Voting Systems Were Shared with Trump Supporters, Election Deniers," *Washington Post*, August 22, 2022, https://www.washingtonpost.com/investigations/2022/08/22/election-system -copied-files-trump; and "Plot to Overturn the Election," *Frontline*, PBS, March 29, 2022, https://www.pbs.org/wgbh/frontline/documentary/plot-to -overturn-the-election.

Charles Shaw shared his interactions with Scott Hall during the 2020 election challenges in an interview with the authors.

Chapter 11: A Threat from Trump

For Willis's remarks at the September 2021 press conference, see "Violent Offenders Will Not Be Released over Case Backlog 'Crisis,' Fulton DA Says," Fox 5 Atlanta, YouTube, September 29, 2021, https://www.youtube.com/watch?v =EsJsvbs-klc.

For Thomas's representation of T.I., and his claims about "the deal of the century," see "U.S.A. v. Clifford 'T.I.' Harris (2008)," Law Offices of Dwight L. Thomas, P.C. website, http://www.dwightlthomas.com/notable_cases.html.

Willis's concerns about Trump's remarks at his Conroe, Texas, rally and her request to the FBI for a risk assessment at the Fulton County Courthouse; see John Wagner, "Georgia Prosecutor Asks FBI for Security Assistance following Trump Comments at Texas Rally," *Washington Post*, January 31, 2022, https://www .washingtonpost.com/politics/2022/01/31/willis-fbi-help-trump-comments.

Chapter 12: A Very Special Grand Juror

Kohrs's account of the grand jury proceedings and the testimony of Graham, Hutchinson, Coomer, Sterling, and Tricia Raffensperger is from interviews with the authors.

Timothy Heaphy recounted the negotiations over granting Willis's prosecutors access to the January 6 committee's evidence in an interview with the authors.

For the visit by Steve Lee, the pastor, to Ruby Freeman's home, see Linda So, Jason Szep, and Peter Eisler, "Exclusive: Georgia Probe into Trump Examines

Chaplain's Role in Election Meddling," Reuters, September 9, 2022, https://www.reuters.com/world/us/exclusive-georgia-probe-into-trump-examines-chaplains-role-election-meddling-2022-09-09.

For the incident at Freeman's home with Trevian Kutti, see Linda So and Jason Szep, "Trump Aide Set Up Meeting Where Election Worker Was Pressured," Reuters, December 21, 2021, https://www.reuters.com/world/us/trump-campaign-official-set-up-meeting-where-georgia-election-worker-was-2021-12-21; Richard Fausset and Danny Hakim, "Inquiry Scrutinizes Trump Allies' False Claims about Election Worker," *New York Times*, November 1, 2022, https://www.nytimes.com/2022/11/01/us/trump-georgia-election-ruby-freeman.html.

The Center for Responsive Politics provided the authors with a breakdown on the Trump campaign payments to Willie Lewis Floyd.

Chapter 13: A True Bill

The account of Willis's meeting with her prosecutors, and her subsequent caution about including some of the individuals recommended by the special grand jury, is based on an interview with Willis by the authors.

For Drew Findling's past comments about Trump, see Bill Rankin, "Atlanta's #BillionDollarLawyer Once Attacked Trump, Now Defends Him," *Atlanta Journal-Constitution*, April 13, 2023, https://www.ajc.com/news/atlantas-billion dollarlawyer-once-attacked-trump-now-defends-him/VI4Z6NLGLFFOX FE2UBJSYX22VQ.

For Findling's background, see Joe Coscarelli, "Atlanta's #BillionDollarLawyer Is Looking Out for Your Favorite Rappers," *New York Times*, February 8, 2018, https://www.nytimes.com/2018/02/08/arts/music/drew-findling-atlanta-lawyer-migos-gucci-mane.html.

For threats to Willis and the staff, see Tim Darnell, "Georgia District Attorney Shares Threatening Email Sent to Her ahead of Trump 'Historical Decision,'" WSFA 12 News, August 1, 2023, https://www.wsfa.com/2023/08/01/georgia-district-attorney-shares-threatening-email-sent-her-ahead-trump-historical-decision.

The account of Willis's wait for the decision of the grand jury and her subsequent use of a body double to throw off would-be attackers was described to the authors by Willis and Jeff DiSantis.

Epilogue: The Mug Shot

Trump's motorcade route through the streets of Atlanta and the "carnival atmosphere" was recounted here: Emmanuel Felton, Fenit Nirappil, and Camila DeChalus, "Along Trump's Journey to Jail, Black Atlanta Residents Mix Outrage with Pride," *Washington Post*, August 28, 2023, https://www.washingtonpost.com/nation/2023/08/28/trump-georgia-motorcade-fulton-jail.

The account of Trump's appearance at the Fulton County jail is based on an interview by the authors with Charles Shaw, the ex-president's bail bondsman. Willis described her letter to Sheriff Labat and her comments to him in an interview with the authors. For the Trump campaign's fundraising off the mug shot, see Alex Isenstadt, "Trump Raised $7.1 Million after Georgia Booking, Mugshot," *Politico*, August 26, 2023, https://www.politico.com/news/2023/08/26/trump-mugshot-fundraising-00113118.

Labat's own comment about Trump's booking being "heartbreaking" can be found at Reeves Jackson, "Fulton County Sheriff Describes What Trump Was Like When Getting His Mug Shot," 11 Alive, September 11, 2023, https://www.11alive.com/article/news/special-reports/ga-trump-investigation/fulton-county-sheriff-describes-trump-when-getting-mug-shot/85-b12676a7-fc23-4879-be8f-320a30a422f3.

For Steve Sadow's comments about RICO being "overused," see Bill Rankin and Tamar Hallerman, "Trump Replaces Top Atlanta Attorney on Day of Fulton Surrender," *Atlanta Journal-Constitution*, August 24, 2023, https://www.ajc.com/politics/breaking-trump-replaces-his-top-atlanta-lawyer-on-day-of-fulton-surrender/Q2BWFNDS2VFCZDC6LAOU5AO444.

A transcript of the Mark Meadows hearing on removal was included by Meadows's lawyers in their appeal of Judge Jones's decision to the 11th Circuit Court of Appeals.

Tanya Miller's comments about Willis were made during an interview with the authors.

INDEX

ABOUT THE AUTHORS

Michael Isikoff is an award-winning Washington investigative journalist and the author of three *New York Times* bestsellers: *Uncovering Clinton: A Reporter's Story; Hubris: The Inside Story of Spin, Scandal and the Selling of the Iraq War* (with David Corn); and *Russian Roulette: The Inside Story of Putin's War on America and the Election of Donald Trump* (also with David Corn). He has worked for *The Washington Post, Newsweek,* NBC News, and Yahoo News and is a frequent guest on CNN, MSNBC, and other networks. He lives with his wife and son in Washington, D.C.

Daniel Klaidman is an award-winning journalist and author based in Brooklyn. He spent more than a decade at *Newsweek,* where he served as managing editor, Washington Bureau chief, Middle East correspondent, and investigative reporter. Klaidman was a key part of the teams that won National Magazine Awards for *Newsweek's* coverage of 9/11 and the Monica Lewinsky affair. He previously served as Ferris Professor of Journalism at Princeton University and is the author of *Kill or Capture: The War on Terror and the Soul of the Obama Presidency.* Most recently he was editor-in-chief of Yahoo News.